a tear in my life
The Brutal Truth

Jarek Ambrozuk

Expanse Media Inc.

EXPANSEMEDIA.CA

Edited by Irene Kavanagh

Copyright © 2018 Expanse Media Inc.
www.ExpanseMedia.ca

a tear in my life: The Brutal Truth / Jarek Ambrozuk

First Edition: October 2018

ISBN 978-1-989309-00-1

To the one who spoiled me,

the one who showed me how to be a better man,

and the only one I ever truly loved.

Contents

Act II: Federal Case

Act III: Immigration Case

One Book—A Thousand Answers

I, Jarek Ambrozuk, do solemnly swear that I will tell the truth, the whole truth, and nothing but the truth, so help me God.

THOSE WERE THE ever so familiar words I was asked to recite each time I took the stand in my numerous court appearances. As it turned out, I took that mantra literally, so that all the speculations, conjectures, and false allegations surrounding the twenty-four-year-old Montana mystery case could finally be cleared up.

In 1982, when Dianne and I fell in love, it was the kind of youthful passion that left no room for reflection or consequences. Like many teenagers our age, we were driven by the freedom the world had to offer, and when faced with our stifling surroundings, we did the unthinkable—we eloped.

It was an exciting plan, as bold as it was innocent, but when tragedy struck at the apex of our seductive adventure, our dreams died along with our future. Left alone to grieve, I would spend decades searching for answers to why I lost the only girl I ever truly loved.

But when I finally returned to where it all began, I found hostility and vengeance in place of understanding and sympathy. My naive belief that I could explain away the reasons behind our whimsical elopement was overshadowed by skepticism and a thirst for retribution. I wanted to believe that the Flathead County authorities would examine the evidence, see the elopement for what it was, and do the right thing—just as the Canadian authorities did.

But they were not that kind of people.

And therefore, their malignant influence and enigmatic conduct in front of the media and the public cannot be sugarcoated, ignored, or excused, if my story is to remain transparent, honest, and accurate.

What this book contains is not only the details of how Dianne and I met, fell in love, concocted our elopement, and eventually executed our perilous plan, but also what happened twenty-four years later when I came back to Kalispell, Montana, to face the presumptuous Flathead County authorities.

As a fugitive in the United States for close to a quarter of a century, I would inevitably face federal and immigration charges as well—because of my alias passport and illegal entry into the U.S., respectively—but neither compared to the witch-hunt by the state prosecutor who was destined to be judge, jury, and executioner.

Over the years, there would be many lives affected, and many tears shed by many people, before the truth could be told. But now it is time to tell all—time for the brutal truth backed only by indisputable facts and evidence.

It would be foolish for anyone to think that what was read in the news—or what came out of the Flathead County justice system—was anything but honest and accurate. There are still many questions, twists, and misinterpreted facts in need of clarification. I hope this book, along with the accompanying www.ambrozuk.com evidence website will, once and for all, demystify our elopement, unravel the twenty-four-year-old Montana mystery case, and finally set the record straight.

CHAPTER TWO

The Day Our World Ended

August 22, 1982

THIS WAS IT: the day we had planned for months. Dianne and I were going to elope and disappear forever.

We had already completed the first phase of our plan—flying a rental Cessna C150 aircraft from Vancouver to Penticton, British Columbia—and were now relaxing on the outskirts of the airport runway until we were ready for the final leg of our journey. For all intents and purposes, everyone believed this was a one-day adventure—a last fling for two eighteen-year-olds before school began—but in reality, we were leaving for the rest of our lives.

Halfway through the day, Dianne went over to the main airport building to use the bathroom in the lobby. When she came back, she mentioned that she had also called home to tell her parents about our safe arrival in Penticton, and that we would be heading back to Vancouver later that afternoon. Our entire charade was based on appearing normal in every possible way, including a phone call if that's what was expected.

Although we had all the plan details worked out, and everything was progressing smoothly, there was always the possibility of something going wrong despite what my ground-school instructor had said about landing the aircraft on water. Dianne and I went over the same scenario for what seemed like the hundredth time, making sure everything was accounted for, and that there would be no surprises during our landing later that evening.

The plane carried twenty-six gallons of fuel, including reserve, and that was well within our limit to find a body of water approximately 400 miles from Penticton. Looking at my flight training aerial maps to locate a sizeable lake that met all our criteria, our most logical destination was Flathead Lake in Montana. It was large in comparison to others, with ample room for landing, and would make it difficult for local residents and weekend campers to spot the aircraft during descent.

Knowing we had less than four hours of flight, our final task was to compute our departure time so it would be pitch black when we were ready to land. With no Internet, and no easy way to get that information without casting suspicion, I casually asked the attendant for the approximate time of sunset during the refueling of the aircraft and was told 9:30 p.m.

Before our departure, there were also a few housekeeping items to take care of. First, we needed to file a flight plan with Air Traffic Control. Unlike our departure from Vancouver, where we tried to appear inexperienced, our return flight warranted a log of precisely what regions we were to fly over on our way back. This detailed flight plan— from Penticton to Vancouver via Princeton, Spuzzum, Harrison Lake, Harrison Hot Springs, Pitt Meadows, and finally, Vancouver—would ensure any search and rescue following our disappearance would be conducted in an area far from our actual destination.

As we intended to land on a lake and, ultimately, would be surrounded by water, Dianne and I changed into our bathing suits while still on the ground. Shedding our wardrobe inside the tiny airplane cabin in mid-air seemed not just inconvenient but much more difficult.

Belongings we had secretly collected for the past several months— supplies, disguises, and clothes now scattered in the storage area behind the seats—were randomly distributed by size and weight into two large green garbage bags we then doubled up and sealed with tape to make waterproof. We left the yellow raft, for use as transport to shore from the aircraft, in its original, clear packaging, with the understanding there would be plenty of time to get it unwrapped and inflated once we were floating on the water surface.

The final task was to unscrew the back panel between the storage compartment and the tail-end of the fuselage, ensuring the air cavity would not hinder the sinking of the plane. Removing the panel also gave us additional space to store the raft and the sealed garbage bag to prevent them from jostling in the back during our final landing approach.

It was close to 6:00 p.m. by the time we got everything organized and ready for departure. With our flight plan now filed, our bathing suits on, and our waterproof bags safely stashed in the back of the aircraft, we were ready to begin the final leg of our journey.

After getting approval from the Air Traffic Control tower, we taxied onto the runway and took off from Penticton Airport on Runway 34 northbound without incident. Once in the air, we altered our course westbound by making a left turn and continuing as if following our flight plan back to Vancouver. Reaching cruising altitude, we maintained this trajectory for another ten minutes, making sure we were clear of the Air Traffic Control tower before deviating south and heading toward Flathead Lake in Montana.

Just as we did on the way to Penticton, we followed landmarks along our new route to the lake. But this time, we intended to remain unseen, plotting a course between mountainous regions with no population indicators and no check points along the way. Flying between mountain ranges with very little civilization, I dropped our cruising altitude from 3,500 feet to below 2,000 feet to remain invisible to radar and avoid visual contact from nearby observation points.

Crossing the U.S. border, we adjusted our flight path to the southeast—flying between mountain valleys of Washington and Idaho—before reaching the state of Montana, using creeks, rivers, and lakes as our navigational markers (see Document: 7400 @ www.ambrozuk.com).

Throughout the day, and during our flight, the weather was perfect with only a few wispy high clouds periodically casting shadows on the ground. Excited and anxious, Dianne and I watched the sun gradually set on the horizon as we made our way toward the designated lake. Continuously looking for landmarks below, we made a game out of who could spot a specific marker on the map first, making time pass by more quickly.

It took us over three hours before we were close enough to see Flathead Lake. By then the sky was practically pitch black with only the moon peering from above, reflecting on the water surface in the distance. Orienting ourselves with the topology below, we could see the large Flathead Lake as well as several smaller bodies of water, namely, Ashley Lake and Little Bitterroot Lake.

Flathead Lake was huge in comparison to the other two, and, therefore, it would take us hours to paddle to shore after exiting the cabin and the plane sinking. To add to the complication, there were also clusters of lights all around the lake perimeter, compounding the possibility that someone would spot us during our landing.

Not wanting to take unnecessary chances, we quickly scrapped Flathead Lake, instead heading for Little Bitterroot Lake, the larger in width of the two smaller bodies of water that appeared to have fewer lights along the shoreline. Although there was always the risk of someone noticing our landing, we could only hope the population around the lake was sparse enough because of the minimum lights visible.

Having the lake picked out, we could finally put away our navigation maps and commence the final preparations for our landing. With Dianne holding the yoke steady, I reached back and placed our aerial maps in the open plastic bag behind our seat before sealing it with electrical tape and a piece of rope to ensure it wouldn't leak if submerged in water.

Throughout the flight, Dianne and I both had our waist seatbelts on. They were made up of two parts: the standard waist seatbelt and an optional detachable shoulder harness used for additional safety. Connecting the shoulder harness to the waist seatbelt was rather cumbersome, requiring that the occupant flip the buckle inside-out prior to clipping the shoulder harness into the latch of the waist buckle. Although the process was convoluted, it was there for a reason, and we both agreed that Dianne should take the extra precaution.

My restraint, on the other hand, was of lesser importance, mainly because I was the one holding the flight controls that would provide me with stability. After some debate about safety versus our aircraft exit strategy, the consensus was that once we were floating on water, I would have more time to devote to inflating our raft if I removed my waist seatbelt altogether. That split-second difference now seems insignificant, but at the time it was sound rationale behind our teenage logic.

Approaching Little Bitterroot Lake, we had everything prepared and were ready to begin our final landing approach. Our bags were sealed, we were in our bathing suits, the two side-door windows were unlocked and open to allow ample water flow into the aircraft once we landed, and it was now just a matter of properly executing the landing.

Guided only by the reflective light of the moon on the water surface, we began our descent at approximately 9:30 p.m. Our aerial maps did not contain contour lines of the lake to indicate depth, but we assumed that landing in the middle of the largest water surface area would prove to be the deepest. Once submerged in water, and buried in mud on the bottom, it would be next to impossible for anyone to find the plane even from an aircraft flying overhead.

I turned off the marker lights on the outside of the aircraft and placed the airplane into a glide by throttling back the engine with fully lowered flaps to decrease our airspeed to approximately 45 mph before trimming the elevators. The air was calm, and with no crosswind, the Cessna cut through the air without much turbulence.

Once close enough to the lake, I turned off the engine to begin our landing approach. Other than the engine being off to maintain silence and the landing surface being water, the landing was a typical textbook maneuver I had repeated dozens of times during my private pilot's training.

Coming in from the northwest, the aircraft quietly gliding on a shallow slope, we began to drop in altitude. The only noise now was the wind whisking by our open windows on either side of the doors. Watching the altimeter needle drop from 1000 feet to 800 feet to 600 feet, my hands stayed firmly affixed on the yoke, holding the plane in a steady descent.

With the flaps still fully down, I began to raise the nose of the aircraft until the stall speed indicator was constant. I remembered that same familiar buzzing sound from the many practice runs and landings during my flight training. The warning indicated the approach of the wing's critical angle of attack that would cause the aircraft to stall and lose lift if exceeded.

Although we came in from the northwest on a fairly shallow angle above the trees, the rate of descent was not sufficient as we were still several hundred feet above the water when we reached the middle of the lake. Little Bitterroot Lake was close to 3.3 miles long, and at the south end, where we were planning to land, it was approximately 1.5 miles wide. Short of stalling the aircraft to stop it from advancing towards the south shore, I began a gentle left turn to prevent us from reaching the shallow end. Using the ailerons to roll the airplane would tilt the left wing down and thus compromise its horizontal orientation, so I made sure to use the rudder only to change direction.

It took several seconds to complete the half circle and reposition the aircraft toward the north as we continued to descend. With the stall warning buzzer loudly piercing our ears, we could clearly see the water reflection as the tail of the plane was just about to touch the surface.

According to instructions provided by David Firth in my ground-school class, the procedure for making an emergency landing on water using a fixed landing-gear aircraft (see Document: 1225 @ www.ambrozuk.com) was straightforward: maintain a minimum airspeed of approximately 43 mph, extending the flaps fully down while placing the aircraft in a nose-up and tail-down attitude; keep a high angle of attack so that when the tail touches the water, it will drag on the surface and further decrease the aircraft speed; when the wheels touch the water, the aircraft will experience a bumpy landing but should float for approximately ten to thirty minutes before sinking.

His instructions may have sounded great in theory, but what happened during our landing was nothing of the kind.

Anticipating a fierce impact, I firmly clenched the steering column to make sure that when the wheels touched the surface, I could fight the water resistance by compensating with the flight controls. But that made no sense from an engineering perspective.

When the two wheels in the middle of the fuselage jackknifed into the water, it felt like the plane had hit a cement wall. No air controls—not the rudder, nor the ailerons, nor the elevator—could counter the dense, viscous fluid to stop the aircraft's forward momentum. As soon as the wheels had penetrated the water surface, the plane went into an abrupt pivotal rotation around its lateral axis. This caused the nose to plunge downward and the tail to rotate up and over itself, forcing the airplane to violently flip upside down almost instantaneously in a 180-degree rotation.

At the moment of impact, Dianne was firmly secured in her seat with a waist seatbelt and a shoulder harness. I, on the other hand, was not wearing any restraints, and thus my momentum catapulted me head-first through the front plastic windshield. The force was so intense that I knocked off the padding from the steering column (see Document: 7152 @ www.ambrozuk.com), possibly with my trailing knee. Being thrust violently forward, I also broke a rib (third from the bottom on the right side, close to the sternum), likely the result of hitting my chest on the steering control handle as I was propelled past the now stationary propeller and into the icy lake water.

The impact with the water was so intense that it took only one or two seconds before I found myself submerged. I could taste blood in my nose and mouth, and my immediate instinct was to find my bearing to the water surface. It was pitch black, and I spun around in a circle, trying to find any glimmer of light to swim toward. It took another few seconds before my buoyancy settled, and I reached the air above the surface.

When I came up, I found myself at the back-left side of the aircraft, facing the tail end of the plane. From my view angle, the left wing was completely submerged with the right-side airfoil extruding at a shallow angle above the water surface.

As I spit out blood mixed with icy water, I yelled, "Dianne! Where are you? Are you OK?"

And that was when I heard the words that would haunt me for many years to come. From inside the cockpit, I heard Dianne call out:

"Jarek, I can't get my seatbelt off!"

She was alive and conscious. The only thing that stood between her and freedom was the safety of the seatbelt. Hearing her voice, I immediately started to make my way to the passenger door. Positioned behind and to the left of the plane, I jumped on the left elevator to get over the tail portion of the fuselage. The Cessna C150 trailing edges and ridges that covered the bottom of the flaps, ailerons, and elevators, cut into my legs, arms, and torso as I tried to reach the aircraft's right-side door.

It would take several seconds before I finally made my way over the fuselage and back into the water. By that time, part of the right side of the wing was already submerged, as the plane continued to fill with water through the open windows and the broken-out windshield.

Desperately trying to reach the passenger door, I grabbed the wing's upward-extruding flap and forcefully pushed it down flush with the airfoil surface. I lunged onto the wing to reach the door latch, and yanked at the door handle several times before it eventually swung outward with a force. The pressure differential between the air in the cabin and the water on the outside of the partially submerged door made the resistance difficult to overcome. When it finally opened, water rushed in violently, as if a dam had been unleashed, adding to the inflow of water inside.

The water pierced my eyes and gushed into my mouth as it rushed around my head and into the cabin. There was so much flow through the door opening I could neither see nor hear Dianne as I struggled to reach in. With my torso partially submerged in the freezing lake, I held the door open with my right hand, while trying to reach Dianne in her seat with my left.

I was sure I would be able to get to her once the pressure equalized around the cockpit door. But that was not to be because *what I thought was the passenger door was actually the pilot's door*. During the impact and my disorientation, I did not realize that when the plane flipped over, the pilot and passenger positions had been reversed, as viewed from the rear of the plane. This inversion not only caused Dianne to be suspended upside-down by her seatbelts, but also put her farthest from the door I had opened.

During the entire time I tried to reach her, the plane continuously filled with water, and the buoyancy eventually gave way to the weight of the aircraft. With the rear panel removed, there was no air cavity to sustain the aircraft above the water line. From the time I had been catapulted through the windshield to the moment I reached and opened the door, it had taken no longer than fifteen to twenty seconds. But that was enough for the aircraft to submerge below the surface.

Watching the plane disappear in front of my eyes while knowing Dianne was still alive inside was indescribably horrifying.

Twenty seconds before, Dianne and I were two of the happiest people on Earth. We were heading off on the greatest adventure of our lives.

But now, the girl I loved—the girl I left home to spend the rest of my life with—went down with the plane in front of me, and there was nothing I could do to save her.

In that one instant, my life was torn to pieces.

Both of our worlds had ended.

Act I: State Case

I who now have nothing,

have my family twice over,

and that is most comforting of all.

CHAPTER THREE

My Life in a Box

August 30 – September 5, 2006
Day 1 – 7

Yesterday was the first day of my second-life reboot; today is the beginning of the end of my twenty-four-year journey home, and I am ready.

AS A FUGITIVE in the United States for the past twenty-four years, it was inevitable my past would eventually catch up, but I always imagined a different scenario for my return.

Early Wednesday morning, Carolyn called as usual to start off our day with a smile. We had been dating off and on for over two and a half years, and that morning was no different. After light-hearted chitchat, I hung up the phone and took Cal, my Blue-Fronted Amazon parrot (see Document: 7511 @ www.ambrozuk.com), outside on his perch to get some fresh air and a bit of sun during the cooler morning hours. Dressed in yellow workout shorts and a T-shirt, I sat down with my laptop at the coffee table in my living room to check emails and work on my ongoing projects.

It was approximately four thirty in the afternoon when I heard my doorbell ring. I walked into the entryway and noticed a gray pickup truck parked in front of my house.

When I opened the door, a man dressed in plain street clothes and holding papers in his hands fervidly asked, "Are you Michael Smith?"

Before I could answer, a second man appeared from behind the shaded small window next to the door and pointed a gun in my face, his arms fully extended. The two men quickly moved me inside. They handcuffed my hands behind my back and pulled out one of my dining-room chairs. As they hovered around me, two more men—who had likely been staking out the backyard in case I got wise and decided to run—walked in through the front door.

All four looked like good ol' Texas boys—clean-cut, in their twenties or thirties. Each wore a white polo shirt with a holstered gun at their side. I didn't know if they were bounty hunters, sheriff deputies, or some sort of undercover cops, but none seemed eager to present their credentials.

Everything happened so quickly in the first few moments that I felt disoriented and unsure of what the chaotic scene meant. As two of the men began searching the house, the others remained at my side and began their interrogation.

"What is your real name?" one of them demanded in a raised voice. "Say it! It will be easier on you!" His aggressive tone seemed puzzling at first, but when I glanced at the papers in his hands with the words "JAROSLAW CZESLAW AMBROZUK" typed in bold letters at the top, everything became clear.

Remaining calm as I processed everything that was happening, one of the men then blurted out, "You're going to jail!"

Over the years I saw enough TV cop shows to be familiar with the constitutional protocols the arresting officers typically followed, but for some reason during my arrest, there would be no Miranda rights read and no charges mentioned.

All they were interested in was reconnaissance as I sat quietly while their wandering partners repeatedly asked, "Is there anyone else in the house?"

"No!" I replied to each of their inquiries, but they insisted on verifying. They swept through the upstairs and downstairs rooms—checking all the bedroom and hallway closets—before conceding I was home alone.

Throughout this entire ordeal I remained calm and not very talkative, responding only when addressed. The only request I made was to bring my parrot indoors because he would inevitably jump off his perch if left alone in the scorching Texas sun. Using a stick from under the cage, they eventually managed to put him back in his cage while we waited for the Plano police to arrive.

Within a half hour, a Plano police officer showed up in his squad car and parked in front of my neighbor's mailbox to take me to the city jail.

Not being allowed to change, I put on my flip-flops lying in the entry way and began the short walk to the car with my hands cuffed behind my back. There was no commotion—no neighborhood onlookers to witness my escort to the squad car—and because the entire operation took only minutes, no media as one of the arresting officers pointed out.

We arrived at the Plano City Jail twenty minutes later. I was taken to the book-in area and patted down before being told to change into a pair of orange pants and a short sleeve shirt.

It would be another half hour before I was instructed to step up to a sheet-metal counter and place my hands flat on the top, while the female officer opposite me began to ask some unusual questions. "What season is it?", "How many months are there in a year?", "Have you ever attempted suicide?" and, "Are you considering suicide now?" They were not the typical questions I had expected, but then I realized they might be the direct result of my calm emotional state during my arrest that set off the red flags.

When we finished, they took my mug shots and asked if I wanted my five-minute free phone call. Eager to call Carolyn and tell her what had happened, I enthusiastically replied, "Yes, please!" before being moved into an isolated cell with a direct line out.

On my first attempt, I got Carolyn's cell phone voice mail and left a brief message telling her that I was in jail, that authorities knew who I really was, and that this was not a joke. But I knew she always had her phone with her, so I tried again and this time I got her live. She remained calm for the most part during our brief conversation, and when her initial shock subsided, she asked how I was doing. I could sense she was trying to remain positive and focused in between her gentle sobs, but in general, I was handling the situation much better than she. This was a long time coming, and now that it was out in the open, my current predicament didn't seem as important as my upcoming first contact with my family after so many years.

During my arrest, I noticed on the rap sheet the charge of negligent homicide, and a $20,000 bond originally set in Montana in 1982. Since my identity had been discovered, I was ready to clear things up, but I preferred to do it on the outside, and asked Carolyn to withdraw that amount from my Merrill Lynch account using an ATM machine.

As it turned out, that would just be wishful thinking, because an hour later I was called out of my cell again to answer more questions—this time by an Immigration and Naturalization Service (INS) agent. Using a regular telephone that sat on the metal counter where I was originally processed, the man on the other end politely introduced himself before starting with carefully phrased basic questions, making sure I couldn't reply with a simple "Yes" or "No."

When he asked for my name, I automatically responded with "Michael Smith," not realizing what that actually meant in my current circumstance. But when he asked who "Jaroslaw Czeslaw Ambrozuk" was, and what country he was a citizen of, it slowly dawned on me where this was heading. I wasn't trying to evade his inquiries or lie about my identity, but after living as "Michael Smith" for so many years, the two were practically synonymous in my mind. In my state of confusion, I wasn't sure what the correct answer was.

The INS agent was persistent and asked again about the citizenship of "Jaroslaw Czeslaw Ambrozuk." I briefly paused to gather my thoughts then replied, "Canada," before pleading the Fifth as the man on the other end continued to pry.

Confused and worried about incriminating myself further, I asked to speak with an attorney. But that was not the cooperative reply he was looking for and calmly said, "If you refuse to answer, I will have to put a detainer on you."

I may have been somewhat disoriented at that moment, but I was rational enough to realize that my fate was sealed the second I picked up the phone, and I simply replied, "I think you already made up your mind about that anyway."

And that, according to the date on the document, was when my immigration detainer was filed (see Document: 3900 @ www.ambrozuk. com), preventing me from getting out, even if I posted my $20,000 state bond.

Less than an hour later, I was transported to the Collin County Detention Facility in McKinney, Texas, by a female officer. After being booked in, I was placed in the infirmary for several days under the watchful eyes of the guards, making sure I wasn't suicidal.

Satisfied I wasn't a threat to myself based on my unusually calm demeanor, they moved me to a cell in maximum security two days later. The pod had individual cells forming a concentric circle on two floor levels. The place was packed and it was loud: people yelling at the guards and at each other, with the occasional song or a percussion ensemble to brighten up the day. Everything one would expect from a maximum-security pod.

Considering the circumstances, I remained complacent in my new surroundings for the most part. I went through much worse after the accident and had learned to adapt, making this more of an inconvenience rather than a hindrance, despite the food being atrocious. The unsightly and repugnant child-size portions seemed more suited for a pig trough than human consumption, but when your stomach is growling throughout the day, you tend to compromise on principles. I didn't know if that was typical of a detention center, but at the very least I expected to lose significant weight over the next few months while on the "Incarceration Instant Diet."

According to the Inmate Handbook, I was entitled to one hour per day out of my cell to either take a shower, use the phone, watch TV, and/or go out on the REC (recreation) yard. Normally, there would be plenty of time to shower, make a couple of phone calls, and still have time to at least watch some TV, but imagine doing all that while in full restraints. For some peculiar reason, each time I left the cell, they insisted on shackling my hands and feet to restrict my movement. As you can imagine, that made phone calls inconvenient. Showers were even more challenging, with only one free hand to wash my hair and body.

Despite the loud noise in the pod, I eventually managed to dial out and speak with Carolyn. Through her sobs and tears, she said she was taking care of my house and my parrot, had already located an attorney whom I would meet with the next day, and even contacted my family in Canada. During our brief conversation, I could tell the shock of my arrest and the local media attention were adding to her emotional distress, but to survive this with minimal scathing, we both needed to remain strong.

Everything seemed chaotic, but there were a few moments of clarity, and on Saturday that saving grace came in the form of a phone call to my parents in Canada. The conversation started with a statement of the detention center's validation process recording, followed by a warning message about the call being taped, before I finally heard my parents' voice. But to my surprise, I had no idea what they were saying.

Growing up, we always had spoken in our native language, but now, after twenty-four years and not a single word uttered in Polish, the language seemed all but foreign. After a brief explanation, we shifted gears and began what was to be the first of many conversations in English. This was the first time we had spoken after so many years, but it felt as if we had never missed a beat.

Our fifteen minutes passed quickly, but in that time I discovered that my sister, Renata, was married to a doctor, had three kids, and lived fairly close to the rest of the family in the Vancouver, British Columbia area. When I left in 1982, she was just fourteen. Now she was a wife and a mother with three kids. How amazing was that? Of course, that made me an uncle, and I could not help but smile in the moment.

My dad also said he not only had prayed for me every day, but the reason they had never moved from the house I'd grown up in was so that one day I could find them. And that is pretty much when I lost it. Tears started pouring down my face, and all I could think of was how lucky I was to have such devoted parents. I'm not an openly emotional guy, but hearing that unexpectedly made me realize how much I had missed them.

My parents, like many European families, always carried themselves with a sense of pride. Growing up, there was constant preaching about how hard they worked so that my sister and I wouldn't have to. They always wanted us to get an education and be successful, and now, hearing about my life, they also seemed proud of my accomplishments. The conversation was brief, but it was great to hear that everyone was doing well and that we would soon be seeing each other in person. It had been twenty-four years since I last saw my sister and my parents, and I very much looked forward to our reunion.

During my subsequent call to Carolyn, I also found out that Tom, my best friend from high school, never became a lawyer as he once had planned. He would have been a great resource in my corner, especially for my state case. Instead, Carolyn found Kevin Clancy, a local attorney referred to us by a friend of a friend.

It was early Saturday afternoon when I was called out of my cell, under full restraints, and escorted to the visitation booth to meet with the attorney. Looking seasoned and authoritative, Mr. Clancy wasted no time introducing himself as he ran down his résumé, disclosing some of the more famous celebrity cases he had represented in the past. His credentials were extensive but more suited to football superstars and their flamboyant lifestyles than an elopement-gone-horribly-wrong case.

Warning that we needed to be careful about our conversation because we were being recorded, he then went off about how the feds and INS are going after people like me and not the al-Qaeda, etc. To make his point, he punctuated his disapproval, "I hope they hear us, those sons of bitches!"

Hearing that, all I could do was look at him and think, *Have you lost your freakin' mind or are you just trying to piss everyone off for no particular reason?* His angry, school-bully attitude served no purpose, and that was when I first began to question whether he was the right attorney to handle my case. Eventually, he calmed down and we moved on to the purpose of our meeting.

There were several complications with my case, beginning with my negligent homicide charge. Since the warrant for my arrest was issued in Montana, I would first need to be extradited, but because he didn't have jurisdiction there, he was opposed to the move.

My identity and passport were his other concerns. Once I got a U.S. passport, it became a federal case, and more charges could follow. Originally, I was concerned only about the negligent homicide charge, but now I realized he was right, and I could potentially face more legal issues.

Although he had some good points to share, it was clear we didn't see eye to eye about my representation and the state case defense strategy. Fighting extradition to Montana and insisting it would be difficult for the state government to prove I killed Dianne was not my idea of defense, and frankly, did nothing but irk me. Perhaps it was his tone of voice, or perhaps because he callously used the word "killed"—echoing what some media outlets were reporting—that I finally stopped him to explain.

"Listen to me, Kevin. This is not about trying to cover things up because I killed somebody. This is about the truth. This has been hanging over my head for twenty-four years and it needs to be cleared up. This is not about murder. This is about two naive kids who fell in love, eloped, and in a middle of it all a dreadful accident occurred that resulted in a tragic death!"

Apparently that got his attention, because at that moment he changed his tone and demeanor. He asked a few more questions about my pilot's license and whether there was any evidence to support our elopement, but this time it was with a more positive temperament. In fact, he became so accommodating that even the $50,000 retainer he originally quoted Carolyn would be considerably less, he said, because of my willingness to be extradited, thereby making his representation in Texas practically obsolete.

On Tuesday, my parents flew down to Texas eager to see me. But our reunion would have to wait because, unofficially, I had refused visitations. According to the reporters who checked with the Collin County Detention Facility, I had no one listed for a visit, which was complete rubbish. Two days beforehand, I had written Carolyn, Brian (Carolyn's brother-in-law), and my friends Kimberly and Ken Sivaraman as my visitation contacts.

It took a while, but I finally connected the dots, and realized why I was singled out and placed in the maximum-security pod with full restraints and a visitation ban. After I was processed and rebooked at the Collin County Detention Facility, following mug shots, a hefty female officer began asking me personal questions, including my height, weight, the color of my eyes, and my citizenship status. And that is when things went south.

Being aware of my circumstances, and not wanting to incriminate myself further, I politely said to the booking officer, "I'm not trying to be difficult but I think I need to speak with an attorney before I answer any more questions." After living under an assumed name for twenty-four years, my request seemed reasonable.

But she was not going to take "No" for an answer. She looked perturbed, turned to the group of officers standing behind her, and, in an irritated voice bellowed, "He's refusing to answer!"

The room went silent for a moment before one, perhaps their superior, addressed me in a commanding voice. "Answer the questions or we'll take away your privileges!"

I once again tried to politely request an attorney, but by then my fate was sealed.

Mistaking my cautiousness about U.S. vs. Canadian citizenship as uncooperative behavior, the booking officers were not going to let me slide without teaching me a lesson, and that's why I ended up in the maximum-security pod under full restraints and no visitation.

In retrospect, it seemed trivial to think I would have a problem differentiating between my citizenship status, but this occurred the same night I was arrested after living under an alias for almost a quarter of a century. Michael Smith was a U.S. citizen, and for all intents and purposes, I was still Michael Smith when everyone started referring to me as Jaroslaw Czeslaw Ambrozuk. Although in the back of my mind I knew otherwise, shifting identity gears that quickly, after living so many years as a U.S. citizen, wasn't as easy as one might think. It was an innocent mistake I would pay a harsh penalty for, but I was still hopeful it could be easily rectified by my new attorney, Leigh Warren Davis.

It was Sunday when I met with the replacement lawyer. He was the friend of the family Carolyn contacted but, being out of town, had been unable to meet, and therefore recommended Kevin Clancy. Our initial conversation went well, and despite splitting his litigation time equally between civil and criminal cases, he appeared confident and knowledgeable as he explained his version of the current facts and events.

Flathead County in Montana had a pending warrant against me for a negligent homicide charge that carried zero to twenty years maximum imprisonment, with the bond set at $20,000. But immigration appeared to be the more problematic case now. They had placed a detainer on me that not only didn't carry a bond but prohibited me from bailing out even if I posted the $20,000 state bond.

And if things weren't complicated enough, he also brought up the federal government and the possibly of "False Statement of U.S. Citizenship" felony charges. There was a chance these would not be pursued because of my exemplary record in the United States, but it was highly unlikely according to the attorney.

I hoped my positive history in the U.S. during the past two decades would be incentive enough for the federal government to look the other way, but like his predecessor, Mr. Davis wasn't very optimistic about my chances—not only with the federal government but also with the state case.

Like Mr. Clancy, he suggested I contest the extradition for the time being so that he could contact not only the State of Montana prosecutor to discuss the case, but also give us time to locate a local attorney in Flathead County.

I wasn't thrilled about the idea of delaying the state case now that my whereabouts were known, and it was all over the news, but I decided to sit tight for the time being.

With nothing to do all day but listen to the excessive noise in the pod, I decided to begin writing a journal to pass time and maintain my sanity. But that proved easier said than done.

For safety reasons, only plastic, flexible BIC pen refills were allowed in the pod, making any prolonged writing painful as my hand quickly cramped up while gripping the tiny writing instrument between my fingers. Fortunately, being a true engineer at heart, I found a solution. Using a long thread from my blanket, I tied the pen to my toothbrush handle for support, and that seemed to do the trick. Classified as an "indigent," I was initially given five sheets of paper to write on, but once my commissary supplies arrived, I began to fill in the details about my new, and hopefully temporary, life (see Document: 7452 @ www. ambrozuk.com).

A few days earlier, I had been enjoying happy-hour specials with Carolyn, sitting on the patio with my Viper parked in front. Now, I was in an eight-by-twelve-foot cell at the Collin County Detention Facility wondering what my future held.

Considering the predicament I had gotten myself into was now out of my control, all I could do was be patient and let the legal system work itself through. I may have been in somewhat of a daze after my arrest, but I could not help wonder what my life would be like for the next few months. The surprising thing was that I was not worried about the outcome of my negligent homicide charge as much as I was ecstatic about finally reuniting with my family after twenty-four years.

It was odd to have my priorities in turmoil, but in that moment that was my reality—a bathroom-sized cell where freedom was limited, but time was aplenty.

CHAPTER FOUR

Waiver of Extradition

September 6 – 19, 2006
Day 8 – 21

AFTER MY LATE-MORNING one hour REC on Wednesday, I got a call from one of the guards telling me that I was going to see the judge. Within an hour, I was in a squad car heading for the courthouse.

Unshaven, with a half-inch long scruffy beard, I walked into the courtroom at 2:00 p.m. under a two-deputy escort. Sitting diagonally from me, approximately ten feet away, Judge Parker was shielded behind his podium, with an officer standing to his right.

When the hearing began, he made several attempts at pronouncing my full name, before he recited my Miranda rights and explained that the hearing was regarding my extradition to Montana.

When asked what I wanted to do, I confidently replied, "I am declining extradition," as per the discussion with my attorney. But that didn't go over well with the judge. Declining extradition would not only require both the Texas and Montana governors to approve my transport—which could take months—but it would also give the media an excuse to speculate (see Document: 2111 @ www.ambrozuk.com).

Curious if I would reconsider, the judge asked again, but I stood firm by my decision. "Your Honor, I currently have an attorney and we're working on establishing counsel in Montana."

He seemed confused. "You have an attorney in Montana?"

"My attorney is local," I clarified, "but as I understand it, he has no license to practice in Montana, so we're trying to find local counsel there before my extradition."

Although this was all the judge needed to know, for some reason I felt I should further explain myself, so I voluntarily added, "This has been hanging over my head for twenty-four years, and I really want this cleared up. But before I get extradited I was told to hold off until we have someone in Montana representing me."

Perhaps not thrilled with my decision, he nonetheless once again verified my refusal before passing down a document for me to sign via the court officer to make it official.

When the hearing was over and we returned to the squad car, I assumed I would head back to my cell, but instead we went in the opposite direction to yet another courthouse that also served as the local county tax-assessor collector's office where I once registered my Viper.

There I was brought before Judge David Ortley, who was dressed in his official courtroom black robe. He looked familiar, but I couldn't place his face until I remembered our encounter at the Collin County Detention Facility a few days before, when he interrupted my attorney visit with Kevin Clancy.

Then dressed in a casual suit, he walked in on us during our first orientation to ask my name and if I was a U.S. citizen. I told him I needed to speak to my attorney before answering that question and got on the phone with Mr. Clancy who advised me to "Plead the Fifth Amendment." The man looked displeased with my response and simply walked off. But now here I was staring him in the face with no idea what his agenda was.

It didn't take long before I was told it was about my bail. My original negligent homicide charge from 1982 was accompanied by a $20,000 bond (see Document: 3001 @ www.ambrozuk.com) but, perhaps to discourage me from posting bail and leaving the custody of the state, Judge Ortley now increased it to $100,000. As I already had an immigration detainer preventing me from bonding out, this seemed redundant. But apparently it was necessary, if for nothing more than to give him additional satisfaction of security before he adjourned the hearing and I returned to the detention facility.

On Friday during our regular daily phone call, Carolyn said that after consulting with her father, a non-practicing attorney himself, they felt Mr. Davis was stalling and didn't seem enthusiastic about finding an attorney in Montana. Instead, she took the initiative and found Patrick Sherlock of Sherlock & Nardy in Kalispell, Montana. Although his now-retired partner was the one with the impressive criminal case history, Mr. Sherlock, by association, appeared like a viable alternative.

Sounding genuinely sympathetic on the phone, he suggested that the case could be dismissed once we went over the evidence, but I remained cautiously optimistic. During his introductory speech, he was quick to point out that he knew the local authorities well and was particularly close to the judge presiding over my case. Not only had he known him for close to forty years but also had attended his wedding. He said this gave him a significant advantage over other lawyers in the area.

He was adamant about beginning my extradition as soon as possible, so when I returned to my cell, I promptly filled out an Inmate Request Form, explaining my current situation (see Document: 4054 @ www.ambrozuk.com) before submitting it to the Jail Case Coordinator.

I remained tentative about Mr. Sherlock based on our conversation, but I believed this to be a step in the right direction, despite my Texas attorney's strong objection to the extradition.

It didn't take long for my paperwork to go through. First thing the following Tuesday, I was picked up by two deputies and transported to the courthouse to amend my extradition stance. When we arrived in court, I was taken in front of Judge James Fry. Wasting no time, he asked for my name and if I had a lawyer. When I explained I did, but that I would have a different one in Montana, he insisted on speaking with my local attorney before we continued with the hearing. It took close to forty-five minutes before they brought me back into the courtroom and the judge confirmed that my attorney, Mr. Davis, conceded to my extradition. I signed four duplicate copies to finalize the paperwork, the judge wished me good luck, and the two officers drove me back to the detention center.

But when I got back to my cell and called Carolyn, there would be more bad news. This time it was about John Bodnar, of JB's Corvette Specialists, who was after my 1981 Corvette.

The car had been in his shop for the past six years because the repairs I had paid for were not done properly. Finding out about my arrest on the news, he now refused to release the car to Carolyn—despite the power of attorney that Mr. Davis had prepared. To make matters worse, he also told her that unless my Corvette was picked up by the rightful owner, he was keeping it.

While confused as to why our power of attorney seemed useless, I was not about to let this man steal my car after I invested upwards of $15,000 for its restoration, with $6,000 of that going to Mr. Bodnar for his repairs. Partly out of principle, I asked Carolyn to find another attorney who could deal with this latest complication.

> *In case you're keeping score, in less than three weeks this was the fourth attorney I needed to hire: Clancy (dismissed), Davis (my current Texas attorney), Sherlock (potential Montana attorney), and now someone to deal with the car repossession issue.*

During Thursday's mail call, I got a letter from Mr. Davis (see Document: 5057 @ www.ambrozuk.com) who, in addition to re-emphasizing his extradition disapproval, also pointed out some good news: the State of Montana would have to prosecute me on the negligent homicide felony as if it were 1982. This meant possible incarceration in a range of zero to ten years, rather than zero to twenty years as it currently stood in 2006. It was a small consolation, but it would come in handy if we ever went to trial.

Hygiene and cleanliness was encouraged in the detention center, but after two weeks of razor denial by the guards, I started to resemble "Brawny Man." I was prepared to deal with the unshaven look, but the constant itching on my face I could have done without. Despite filling out an "Inmate Medical Charge Sheet" for my "Clipper Pass," they would not give me a razor because I was housed in the maximum-security pod. As an alternative, the nurse suggested I get a shave and a haircut from the detention center barber. A pretty good deal for ten bucks, but done only once a week, on Mondays.

During my call to Carolyn on Saturday, I also found out interesting details about my arrest—the watering ticket citation I got from the City of Plano for using my sprinklers on the wrong day was just a setup. The sheriff's deputies—or whoever they were—moved the notice from my neighbor's door as bait. When they saw the notice gone from my front door knob, it was their signal that I was home. Carolyn said they had tried arresting me twice before: once when I was at my orthodontist, and again on Monday when I was playing racquetball. Whatever happened to simply calling my home phone to see if I answered?

I suppose I should have considered myself lucky that the timing of the arrest worked out as it did. If they had waited just a few more days, they would have found me with four of my front teeth missing. After months of deliberation and several visits to the orthodontist, I was about to commit to gold-plated braces from Germany that would require four of my teeth being pulled. Can you picture my mug shots, or how I would look when talking to the judge with four missing teeth? Worse yet, what would have happened if the orthodontist had installed the braces before I got arrested? Would they have let me out every two weeks for an adjustment? An interesting dilemma I'm happy to have avoided.

After my one-hour-out on Sunday morning—when I was finally allowed to take a shower without shackles—I returned to my cell and spent the rest of the day silently deliberating my arrest, trying to figure out who had turned me into the authorities.

There were only four people who were close to me and knew about my past. I had told Carolyn and my best friend Kim over a year and a half before, so the timing seemed illogical. I dated Carolyn for years, and although we broke up for a while, we were back together again, so that didn't make any sense. Kim and Ken were a possibility because of our parting ways in the last few weeks over disagreements surrounding a possible future business venture. But after six years of a close friendship with Kim, I found it difficult to believe they would be responsible.

And therefore, through the process of elimination, all my deductive reasoning pointed to the only person who was angry and spiteful enough to do such a thing; the only one with an incentive to be so insidious—and her name was Genea.

Although this was simply speculation while in the Collin County Detention Facility, my hypothesis would be confirmed after I was extradited to Montana and given the stack of evidence that surrounded my case. There I would find the undeniable proof of confirmation.

CHAPTER FIVE

Innocent Days of Bliss

1963 – 1973

I WAS BORN on July 22, 1963 to Tadeusz and Halina in the small town of Kłodzko, Poland. Located in the southwest corner of Poland next to the Czech Republic border, Kłodzko paled in comparison to the larger cities around the country, but it had its appeal. As with many towns in Europe, it had castle ruins shrouded in legends and mysterious, impregnable fortresses. But it also had suburbs where many of the townsfolk lived, including my family. It was there that I grew up and spent the first ten and a half years of my happy childhood (see Document: 1014 @ www.ambrozuk.com).

My parents met in 1960 at a church social gathering, and were married a couple of years later. At the time, my father was a truck driver working for a local company; my mother worked in an office until I was born. Following the customs and traditions of a Catholic family, my mom would eventually take on the role of raising children at home while my dad supported our family on a single, modest salary.

While my mom's family lived within the vicinity of Kłodzko, my dad's relatives, including his only twin sister, were in Białystok, a large city in the northeast corner of Poland, adjacent to the Russian border. We would visit them on occasion, but my life as a preschooler generally revolved around my maternal relatives, with plenty of kids my age to play and share toys with.

My parents rented a house close to my elementary school (see Document: 1017 @ www.ambrozuk.com), but we spent most of our time at my grandparents' home, thirty minutes walking distance from where we lived. My grandparents' house was old and rundown, but cozy, and there were always lots of things to do and explore. Among the crop fields the local residents used for growing vegetables, like potatoes and cucumbers, there were also cherry and apple trees to climb and fill up on during the harvest season.

But the most exciting place to hang out was the valley behind the plowed fields. There were fields of grass where cattle grazed and a small pond that had an island with a large tree at its center.

During the dry season, when the water subsided, a small pathway emerged, and we could reach the island without getting our feet wet. My friends and I spent hours at a time on that island, chasing colorful dragonflies and entertaining frogs that jumped between the few lily pads scattered in the shallow water.

The pond was full of wonders during the summer months, and even more so during winter, when the water froze and the amphibians that once croaked with excitement now silently rested in hibernation under the ice. Bundled in warm winter clothes, my friends and I often visited the icy pond to observe in amazement the seemingly lifeless frogs that were sure to return in the spring.

Between building snowmen in winter and racing the hand-carved tree bark sailboats in the summer, we kept busy without the need for extravagant toys. We rode bikes, roller-skated, and played soccer when the weather permitted, and every now and then got into innocent trouble all in good fun.

Running around with my friends was always enjoyable, but my fondest memories of that early age were with my family. I loved the home cooking that came from my grandma's kitchen almost as much as the hot, fresh bread and buns she bought at the local bakery each morning at 4:00 a.m. and had waiting for me when I got up.

To make ends meet, my grandparents bought necessities at the nearby local store, but the rest of the produce they grew themselves. There were always fresh eggs from our poultry on the table, and on occasion, I helped my grandfather catch a chicken or a rabbit before he prepared it for that special Christmas or Easter dinner.

Along with the rest of my friends in the neighborhood, I started elementary school at the age of seven. Dressed in a standard black uniform with a white-collared shirt, I enthusiastically headed off to school every morning (see Document: 1002 @ www.ambrozuk.com). There was always homework to do when I got home, but with my mother's patience, I would always be prepared for the next day.

While my mom took care of the kids, my dad looked for ways to make ends meet and improve his family's lifestyle. Working fourteen-hour days—first as a truck driver and eventually a taxi driver—didn't give him much time to socialize, but he was at church every Sunday with his family. Like 95 percent of Catholics in Poland, we were quite religious and strictly abided by doctrine of the church.

But unlike the repetitive Sunday masses, the holidays were always memorable in our little family circle. During Easter, and especially Christmas, everything was festive, whether at our house, at my grandparents', or at one of my mother's siblings' homes. Each year, all the kids waited what felt like forever until St. Nicholas came and we could open the presents under the tree (see Document: 1003 @ www.ambrozuk.com). During those holidays, with the joyous mood in the air, all the best plates and cutlery came out, as everyone ate the gourmet dishes that took days to prepare, while toasting with the best vodka money could buy.

Although Poland was still under Communist rule at the time, with things like meat and deli products scarce, everyone constantly looked to improving their way of life, including my father. It was through his uncle in New Westminster, British Columbia that he would eventually get the opportunity for us to migrate to the West.

During my Great-Uncle Joseph's visit to Poland, I listened to dinner conversations about how amazing Canada was. One could walk into a store to buy Levi jeans, and everyone could afford a car if they so wished. The tales seemed almost too good to be true, and I could only imagine the wonders that the other side of the world had to offer.

Invited to Canada on a work-permit visa, my father boarded a cruise ship in Gdańsk and sailed for ten days to New York before flying to Vancouver. As an immigrant, he initially worked at a small automotive brake shop before moving on to become a mechanic at a large trucking company, from where he would eventually retire.

My mother, on the other hand, took care of my sister and me with the help of my grandparents. During his absence, my father sent letters and called us once a month at the only phone in the neighborhood—the coffin-maker's shop located behind my grandparents' house. There was lots of catching up during those expensive twenty to thirty minute con- versations— everything from an update on his progress in Canada to how things were going back home. But my favorite part was always the promise of a surprise package that arrived during the holidays. Among the canned ham, there was often candy, chocolate bars, or the Quik Chocolate powder mix that I waited for with anticipation.

In my father's absence, my family managed the best we could with the money my dad periodically sent via Western Union. Back then, the exchange rate between the Canadian dollar and Złoty was significant enough for my mother to devote herself to raising us, rather than work- ing a full-time job to make ends meet.

Because religion played a big part in our life, once I was old enough, I began serving mass as an altar boy, not only multiple times every Sunday, but during the special weekly masses throughout the year. My favorite time of year was always during Christmas, when the priest, along with two altar boys, walked from house to house every night to bless each home and its residents. The white powder snow that blan- keted the roads and sidewalks during our nightly treks often reminded me of the picturesque landscape on a postcard.

Maturing from a preschooler to a ten-year-old under the careful guidance of my mother and grandparents, I spent much time with my family over dinners, listening to their stories of politics, religion, and their past. One of my favorites was about my grandfather and his brush with death while a prisoner during World War II. During the Holocaust, Hitler and the Nazis killed between five and six million Jews, and close to two million non-Jewish Poles. The fact that my grandfather managed to escape their clutches was nothing short of a miracle.

He was taken by the Nazis to Auschwitz—a concentration camp— for extermination. Spending several months in the camp with his life hanging by a thread, he got a break when the guards picked him, along with three others, to investigate the smell that was coming from the sewers. Unclear if it was bodies or dead animals decomposing, the four prisoners entered the sewer maze to locate the stench. Heading in various directions, each took a tunnel to inspect—and by a sheer stroke of luck, the one that my grandfather was searching had a manhole that led to street level. He climbed the ladder to the top and lifted the cover slightly to see if there were pedestrians nearby. Crossing himself, he climbed out into the street and eventually made his way back home.

Such heartfelt stories had a profound impact on my young life, just as much as the possibility of moving to the western world to start anew. Because of Canada's immigration laws and Poland's red tape, my dad's sponsorship would take almost three and a half years to complete. In the meantime, there were preparations to be made, including learning English.

The idea of picking up a few words before we left for Canada seemed prudent, but in reality we made little progress. After almost a year of one-hour-per-week English classes, our vocabulary was limited to a few basic words and the ability to count to twenty, topped only by our unprecedented rendition of the classic New-Canadian song, "My Bonny Lies over the Ocean."

But all that seemed insignificant when our visas arrived, and my mother, my now five-year-old sister, and I boarded an airplane in

Warsaw on a direct international flight to Canada. For a ten-and-a-half-year-old coming from a small town, the thirteen-hour flight—my first!—was exciting. But it would pale in comparison to the wonders I would see and experience after we landed at YVR airport in Vancouver, British Columbia.

CHAPTER SIX

The Lynch Mob Awaits

September 20 – October 4, 2006
Day 22 – 36

AFTER WAIVING EXTRADITION, on September 20, I got a call from a Collin County Detention Facility officer on my intercom telling me to pack up all my belongings because I was going "ATW" (all the way), as they later clarified. I was told to place all my personal belongings in a clear plastic bag. Other than the clothes on my back, anything else from the detention center would go into my bed sack.

Two officers showed up twenty minutes later and placed me in full restraints. They took me to the checkout desk where I changed into my yellow shorts, shirt, and flip-flops that I had been wearing when I came in. A female officer motioned for me to sign off on the release of my property before giving me an eighty-dollar check for the balance of my commissary account.

When all the check-out formalities were completed and the rest of the release papers signed, a tall, fairly stocky gentleman dressed in street clothes walked up and introduced himself as Michael Meehan, the undersheriff of Flathead County. In a firm voice, the deputy explained, "I'm here to take you back to Montana. If you try to run . . .," he paused briefly to get my attention, "I will do whatever is necessary to stop you. Do you understand?"

"Yes, sir!" I confirmed, before the deputy re-shackled me using the irons he brought in a small black bag. He first placed a thick leather belt around my waist before attaching my handcuffs to it and placing leg irons around my socks.

Fully secured, we drove to Dallas-Fort Worth airport and arrived at approximately 1:30 p.m. Because of security, we were the first to board the aircraft at around 4:30 p.m. and made our way to the last row, occupying seats 25A and 25B. When we landed in Minneapolis two and a half hours later, we transferred to a different airline that was on the other side of the airport. The trek through the airport walkways was painful as I shuffled my feet in irons like an old man, with onlookers staring, before reaching the departure gate.

Waiting to board the aircraft, I declined an offer of food from the deputy, as it would have been awkward to eat in front of others in the lobby while in handcuffs. Instead, I asked to use his cell phone to call Carolyn and let her know I was on my way to Flathead County, Montana.

Once in the air, we made a stop at Great Falls International Airport, Montana to unload and pick up new passengers before heading to our final destination, the Kalispell Airport. Our last leg took less than an hour and once everyone disembarked, we walked out into the lobby where two other officers in brown uniforms were already waiting for our arrival.

I was big news in the little town of Kalispell, where the twenty-four-year-old mystery was about to unravel. Along with local spectators, the media were gathered in the main lobby straining to get a glimpse at the fugitive who had eluded the Flathead County authorities for so many years.

As we slowly descended the escalator towards the inquisitive mob, I could hear the rapid fire of snapping camera shutters from the reporters gathered in the crowd. There was a big video camera suspended on one man's shoulder and a large boom microphone overhanging the crowd, waiting to capture every sound that came out of my mouth.

Once on the ground floor, the crowd quieted as I was motioned by one of the officers to head toward the SUV parked just outside the airport exit doors. Still approaching in silence, a female reporter pointed her microphone at me and asked, "Do you have anything to say?"

"Not right now, ma'am," I said, as I continued my slow walk through the crowd toward the SUV.

Not satisfied, she tried again with a more direct approach. "Do you have anything to say to Dianne's parents?"

Briefly glancing in her direction, I reiterated "Not right now," and continued toward the exit doors.

This was neither the time nor the place to make statements to people who were there just for sensationalism. There would be plenty of time for that later. Over the years the media, along with the outspoken Sheriff Dupont of Flathead County, made plenty of accusations about what happened during the night of the accident. The only way to clear this up now was to have my day in court.

When we eventually arrived at the Flathead County Detention Center (FCDC), I was escorted into the main lobby area for booking. Unlike the McKinney, Texas detention facility that housed approximately 1,000 inmates, here the capacity was closer to 100, and seemed much more personable.

The first thing they did was remove my restraints and pat me down, explaining that everyone there moved around the facility un-cuffed, with their hands cupped behind their back. I was offered the option to take a quick shower before being given my new wardrobe: an orange long-sleeve, sweater-like shirt with "Flathead County Jail" printed in white on the back, a pair of blue sweatpants with the same label printed on the left leg, and a pair of pink socks along with burgundy shower shoes. But unlike the Collin County Detention Facility, there would be no underwear option—whether offered, or for purchase; here "commando" was apparently the standard.

By then it was already 1:30 a.m., and the officer in charge said I would be booked the next day because of the late hour. They moved me to a temporary private cell around the corner for the night.

When I walked in, it was obvious that the "Texas hospitality" I'd been subjected to for the past three weeks was over. On the metal desk was a tray with some human-grade food already waiting. In between the two Nathan's type hotdogs and buns, complete with ketchup and mustard, there was a large portion of French fries, a scoop of potato salad, and pudding. A pint of milk was resting next to the tray. It didn't look like a meal at a detention center—it was more like a picnic spread that one would gladly eat with their family on Sunday; a hearty meal that I very much appreciated.

Next morning, after breakfast, I asked to use the telephone and called Carolyn, my sister Renata, and my parents. My family was very excited to hear I was within driving distance from Vancouver and vowed to see me soon. I was on the phone for what seemed like almost an hour before I made my last call to my lawyer, Patrick Sherlock, who planned to see me later in the day.

After my sack lunch at noon, one of the female officers began my book-in process when, halfway through, we were interrupted by the arrival of my attorney. Taking the elevator to the visitor area on the first floor under a guard escort, I met with Mr. Sherlock in the second passthrough booth. From behind the Plexiglas, I immediately recognized him from his Internet profile and photo that Carolyn sent.

He was a tall, willowy man, sixty-three years of age, with a pleasant grin on his face when I walked into the visitors' booth from the other side. We exchanged pleasantries before getting to the business at hand—the Retainer Agreement he brought (see Document: 5101 @ www.ambrozuk.com). I imagined in a small town like Kalispell there weren't too many clients who dropped $30,000 cash in his lap often, so he appeared quite enthusiastic going over the contract conditions, including his $250 hourly rate for any additional expenses like travel.

No matter what the outcome of the case, he was to keep the full retainer, and conservatively estimated, it would cost upwards of $120,000 before I was back in Canada. It was not an easy pill to swallow, but being a hopeless optimist who still thought the case would be quickly dismissed once I explained the events of the accident, I signed the contract, and we moved on to the negligent homicide charge and what to expect next.

Pulling out a two-page Court Procedures document from his folder (see Document: 4101 @ www.ambrozuk.com), we went over the judicial steps typically followed in court: Initial Appearance, Bail, Arraignment, Trial, Sentencing, Appeal and Post-Conviction Relief, and Sentence Review Board explanations. But most interesting was the preliminary hearing document— a line had been drawn through the paragraphs with hand-written notes "to District Court" and "Filed Direct" circled at either end. A preliminary hearing was defined as one that determined "whether or not there is sufficient reason to believe or probable cause that a crime had been committed and that you may have committed same." After reading the definition, this seemed like the perfect opportunity for me to tell my story in front of the court. After they heard all the details and looked closer at the evidence, I was sure they would be forced to reevaluate the charge, conceding that this was an innocent elopement gone wrong. But now I was confused about Mr. Sherlock's handwritten notes. I was new to the judicial lingo and court-procedure protocols, but it appeared that he was planning to waive my preliminary hearing altogether.

When asked to clarify, he explained that this step was usually skipped to save a week or two of court proceedings so that we could move directly to the arraignment. You would think that my own attorney would look for every opportunity to dismiss the case, but rather than acknowledge my concerns about forgoing the preliminary hearing, he cut our debate short and excused himself because he was late for another appointment. I was left confused and disappointed.

I would not see him again until Friday when we appeared in front of Judge Stewart E. Stadler for my initial court appearance. The room was packed when I walked into the courtroom on the third floor and joined Mr. Sherlock who was standing in front of the judge's bench.

To begin the hearing, Judge Stadler made a few introductory statements before confirming I could read English and follow along without him having to read the entire document. He advised me of my rights and being entitled to legal counsel if I couldn't afford one—despite seeing Mr. Sherlock beside me—before asking if I was waiving the preliminary hearing.

By now, Mr. Sherlock had had some time to think about our conversation of the previous night and possibly change his mind, but he appeared to be a man who didn't like to rock the boat and simply went along with the judge.

Content with our cooperation, Judge Stadler brought up the bond. According to Mr. Sherlock's document definition, "Under Montana Law, nearly all persons are entitled to bail except in capital cases, because all persons charged are innocent until proven guilty." Twenty-four years ago, my bond had been set at $20,000. The previous week Judge David Ortley in Collin County, Texas had increased that to $100,000. But all that became null and void when Judge Stadler dismissed those judgments and set "No Bond" to prevent me from bailing out. With no dispute from my attorney, the judge then asked if either of us had any questions. After Mr. Sherlock responded with, "None at this time," the judge adjourned the hearing.

When I met with Mr. Sherlock again a half hour later and asked why he opted out of the preliminary hearing after our discussion, he still had no explanation other than to remind me that it was usually done that way to save time. Seeing my disappointment, he said we could still ask for a preliminary hearing either through Judge Stadler or the judge who would be handling my arraignment. I was no attorney, but it seemed that we'd just missed the optimum time to force the judge's hand. With the media and all the townspeople watching, Judge Stadler would have had no choice but to grant us the hearing. Now we would have to depend on motions filed in court just to try and convince the prosecutor and the judge to grant us the hearing again. A hell of a strategy from a lawyer who not too long ago sounded very much in control of my case and the Flathead County justice system.

But he was all I had for now, so we spent our remaining time going over the details from the night of the accident. Although he appeared intrigued while I explained our elopement plans, he didn't seem as pessimistic as Sheriff Jim Dupont, who casually approached us to introduce himself when we were leaving the visitors' booth. Dressed in his brown county sheriff uniform, we shook hands before he began what felt like an interrogation about the accident and the recovered aircraft.

Deputy Jim Dupont was the county investigator presiding over the case in 1982 and since then had managed to elevate himself to the status of sheriff. He said there were still pressing questions on his mind about the unsolved case. He had spent twenty-four years criticizing me in front of the media while he made excuses for his own shortcomings (see Document: 7500 @ www.ambrozuk.com), and even went so far as to call me an S.O.B. in a 2005 *Daily Inter Lake* newspaper article (see Document: 2201 @ www.ambrozuk.com).

Calm, yet inquisitive, he questioned me extensively about the passenger door, and whether it was opened before the aircraft sank. He said the investigation showed the door was closed. But until I saw the evidence and the recovery photos to confirm what actually happened, I could only tell him what I remembered. There was no doubt in my mind that I opened a door trying to get to Dianne, but his look was evidence enough about his doubt. He had been working on his theory for the past twenty-four years, and there was very little I could say now to dispel his false speculations. There may be two sides to every story, but there is only one set of facts based on evidence. Until I saw the 1982 RCMP and Flathead County investigation reports, and looked at the video and photos taken during the aircraft recovery, it was my word against his.

We spoke for less than ten minutes, and when we were about to part ways, he said something startling. He suggested that everyone— he, Mr. Sherlock, the prosecutor, the judge, and I—should all sit down to discuss the details of the case before it got to court. Surprisingly, that sounded a lot like a preliminary hearing, and I wholeheartedly agreed. After so many years, it was the opportunity I had been waiting for. Despite coming from the mouth of Sheriff "Buford T. Justice" of Flathead County, I remained optimistic that the misunderstanding surrounding the accident would finally be cleared up.

Feeling encouraged about the case outcome, my spirits were elevated even moreso on Saturday, September 23, when I finally got to see my baby sister and her family during visitation hours. Even in the pass-through booth behind Plexiglas, they all looked amazing in every sense, especially my niece, Angelina (see Document: 7308 @ www. ambrozuk.com), who was the cutest little thing I had ever seen. She would occasionally poke her head from behind the door, as if playing peek-a-boo. It took a few minutes to get over her shyness, but she eventually sat on the counter next to the window and helped my sister with the family picture slide show. Renata's husband and my two nephews briefly took turns to say a few words, but most of the conversation through the telephone handset was between my sister and me.

As I watched them and listened to their stories from the past, I couldn't believe my little sister was all grown up with three incredible kids. Up until then, I didn't mind or care about being detained, but when I saw my family and realized what I was missing, I was eager to wrap things up and get back to Canada so we could catch up on all the things we had missed over the years.

Seeing Renata and her family, even through Plexiglas, was exciting, but that evening things got even better when I finally saw my parents after twenty-four years. They drove their motor home over 1,100 kilometers (approximately 700 miles) from Vancouver to visit me, and I was ecstatic.

It was an emotional reunion in the full-contact visitor booth, with hugs, tears, and photos, as we sat down to a long-overdue conversation about our immediate family, our distant family, and our lives. They both looked healthy and fit. I was amused that they often drove their RV across the country like regular retired people. I had missed so much of their past, but now that I was back, I was sure things would only get better. My current inconvenience was temporary, and it was just a matter of time before I was back in Canada, spending time with them, my sister, and her three adorable kids.

That same evening I was also assigned a permanent cell. Because of my high-visibility case, the booking guard said I would not be housed in the general population area, and instead placed me in a separate section of the detention center. It had all the amenities of a regular home, including a shared main area, complete with shower, two-seat metal dining table, telephone, and small color TV (see Document: 4100 @ www.ambrozuk.com). It wasn't much, but it was a hell of a lot better than the Collin County Detention Facility, and I had no complaints.

On Sunday, everyone said goodbye before they drove back to Vancouver that afternoon. But it would be Renata who came for our last visit and picked up where we'd left off the day before. Over the last few weeks, it had been delightful talking to my parents every day on the phone, but with Renata I seemed to share a much closer bond.

Twenty-four years ago, we were teenagers—five years apart and with very little common interests. Since then, she had grown up and was literally my lifesaver, dealing with the attorneys, managing my personal affairs, and taking care of everything else in between. We talked several times a day and each time our conversation flowed as if we had been best friends for years. I was so proud of my sister and couldn't be happier to have such a positive and kind sibling looking out for my best interests.

CHAPTER SEVEN

State Arraignment and Bond Hearing

October 5 – 10, 2006
Day 37 – 42

IT WAS NINE o'clock in the morning when I walked into the court-room for my arraignment. The place was filled with reporters, cameras, and several other attorneys and their clients who had business in court.

Judge Katherine R. Curtis—or Kitty—presided over the proceedings and began as soon as she took her seat at the bench.

Mr. Sherlock and I had gone over the arraignment process and the ACKNOWLEDGEMENT OF RIGHTS paperwork the previous night (see Document: 3206 @ www.ambrozuk.com) before he submitted the document to the court earlier that morning. When we were eventually called to the defendant's table, the process was quick and painless.

Judge Curtis briefly went over the specifics outlined in the document: was my name Jaroslaw Czeslaw Ambrozuk, did I know what the charge was against me and, of course, what was my plea?

To the latter, Mr. Sherlock replied, "The defendant pleads not guilty, Your Honor."

Accepting our plea while shuffling through documents lying in front of her, the judge scheduled the omnibus hearing for January 31, 2007 and the pre-trial conference on February 7, 2007. The trial date was set for March 12, 2007.

My arraignment took less than fifteen minutes, and after a quick trip to my cell, I met with Mr. Sherlock to go over the particulars of my scheduled bond hearing later that evening.

In general, he was against a defendant testifying at his own bond hearing because 80 percent of the time it worked against him. In my case, he was willing to make an exception. We went over the basic questions scribbled on his yellow notepad that he would ask when I was called to the stand: age, marital status, level of education and the degrees I had achieved, what I did for a living, and what happened during the night of the accident. His strategy was to minimize the cross-examination from the prosecutor by asking any relevant questions himself. But I was confused why things like the accident would even be mentioned at a bond hearing. When I asked what that had to do with setting the bond amount, Mr. Sherlock, once again, had no clear answer before the guard knocked on the visitor-booth window to remind us about the court time.

The bond hearing was in the same courtroom as my arraignment earlier that day, with Judge Curtis again presiding. This time there were far fewer media present, and only Mr. Sherlock gave an interview to the local reporters standing in a semi-circle outside the main exit doors.

The judge briefly scanned the MOTION FOR SETTING OF BOND AND NOTICE OF MOTION document that my attorney filed (see List: 9560 @ www.ambrozuk.com), before calling me to the stand to testify. We went over the rehearsed answers with Mr. Sherlock, before the lead Flathead County District Attorney, Ed Corrigan, began his Perry Mason-like cross-examination.

Mr. Sherlock had earlier described the prosecutor as someone who didn't like publicity and media attention, but what I saw now was nothing of the kind. He appeared neither timid nor reserved.

He began by questioning whether or not I had mourned the loss of Dianne. "You say you're grieving so much over the loss of the love of your life, but you're in Florida at the beach having fun. That doesn't seem like it's real tough for you, does it?"

They were tactical questions designed to provoke, and each was as strange and out of context at a bond hearing as the next. "If you were so distraught, why were you in England and Japan having a good time at the race track?" he continued, referring to my recent projects with Honda.

They were all valid questions, except that everything he was referring to happened at least twenty years after the loss of Dianne. Twenty years seemed like ample time to move on after grieving, even for a determined prosecutor. And that's when I realized his game—it was all about vilifying me as someone irresponsible and without compassion. I was warned by Mr. Sherlock that unlike a preliminary hearing or a trial, hearsay was admissible at a bond hearing, and Ed Corrigan had no problem exploiting it.

Following a pattern, he then brought up the twenty-four-year-old phone transcript between my friend Tom and me that was recorded two weeks after the accident (see Document: 3111 @ www.ambrozuk. com). "I feel like a murderer," he quoted, insinuating that the plane crash and the drowning were deliberate. It was completely out of context and without consideration for the shock and the irrational state I was in at the time. His carefully chosen excerpts reflected my traumatized state-of-mind rather than what Dianne and I truly shared, but to the prosecutor, it was fair game.

Despite his provocation, I tried to remain calm. "I didn't say I *was* a murderer. I said I *felt like* a murderer." To counter his cleverly thought-through tactic, I quoted a couple of my own from the transcript: "..., but you know, we're, we just got so close." and "It felt like half of me died when Dianne died."

That was enough for him to change gears and turn to my net worth, including my Pontiac Firebird, Dodge Viper, house, and the two lake-front lots. The cars and my house were public knowledge, relayed in many newspaper articles, but how did Ed Corrigan know about my two lots on the lake? The only person I had told about those after my arrest was Mr. Sherlock during our discussion on how to transfer the house title to my real name.

During the prosecutor's cross-examination, I calmly answered all his questions and ignored what sounded like provocation to stir my emotions, but when he brought up my father and how he was a millionaire who owned a fleet of Ryder Truck Rental trucks, I had enough of his nonsensical fabrications.

"Where are you getting this information from?" I asked.

He looked up at me, pointed at Mr. Sherlock who was sitting at the next table over with his head slouching, and said, "From your attorney!"

I was stunned.

And so was Mr. Sherlock, who remained seated with his head buried in his doodles—guilty as charged! Like a child caught stealing from the cookie jar, he remained speechless and denied nothing of the prosecutor's accusations. I'd paid this man $30,000 to defend me, and I felt betrayed. I couldn't understand why my attorney was aiding the prosecutor by divulging information I believed was private under the rules of client-attorney privilege.

But Ed Corrigan wasn't through. Sounding almost gleeful, he informed the court that Merrill Lynch—the financial institution where most of my personal and corporate money, stocks, and retirement accounts resided—was currently in the process of freezing my assets.

This was the first time I'd heard about Merrill Lynch seizing my accounts. If true, the news was disturbing.

When the prosecutor rested, the focus turned to Judge Curtis and my legal documents, including my U.S. passport. She asked about their whereabouts: "Are they in your possession? Does your family have them? Or are they with friends for safekeeping?"

I had no idea who had my legal documents, but I suspected they were probably with one of my friends. I respectfully answered all her questions to her satisfaction before she motioned for closing remarks from the prosecutor and my attorney.

Corrigan summarized the prosecution's position. "Because of all the resources Mr. Ambrozuk has access to, I recommend bond be set at $500,000."

Mr. Sherlock followed with, "The original bond was set at $20,000, and the defense thinks this seems reasonable. But I leave it to the judge to decide what is fair."

Taking both sides into consideration, Judge Kitty Curtis split the difference, setting my bond at $250,000, with the condition that once I posted bail, I return all my identification documents to Flathead County before I would be allowed to leave.

Disappointed, I returned to my cell and immediately called Carolyn and Renata to tell them the bad news. Despite my frozen assets, the $250,000 bond was still doable if I really wanted out. My parents were ready to mortgage their home to get the money, but I told them that would not necessarily guarantee my freedom.

I still had an immigration detainer that would kick in as soon as my bond was posted, and that meant I would automatically be placed in ICE custody. Because there was a very good chance they would deport me back to Canada, I would have no way to resolve my state case and therefore forfeit the $250,000 bond.

It was the classic tug-of-war decision between potential freedom *versus* money. Although I had the option, my family and I ultimately decided that clearing up the state case after all these years was more important than my immediate release from Flathead County.

It was late Friday evening when Mr. Sherlock finally showed up to talk about Ed Corrigan and the bond hearing. He'd been told the prosecutor was originally considering a suspended sentence for my negligent homicide charge, but after talking to me on the witness stand, he wasn't sure what to think. Even in a newspaper article after the hearing, Corrigan told a reporter that he was keeping an open mind because of my attitude and responses to his questions.

While that all sounded like political bullshit designed to appease the public, it was becoming clear that I was not dealing with someone who would be honorable and unbiased.

To that extent, Mr. Sherlock was happy to confirm my suspicions. Ed Corrigan had already been reprimanded multiple times by the Montana Supreme Court for unethical conduct, including once, a few months before, against Mr. Sherlock himself. Although the Montana Supreme Court allowed only one instance to be published and used as a reference, the repetitiveness of the prosecutor's poor judgment and case manipulation spoke volumes about the man who was now trying to exploit our innocent elopement.

CHAPTER EIGHT

The Merrill Lynch Saga

October 11 – 17, 2006
Day 43 – 49

IT WAS OFFICIAL: just as Ed Corrigan had said at my bond hearing, Merrill Lynch had frozen all my assets, and Carolyn verified it.

Merrill Lynch—a financial institution I also used for my basic banking needs—had, without so much as a court order, denied me access to my own money. A couple of weeks before, I'd signed their form giving Carolyn the authority to use my account to pay bills and post the $250,000 bond (before we decided not to go that route). Now they refused to give her access to my account as a co-signer. Worse yet, even I was unable to get to my own money and investments in my personal and corporate accounts.

It seemed unbelievable they and their attorneys could actually deny me access to my own money and stocks. But there was nothing I could do about it other than hire *another* attorney to contest this outrageous behavior from what I once considered to be a reputable financial establishment.

Walter—a friend of my family who I'd known twenty-four years ago in Vancouver—and who, unbeknownst to me, now lived just a few blocks down the street from Carolyn's parent's house in Colleyville, Texas—stepped in with much-needed aid and advice. After my arrest, he contacted my parents and offered to post my bond until they could arrange financing through their bank. But more importantly, he also recommended a local civil attorney to help with the Merrill Lynch fiasco. He'd hired Bob Cohen previously on a personal matter, and said that he was a real "street fighter."

If you're keeping score, we're up to five attorneys: Clancy (dismissed), Davis (Texas), Sherlock (Montana), still to be determined Corvette release attorney, and now Mr. Cohen to deal with Merrill Lynch.

After a quick discussion, we agreed that Carolyn should contact Mr. Cohen the next day, but for the time being we had other fires to put out. The Merrill Lynch checks she wrote to pay for my house utilities had all bounced, and I had no choice but to ask my family to step in again.

With a new attorney to deal with Merrill Lynch, there was no reason for Mr. Sherlock to continue contacting their legal department in Montana. When I asked that he stop and concentrate on the negligent-homicide charge, he seemed disappointed with my decision at first but eventually backed off.

It was at that point he also told me he would be gone for the next couple of weeks, celebrating his wife's retirement in New York. It was clear that neither the prosecutor nor the judge had any intention of resolving the case quickly. Ed Corrigan was holding out with the plea bargain negotiations until we got closer to the trial date. And Judge Stadler, along with the rest of the court appointees, had their political career to think of. With their reelections coming up the next month, they had no intention of making any rash decisions that could potentially stir up unfavorable opinions with voters.

His reasoning made a lot of sense, although I couldn't understand why he still dodged my requests to file the court documents for a preliminary hearing.

The more time we spent together, the more I felt he was not acting in my best interests. First, there was the preliminary hearing blunder. Then, every time I asked if he had gone through all the evidence, he said he hadn't. Being familiar with the case facts would not only decrease the amount of questions he had for me each time we met, but it would also allow him to be better prepared when the judge pulled him over in the hallway for a water-cooler chat, which, according to Mr. Sherlock, was often.

That's the difference between an engineer and a lawyer: one reads the stack of evidence the first day he gets his hands on it; the other just wings it.

CHAPTER NINE

Welcome to Canada, Eh!

1974 – 1980

ON MARCH 26, 1974, we walked out of the arrival gate at YVR, where my dad and his uncle were waiting for my mom, my sister, and me with a bouquet of flowers and a couple of toys to welcome us to Canada. Coming from the suburbs of an old small town, everything seemed newer, bigger, and brighter as we drove from the airport to our new home.

By then, my dad had already bought a house in Burnaby—renting out the main floor—so we initially settled into the small basement suite. The place was quaint but crowded for a family of four, underscoring the need for us to eventually relocate to the upper floor where my sister and I would get our own rooms.

Like typical tourists, during the first month we spent much time sightseeing—visiting many popular Vancouver attractions, including the Stanley Park Aquarium and Queen Elizabeth Park with its famous botanical gardens. But to me, the most spectacular were the malls and the stores filled to the brim with clothes, electronics, and groceries. I was in awe the first time we walked into a grocery store. There were aisles after aisles of goods that I once could only imagine. Life in Poland at that time was challenging. The cost of food was high, and it was scarce. I was used to seeing three or four sausages hanging on a deli rack, with perhaps a few meats and cheeses lying behind the counter glass to choose from. But here I saw fruits like pineapples and mangos that I'd only read about in books! In my wildest dreams, I could not imagine such exotic variety. The only thing missing among this abundance was my communication skills.

Although the tenants living above us were from Austria, their children were born in Canada and became instrumental in my first introduction to the challenges of the English language (see Document: 1201 @ www.ambrozuk.com). Being of similar age, we spent hours building forts in the backyard, riding bikes, and playing board games as I struggled to grasp the language basics. My hand gestures were eventually replaced with words that were good enough to get by among friends, but school was a different matter.

Wanting to drop me in the water to sink or swim, my father unsuccessfully tried to campaign the elementary school principal down the street from our house to let me enroll. Instead, I would spend the next half year in a "New Canadian" class learning the basics of English, including vocabulary and pronunciation. Not yet eleven years old, I took the bus every day to my new school and learned all I could from my new teacher, Ms. Alishuran—a young instructor with lots of patience who divided her time among a handful of students from all corners of the world. There were kids from India, a brother and sister from Brazil, and Asian children who sat with me in a circle on the floor as she stressed the proper pronunciation of syllables and words by repeatedly pointing out the correct position of our lips and tongue, using her own fingers and hands.

By September, I showed enough progress to be reintegrated into the neighborhood elementary school, but until I fully mastered my English reading and writing skills, the principal insisted on placing me two grades behind. Keeping up with the class for the next couple of years, and learning from friends during our after school extracurricular activities, I brought my English level up to the point where I would skip the last year of elementary school entirely and head straight into Moscrop Junior High School the following year.

There I spent the next three years on the school honor roll, even though in the classroom I had evolved into an ostentatious teenager. Pushing the boundaries, I eventually mastered the art of humor and became the "class clown," often disrupting the classroom with a bird call or a witty comment. Most teachers found my behavior nothing more than irritating, but there were a few exceptions. My antics would eventually land me in the principal's office no less than eight times during my last semester of junior high. I was warned that if it happened again, I would not be allowed to graduate. I may have been brash, and perhaps looking to establish my own identity, but I was smart enough to realize the seriousness of the situation and finished out the year without further incidence.

Along with my academics, I also excelled in sports, including playing rugby for two years, wrestling, and participating in several track-and-field events during my tenure at Moscrop High. My career in wrestling ended abruptly when I broke my arm during practice and had to wear a cast for six weeks. Being naturally athletic, I collected numerous ribbons and metals during those years at various high school track-and-field meets, despite rugby being my only devotion to practice.

I also did my share of socializing after school and on the weekends. Moscrop Junior High was divided into three basic clans: the jocks, the potheads, and the rest of us. The jocks were strictly into sports, with parties and get-togethers that, in most cases, lacked excitement. The potheads were the self-proclaimed "cool dudes" who wore thick lumberjack flannel shirts and hiking boots to school during the summer—but their parties were always festive and entertaining. The majority of the students, though, fit somewhere in between, including my friends as we maintained our neutral stance that allowed us to seamlessly go between either extreme.

By now I had managed to make a few friends in high school but still lived a double life because of my ties to the Polish community. During the week, I spent the majority of my social time in my neighborhood with the local high school kids, but on Wednesday nights and on weekends, I joined the hundreds of Polish immigrants who congregated around the church and its community halls to continue our native traditions and heritage.

Wednesday nights, my sister and I attended Boy Scout/Girl Scout meetings in the school building adjacent to the church. Meeting in separate classrooms based on gender, we went over troop discipline and responsibility with our leaders during the first two hours before adjourning to the gymnasium for an hour of friendly co-ed volleyball or floor hockey games.

But the highlight of the week was always Sunday when my parents, my sister, and I dressed in our best clothes and headed to church to attend weekly Catholic mass. The Polish church was always filled with congregants who, after the service, gathered outside to mingle with their acquaintances and make plans for dinner.

Many of my parents' friends also had kids my age, and that is where the fun usually started. Leaving the adults to their political talk over vodka, we spent the day hanging around the house shooting pool, playing games in the basement or, if one of the teenagers was old enough to drive, taking off to paint the town.

In the summer, during those sunny afternoons, we would load up and head to exciting destinations around Vancouver. Stanley Park or the beach was always an option, but if that didn't suffice, there was always a drive-in movie to consider.

Between school and Polish community activities, I had plenty of things to do and many friends to hang out with, but none of them would become as important as Tom—a landed immigrant himself who would eventually become my best friend.

CHAPTER TEN

The Proof Is in the Pudding

October 18 – November 2, 2006
Day 50 – 65

ON OCTOBER 26, I finally received a copy of the memorandum, MOTION AND ORDER FOR A PRELIMINARY HEARING (see Document: 3211 @ www.ambrozuk.com) from Mr. Sherlock's office in the mail. It called for the court to either dismiss the negligent homicide charge or have a preliminary hearing remanded to the Justice Court. By the time I got the packet, Mr. Sherlock had already left for his two-week holiday, but at least my three weeks of nagging persistence paid off. Most likely, it was a case of "too little, too late," but at least it was officially filed with Flathead County, and now the ball was in their court (no pun intended).

After debating for weeks, on Sunday, my sister Renata called Dianne's parents, the Babcocks, to introduce herself and talk to them about Dianne and me, our relationship, and the details of our elopement. We both thought it best to contact them unofficially and offer an opportunity to answer any questions they may have had over the past twenty-four years. Being proactive, I prepared some key points for Renata to share about Dianne and me. It was my family's first contact with her relatives since the accident, but I knew the day would come when I personally would have to explain our relationship to them, the reasons behind our elopement, and the details of what happened that night. Whether they wanted to speak with me was a different matter, but

I had long felt the need to offer them the opportunity if it would bring some degree of closure.

Renata told me the conversation with Dianne's father was cordial. Mr. Babcock was still in disbelief that Dianne had eloped with the intent to leave her life and family behind. Much of their discussion echoed my attorney's conversations with Ed Corrigan, who all but insinuated that this was a kidnapping rather than an elopement. Since my arrest, Dianne's father had also received a letter from the prosecutor regarding my negligent homicide charge, but had not yet responded and was maintaining a low profile to avoid the media.

During their conversation, Renata learned that Dianne's mother had since passed away. On route to visit Dianne's grave several years earlier, Mr. Babcock and his wife were in a car accident with a bus. Shortly thereafter, she died in hospital from severe injuries. She had been a kind and gentle woman, and I was deeply saddened to hear of her tragic death that also had been caused by an accident on August 22, the date I lost Dianne.

Throughout their conversation, Renata said Mr. Babcock didn't seem spiteful nor was he seeking retribution. But he was in no way ready to call the prosecutor and insist he drop the case to prevent the media spectacle that was beginning to unfold.

When Mr. Sherlock finally showed up on Monday after two weeks' absence, he brought with him a fourth version of power of attorney to sign—this one to get my Corvette back.

After my arrest, instead of properly completing the 1981 Corvette repairs I had already paid for, John Bodnar had decided to confiscate it. The car sat in his shop for over six years while he repeatedly failed to complete the restoration as agreed. There were misaligned panels, large chips clearly visible in the brand-new paint job, and during the last inspection, there also appeared to be missing parts: carpet, door panels, and other console and dashboard pieces (see Document: 3612 @ www. ambrozuk.com).

I had invested over \$15,000 in the car project—with over \$6,000 of that going to Mr. Bodnar—so I was not about to let him confiscate my car on a technicality. Through some personal contacts, Carolyn found and hired our next attorney, Robert Palmer, who then sent a petition letter to Mr. Bodnar and his attorney (see Document: 3603 @ www. ambrozuk.com), forcing them to cooperate legally. Their response was to request yet another power of attorney.

I don't know what I found more ridiculous—signing multiple powers of attorney that appeared to carry little legal authority, or dealing with an opportunistic shop owner who was looking for a loophole to keep my car. The Corvette issue was distracting, but it was only one of several mini-battles I was forced to fight while dealing with more pressing legal matters.

On Tuesday, during his next visit, Mr. Sherlock brought the rest of the case evidence that I still had not seen—specifically the more than 100 photographs taken in 1982 when the aircraft was being recovered from Little Bitterroot Lake. Some of the 8½ x 11 glossy photos (see List: 9585 @ www.ambrozuk.com) were of the equipment used to search for and recover the plane, but a handful showed the details of the aircraft itself.

We went through them one at a time, after Mr. Sherlock removed several of the explicit pictures of Dianne still strapped in the seat by her seatbelt. Trying to keep my emotions in check, we flipped through each one while the attorney continued to ask questions surrounding the night of the accident and what had happened during those critical seconds when the aircraft wheels touched the surface of the water.

Up to that point, all I had was my memories backed only by the stack of case evidence I had been given a few days prior. But the photographs proved invaluable, validating everything I had been saying since the day I arrived in Kalispell.

I remembered many things from that night, but the details surrounding the few seconds it took the aircraft to penetrate the water, flip over, and capsize still needed further clarification. Mr. Sherlock and I often discussed those critical moments during our meetings, but here was concrete visual evidence that even he could not dispute. There was the removed back panel behind the storage compartment (see Document: 7148 @ www.ambrozuk.com), the broken-off padding on the pilot's side yoke (see Document: 7152 @ www.ambrozuk.com), the aircraft's missing front windshield that had been clearly broken outward (see Document: 7156 @ www.ambrozuk.com), and the inexplicable damage to the top of the aircraft tail fin (see Document: 7167 @ www.ambrozuk.com).

Since the beginning, Mr. Sherlock had been blindly repeating what the prosecutor and Sheriff Dupont fed the media regarding the accident: that I landed the aircraft on the water, grabbed a garbage bag with all our belongings—including Dianne's non-existent purse—and exited the plane through the pilot's door without helping her or caring about her welfare. No matter how many times I tried to explain I had been catapulted through the front windshield when the aircraft wheels jack-knifed into the water, he always reverted to what he had been told by Sheriff Duport. Now that there were photographs supporting everything I said, he had a problem retrofitting the new evidence into his theory.

Mr. Sherlock and I talked extensively that evening about the accident details, but I could see even the hard visual proof of photographs were not enough to change his bias. It now seemed there was doubt in his mind, but he wasn't about to accept my explanations that easily. Twenty-four years of Sheriff Dupont spreading nonsense in the media could not be wiped away by a few conversations. I remained patient, letting my attorney mull over the visual evidence to see if he would eventually realize the error of his assumptions.

CHAPTER ELEVEN

You Want a Preliminary Hearing?
Good Luck with That!

November 3 – 12, 2006
Day 66 – 75

OVER THE PAST five weeks, I had been enjoying daily conversations with Carolyn, my sister, and my parents, but at $17.30 and $19.38 per call to Carolyn and my family, respectively, the reality finally hit the fan. Between September 1 and 23, we were billed $2,300 just for calls to Carolyn in Texas—with most likely a larger bill still to come for the international long-distance calls to my family in Canada! Talk about a racketeering scam.

EVERCOM, the company that provided the telephone service in the detention center, may have had a captive audience, but, fortunately, we found a workaround to their extortion. Carolyn ordered a cell phone from Alltel with a local Montana number that she could forward to her cell phone. Similarly, Renata got Verizon's North American plan that also allowed her to get a local Montana number. In both cases, the result was the same—I would dial a local Kalispell number, cutting each of our fifteen minute conversations to just $2.90.

Mr. Sherlock showed up Friday afternoon and brought with him the prosecutor's response to his MOTION FOR PRELIMINARY HEARING OR IN THE ALTERNATIVE MOTION TO DISMISS (see Document: 3210 @ www.ambrozuk.com). As expected, the district attorney denied both requests (see Document: 3212 @ www.ambrozuk.com), citing there was no statutory provision allowing the option of a preliminary hearing once the state had initiated proceedings by filing directly with the district court.

What did that mean?

It meant Mr. Sherlock looked incompetent because when he had had the chance to force the court to grant us the preliminary hearing at our initial appearance, he waived my rights, and now the prosecutor and the judge were not going to be cooperative.

With regard to dismissing the case, Ed Corrigan also noted that only a mere probability that an offense had been committed needed to exist, and therefore the dismissal of the case should be denied as well. Of course, the final decision rested with the presiding judge, Stewart E. Stadler, so Mr. Sherlock prepared a reply memorandum: REGARDING COURT DENIAL OF REQUEST FOR PRELIMINARY HEARING AND MOTION TO DISMISS (see Document: 3213 @ www.ambrozuk.com), to counter the prosecutor's denials.

I didn't have a law degree, but all these orders, rationales, and rebuttals seemed like a waste of time. With Mr. Sherlock's minimal criminal experience, Ed Corrigan was not about to let himself be undermined by an appellate attorney in one of the biggest cases in Flathead County history. He had the law behind him and was frankly too clever for Mr. Sherlock, who always seemed to be one step behind the shrewd prosecutor and the gang of judges with their political careers always on the line.

Although the court's rebuttal was disappointing, it was expected. But what Merrill Lynch's attorneys came up with to justify freezing my accounts strained credulity. When David Zwerner, Bob Cohen's partner in Texas, spoke to Daniel Spectre, an attorney for Merrill Lynch, he was told that it was the Patriot Act, money laundering, and possible ties to terrorist activity that prompted their actions. Merrill Lynch had all my check deposits and company payroll stubs to verify where all the money came from, so their excuses were nothing more than corporate horseshit. But unfortunately, the highly paid, clever Merrill Lynch lawyers were running the show, giving us no choice but to continue with the "David vs. Goliath" battle. No doubt President George W. Bush and the U.S. Congress would be proud to see their Patriot Act used so frivolously.

Despite the Merrill Lynch absurdity, there was much better news to lift my spirits as the weekend approached.

On Saturday morning at 4:00 a.m., on the spur of moment, my sister got into her car and started her trek to Kalispell, Montana for a visit. The ten-hour drive put her on track for Saturday's visitation, but her car broke down somewhere near a small town in Washington State. Undeterred, she got a local mechanic to tow her vehicle to his shop. From there, she hitched a ride with the mechanic's brother to Spokane, where she rented a car and was back on the road to Flathead County. By the time she arrived at the detention center, there were only two hours left for visitation and they were both full. After all she went through, that was not the news we wanted to hear. But we simply laughed it off and spent the rest of the night talking on the phone, waiting to see each other next morning.

In the months since my arrest, Renata and I had grown so close, albeit fifteen minutes at a time. Both of us were surprised by how similar our personalities were despite being separated for almost a quarter of a century. We were like "stare baby" (old hags in Polish), who could yap non-stop about any topic for hours. If this were possible through Plexiglas and a telephone call, it was inevitable that our bond would only grow stronger once we were officially reunited in Canada.

CHAPTER TWELVE

The Federal Detainer and Charge

November 13 – 22, 2006

Day 76 – 85

THE TRIFECTA OF U.S. Government charges was now complete. On Monday morning I got news about the detainer (see Document: 3705 @ www.ambrozuk.com) and arrest warrant from the federal government, charging me with the commission of the following offense: FALSE STATEMENT IN APPLICATION AND USE OF PASSPORT, dated October 12, 2006 (see Document: 3701 @ www.ambrozuk.com). The good news was we now had something tangible to work with and could begin a search for the next lawyer—an attorney in Texas who specialized in federal criminal cases.

> *If you're keeping score, we're up to six attorneys: Clancy (dismissed), Davis (Texas), Sherlock (Montana), Palmer (Corvette release), Cohen (Merrill Lynch), and now another lawyer to deal with the passport charges.*

As usual, Mr. Sherlock offered to help from Montana with the federal charge groundwork, but after seeing his performance in court and realizing that, like the Merrill Lynch case, he had no jurisdiction in Texas, my decision seemed simple—thanks, but no thanks!

During his visit on Monday, he casually mentioned running into Judge Stadler at the courthouse. The judge told him, unofficially, that he planned to deny our request for a preliminary hearing. Not unlike the prosecutor, Judge Stadler thought Ed Corrigan, not he, should agree to the preliminary hearing. It was the classic "it's not me, it's him" game as they passed the baton between themselves while Mr. Sherlock stood helplessly on the sidelines, resorting to the only strategy he was comfortable with—manipulating his client into taking a plea.

I understood that he was not a criminal attorney *per se*—that was his business partner's strength, as we later found out—but I did not appreciate being coerced into a plea that I stood firmly against. Even within the ACKNOWLEDGEMENT OF RIGHTS that was eventually filed in court (see Document: 3217 @ www.ambrozuk.com), there was a clause 8) that stated "*I have not been threatened, coerced, forced, intimidated, or influenced in any way*" with regard to my plea agreement. But to Mr. Sherlock, that affidavit seemed almost inconsequential, as long as it was done subtly.

Rather than going to trial, his tactic was to wear the client down until he eventually agreed to whatever was offered. But how do you accomplish that when you know you're not supposed to coerce or influence your client? His solution was to continuously question our elopement and pepper me with what he thought were comparable examples so that, eventually, I would crack and cooperate. One of his more astute scenarios was comparing our accident to a passenger getting killed by a driver whose car hit a tree. Although in both instances the passenger may have perished, there was a distinct difference between the two. Going from point A to point B with the passenger expecting to arrive safely at their destination, was not the same as two people who both made a conscious decision to elope in an aircraft and land on the surface of the lake, knowing perfectly well that it was dangerous.

Being voluntary participants in a risky stunt is no different from a passenger who performs a tandem skydive, a climber who attempts to reach the summit of Mount Everest, or an X-Games motocross biker who takes his life into his own hands when scaling the side of a mountain. The difference between those examples and a car driver hitting a tree is that in the latter, the passenger is not aware of the impending danger. You can't take a pear, paint it red, and pretend it's an apple. But despite my logical counterarguments, such rationale continued to elude my attorney.

On Wednesday, making it official and siding with the prosecutor regarding the preliminary hearing decision, Judge Stadler filed his own ORDER AND RATIONALE (see Document: 3214 @ www.ambrozuk.com) that said, in part, "...*these facts clearly establish, as required, the probability that the Defendant committed the offense of Negligent Homicide.*"

He may have delivered on his unofficial water-cooler promise to my attorney, but the obvious question was: did the facts as stated clearly establish negligent homicide, or was that what the preliminary hearing was supposed to be for?

CHAPTER THIRTEEN

The Tom and Jerry Show

1977 – 1981

DURING MY ADOLESCENT years, my life at home was stereo-typical for the time—pleasant enough and with all the basic necessi-ties provided. The only thing missing to round out our household was a *Leave it to Beaver* family atmosphere. There was always a three-course meal on the table when my father returned from work. But when we all sat down to eat dinner, rarely did we have the friendly conversations about how our day was, what happened at work, how our school-day went, or did I win the rugby game. Back then, that seemed to be the norm. There weren't many helicopter moms get-ting involved with their kids' daily activities or wondering about their emotional state.

Being of Polish descent also had its own set of challenges com-pounded by prejudice from kids at school. Bullying was something you rarely brought up to adults and simply took care of yourself. When they called you a "Polack," you defended yourself in kind with an appropri-ate response in the heat of the battle. And when it was over, you were that much stronger for it.

But that is not to say our parents weren't involved in our lives and tried their hardest to provide the best environment. I considered myself one of the luckier ones because, despite their rigid stance on some ide-alistic rules, my parents were very much accommodating and generous.

At the age of sixteen, I had a hand-me-down blue 1967 Ford Meteor at my disposal, always a few dollars in my pocket for spending when out with my friends, and was even fortunate enough to endure several years of private accordion lessons. But the envy of most kids my age was my private pilot's license paid for entirely by my parents. The accordion lessons were somewhat of a disappointment, as I aspired to play synthesizer in a rock band rather than polkas at the Polish community (my father's idea of a compromise). But the pilot lessons were well appreciated since they were the first stepping-stone to becoming an airline pilot.

It was during my first year at Moscrop Junior High when I met Tom Pawlowski, also a transplant from Poland. Tom's parents were good friends with my family, so naturally we spent a lot of time together during their frequent social gatherings.

Initially meeting at church on Sunday and during our regular Boy Scout meetings on Wednesday nights, our get-togethers would soon extend beyond our families and the Polish community. Having similar interests and living only thirty minutes away, we quickly bonded and began spending much time together, including playing sports, periodically venturing out to a movie, attending the occasional concert, or simply browsing for some offbeat, little-known band at a record store.

Like many kids our age, music was a big part of our lives. It was through Tom that I would eventually expand my genre past mainstream tunes playing on the local rock stations in Vancouver. We spent countless hours talking about bands like Pink Floyd, AC/DC, UFO, Black Sabbath, and Judas Priest as we carefully dissected each lyric in search of their deeper meaning. Whether listening to albums in his bedroom, bellowing out Deep Purple's "Child in Time" chorus at the top of our lungs at a bus stop, or counting the pauses in Uriah Heep's "The Park" song, our affinity for mutual interests only grew with time.

Moscrop was a junior high school back then, and when the opportunity presented itself to transfer schools at the end of my tenth grade, I convinced my parents to let me finish my last two years at John Oliver

High School rather than attend the default Burnaby Central High. John Oliver was not only larger, but it was also where many of the Polish kids from our community went, including Tom.

Despite being a senior, we managed to take several elective courses together—including French and an Electronics class—partly because we both needed them to graduate, and partly for selfish social reasons. Already spending much time together outside of school, with the added classroom interaction we eventually became known to many as "Tom and Jerry," not unlike the two inseparable cartoon characters.

Although neither of us ever did drugs nor smoked pot, on occasion we did find ourselves with a twelve-pack of beer, or a bottle of vodka and orange juice to lighten the mood. Whether it was at a weekend party with friends, or just hanging out by ourselves while getting philosophical about school, teachers, politics, religion, the Polish community, or our parents, it was just kid stuff that always ended on a positive note.

Periodically serving mass at church in a scout uniform, and participating regularly in the Polish community holiday events, Tom and I also aspired to the occasional weekend or holiday outing. Because of the varied age groups in the Polish Boy Scouts, we would often join the older university students in extracurricular activities outside of school. There were weekend hiking and skiing excursions in the local mountains, sailing in the Boy Scout-owned, sixteen-foot sailboat, playing floor hockey at the university gym and, of course, the Simon Fraser University toga parties that we, as minors, could attend because of our brethren chaperones. It was exciting to be part of something that very few kids our age were privy to.

But the most anticipated event each year always took place in the middle of summer—the two-week Boy Scout camping trip. The co-ed camp was either local—where Polish scout troops from places like California would join us—or, in the alternative, we would travel to their home towns of Toronto or Winnipeg. This not only provided a change of scenery, but also allowed us to spend several days after camp with local families while touring their town (see Document: 1207 @ www.

ambrozuk.com). During those youthful years there were badges to earn, competitive games to play, and skits and songs to perform around the campfire in the evening. But there were also some memorable "covert operations" for the older crowd after the lights went out. Boys will be boys, with the girls not far behind, when it came to a bit of innocent fun after dark. Every year there would be plenty of memories to reminisce about, with a few hickeys sprinkled in between.

Although Tom and I were practically inseparable during my first year at John Oliver, once he graduated, things slowed down considerably because of his university studies and the Canadian Reserves he joined on the weekends. We would still see each other periodically, but our time together would eventually be limited to a few of my graduation parties and the occasional get-together to discuss his law courses, or the latest from my private pilot's ground-school class.

Although there was a lot going on in my life at the time—family, school, sports, friends, my pilot's license—I kept up with my studies, attended all my classes, and completed assignments as required. As a senior, I even excelled at some, including mathematics and a few of the technical electives.

But during those final years of high school, life was slowly changing for both Tom and me. No longer was everything about academics; gradually, it was becoming more about individuality, status, parties and, of course, girls.

CHAPTER FOURTEEN

Happy (South of the Border) Thanksgiving

November 23 – December 3, 2006

Day 86 – 96

AFTER THREE MONTHS in detention centers, I continued to remain positive about my case outlook. In general, I was doing surprisingly well, not only mentally but physically. Much of the credit for keeping my spirits up was due to my daily communication with Carolyn, Renata, and my parents. But the Flathead County Detention Center also contributed to my wellbeing with some unexpected perks.

On Thanksgiving, they treated everyone to a holiday meal of traditional, mouthwatering Montana cooking. According to the guards, this was typical of Thanksgiving and Christmas. The feast consisted of real turkey with stovetop stuffing, mashed potatoes covered with gravy, sweet potatoes, cranberry sauce and, of course, carrot cake.

But it wasn't just the food, and the daily access to a TV and a telephone, that made the confinement bearable. It was also the humorous conversations with the other detainees that provided the well-appreciated comedy relief, especially when out on REC.

Every day we were allowed an hour on the twenty-by-thirty-foot outdoor courtyard surrounded by four twenty-foot high concrete walls, with fresh air coming from the steel wire-mesh roof open to the sky above. After breathing the stale cell air for twenty-three hours a day, it was refreshing to either walk around and stretch my legs, or shoot some hoops with my cellies. During those well-appreciated outdoor breaks, I heard many colorful stories from individuals who always managed to put a smile on my face with their wild escapades, history cases, and brushes with the law.

But not everything was always so entertaining. On Monday afternoon, Mr. Sherlock showed up again, looking for a new angle to demystify the reason for my negligent homicide charge. Up to that point, he could only explain it as a collection of circumstances: the elopement, the landing of the aircraft on the lake, Dianne being unable to remove her seatbelt, my inability to help her, etc. But that day, he came prepared with a new arsenal based on his water-cooler discussions at the courthouse.

According to his sources, the felony was the direct result of not properly landing the aircraft on the lake. Because the right wing was damaged (see Document: 7166 @ www.ambrozuk.com), the authorities speculated I had attempted to turn right while in a glide above the water, and that was what triggered the inevitable accident. Their theory was based on the wing hitting the water first, and thus causing the damage to the airfoil, which, in turn, forced the nose of the aircraft to lunge forward, damaging the cowl of the engine (see Document: 7163 @ www.ambrozuk.com).

It was a fine theory except for some minor details that didn't fit their assumptions, primarily, the damage to the aircraft clearly visible in the photographs.

I spent five years studying aerospace engineering, taking courses ranging from "Analysis and Design of Flight Vehicle Structures" to "Flight Dynamics," and yet I was being challenged by my attorney and his merry men with no formal education or professional experience in the aviation industry. Every one of them seemed to be convinced that only they had the answers. But even though they had access to all the evidence, including the recovery photos, their laymen speculations and explanations simply didn't account for all the aircraft damage.

Here's why.

First of all, our landing on the lake was executed exactly how my ground-school instructor, David Firth, had meticulously explained if we ever found ourselves in an emergency and had to land on water.

Second, the aircraft didn't make a right turn—it made a shallow *left* turn to avoid getting too close to shore. I was seated on the left side of the cockpit, so it was only natural that I turn into the direction where I would have the best field of view.

But most importantly, the damage to the right wing was not caused by making a right turn as my attorney had insisted. It was caused by the abrupt pivotal rotation of the aircraft around its lateral axis when the wheels dug into the water. When an aircraft is in a glide, the fuselage and nose are elevated upwards to maintain altitude at low speeds. With the wings mounted high above the cockpit, it would be impossible to make such a steep turn so that the right wing would hit the water first without stalling the plane.

Therefore, the only plausible explanation for the right wing damage was due to the abrupt aircraft rotation around its rear landing gear that acted as a pivot point. As soon as the two wheels underneath the cabin touched water, the aircraft's forward momentum transferred into a 180-degree rotation around the now stationary rear wheels, causing the aircraft to instantaneously lunge forward and flip over.

If you still can't envisage or appreciate the forces involved, stick your hand into the water when you're in a boat going 45 mph, and you'll see it more clearly.

Because of the aircraft's steep angle of attack, the only ambiguity was whether the wheels or the bottom of the tail touched the water surface first. In either case, the wheels would have ultimately acted as an anchor for the aircraft, violently rotating the fuselage 180 degrees over itself, thus causing the substantial damage not only to the bottom of the engine cowling, but also to the right wing as it fiercely spun around and hit the water.

No matter what the theory, the complete damage to the aircraft had to be accounted for if it was to be a viable explanation. And that was why Mr. Sherlock and his sources, including Sheriff Dupont, a novice pilot himself, could not explain things like the broken outward windshield (see Document: 7156 @ www.ambrozuk.com) and the damage to the top of the aircraft's tail fin (see Document: 7167 @ www.ambrozuk.com). Despite being unable to account for such unequivocal anomalies, like fastidious, stubborn old men, they were determined to stick with their original theory based on false assumptions, inadequate investigation, and bias. They were insistent that I had not been catapulted through the front plastic windshield, and the aircraft never flipped over.

As often was the result, our Socratic debate that day ended in a stalemate, but before leaving, Mr. Sherlock made two suggestions which he said could improve my odds if we ever went to trial. The first was to hire a local psychologist to evaluate not only my current mental state, but also the trauma I had suffered twenty-four years ago. Initially, I opposed the idea but eventually agreed after Carolyn's sister Jenny, a school counselor, suggested it would explain some of my feelings and comments after the accident.

His second proposal was to suppress the taped phone conversation between Tom and me that took place two weeks after the accident (see Document: 3111 @ www.ambrozuk.com). He had done this once before in a similar case, he said, and it was eventually thrown out because of lack of evidence. Although I understood the reason for wanting to suppress the phone tap, thereby eliminating further exploitation by the prosecutor during a trial, I did have a few reservations. Unlike Mr. Sherlock, who still hadn't read the seventy-five-page transcript, I *had* read it several times over. By doing so, I realized that despite the few remarks Ed Corrigan had already taken out of context during my bond hearing, our conversation would clearly show my shock and emotional devastation surrounding my loss of Dianne. And that, I thought, would be a good thing for everyone, including the jury, to see and hear.

But Mr. Sherlock was insistent. So, for the time being, I agreed to his strategy, letting him do more research to see if it was even possible.

Despite the ongoing challenges with my attorney, that weekend turned out to be quite entertaining, not only because of a visit from Renata, and Carolyn ,who flew up from Texas, but also because of interesting gossip I learned about from one of the guards.

Sunday afternoon, one of the more unreserved officers told me that after my arrest, Sheriff Jim Dupont—or "Hollywood" as some of the deputies called him in Flathead County—was so ecstatic about my capture that he actually threw a *soiree* in my honor. He was so excited about finally getting closure to the only unsolved mystery on his record, as one of his undersheriffs would eventually confess (see Document: 2245 @ www.ambrozuk.com), that he threw a bash in the detention center, complete with food, drinks, and party cakes.

It was a wonder how that man ever got to the status of sheriff after exemplifying such professionalism throughout his career.

CHAPTER FIFTEEN

Saving Detainees, One Soul at a Time

December 4 – 14, 2006

Day 97 – 107

AFTER A RELATIVELY quiet few days in the FCDC, I decided on Monday night, largely out of boredom, to attend church. For safety and control reasons, only detainees from the same cell were allowed to congregate together. That evening it would be me and Bill, a carefree young man who was as ornery as he was likable.

They called it church, but it was really just a random "man of the cloth" who came in once a week to talk in the conference room with anyone willing to listen. A couple of weeks before, it was a Catholic man, but that evening, Burt showed up—a man who simply referred to himself as Christian. He said he had changed religions several times over the years before settling on the generic title.

After a brief introduction, Burt quickly jumped into the King James Bible, sharing his interpretation of Adam and Eve, Noah's Ark, and the crucifixion of Christ. Being a Catholic who had served as an altar boy for years, I was well versed in the many stories and quotes from the Bible, but when he brought up aliens who came from the sky to corrupt people, that was when he lost me.

"That was why God decided to cleanse the earth," he preached with conviction. I was surprised to hear aliens and God in the same sentence, but Burt was willing to put a new spin on old Bible stories. A devoted Christian who once was saved himself, he went on to explain about the unity of man and woman, condemning the idea of a man coveting another man, or the union of two women.

And that was when the always unpredictable Bill enthusiastically jumped in. Maintaining an innocent look, he naively confessed, "But I like being with two girls!"

It was a "deer in the headlights" moment for the stunned Burt, as he searched for a rebuttal that never came. Instead, he brushed off the blasphemous comment and moved on to a new topic. But by then it was obvious that no one was going to be saved that night. I was born a Catholic and will most likely die a Catholic; to me, that night was less about being "saved," and more about entertainment, and for the most part, the evening didn't disappoint.

On Tuesday, when I met with Mr. Sherlock about my federal case, he was under the impression they were going to throw the book at me because of the current government's conservative position. But when I spoke to Carolyn the next day, she had been told by an attorney who actually knew Mr. Shipchandler, the U.S. federal prosecutor handling my case, that out of all the U.S. district attorneys, he was one of the most reasonable and fair. That sentiment was further echoed on Friday when Mr. Sherlock talked with Mr. Shipchandler, who sounded cordial and sympathetic rather than someone looking for blood.

According to the federal prosecutor, my base passport offense was at level eight, but because I committed the crime, four more points would be added. If I decided to plead guilty to the passport charge, two levels would be subtracted for taking responsibility, thus bringing the total down to level ten.

Looking through the Federal Sentencing Guidelines Table that Mr. Sherlock brought (see Document: 3751 @ www.ambrozuk.com), and noting I had no prior felonies, my charge fell into Column I of the Criminal History Points Category. When cross-referenced with a level ten offense, the sentencing table put me in Zone B, with an incarceration period of six to twelve months. Although that sounded serious, the sentencing guidelines were just that—guidelines—and the presiding federal judge would make the final decision that could range anywhere from maximum prison time to probation only.

Probation sounded promising, even though Mr. Sherlock went off on one of his hypothetical tangents that once again made absolutely no sense. He first suggested switching the state and federal cases, thereby minimizing my federal sentencing recommendation because I wouldn't have any prior felonies counted toward my criminal points. Then he pointed out how I could more effectively deal with my state and federal charges if I wasn't incarcerated.

Both of these scenarios sounded really good, except for the necessary cooperation of not only the state and federal prosecutors, but also the immigration judge. And that was never going to happen.

After spending over 100 days in the detention center listening to this man's impossible possibilities, I started to feel as if we were going in circles. Perhaps that was his strategy: to confuse, frustrate, and discourage me to the point where I would eventually agree to any plea bargain that he and the prosecutor inked.

It might have been wishful thinking, but at that moment I was hoping to still get my money back.

CHAPTER SIXTEEN

The Secret: My Answer to Salvation

December 15 – 24, 2006

Day 108 – 117

UP TO THAT point, the Federal Eastern District of Texas had only charged me with illegal application and use of a passport, but on Friday, Mr. Sherlock came in to tell me they were now considering filing a second social security charge. He gave no explanation behind the possible new charge, other than to suggest Mr. Shipchandler had changed his mind about being lenient.

If that wasn't bad enough, he went on to say Ed Corrigan was now considering not only filing an additional criminal mischief charge, but also re-filing the airplane theft charge as originally filed and later dismissed by the Flathead County authorities twenty-four years before (see Document: 3001 @ www.ambrozuk.com).

Because both of the prosecutor's threats seemed not only ridiculous but baseless, I had a few obvious questions for Mr. Sherlock:

1) *If the theft charge was already filed and dropped in 1982, how could they re-file it?*

2) *Sol-Air Aviation, the company that owned the aircraft, was no longer in business. Who was now the complainant?*

3) *Hadn't the insurance company already paid Sol-Air Aviation for any damages?*

4) *If the aircraft and the rental company were both from Canada, why was the State of Montana asserting jurisdiction? Shouldn't that be handled by Canadian authorities?*

After a lengthy pause and some deep thought, he responded with his typical vagueness: "I don't think Judge Stadler will let the prosecutor re-file the theft charge, but he could win the criminal mischief charge."

In other words, it was a "definite maybe."

After months of frustrations, I wasn't sure what to believe, or think, about this man anymore. I had heard so many contradictory statements from him throughout the previous three months, I stopped worrying about things that might not ever happen. But it bothered me that my attorney seemed so wishy-washy about everything, whether on purpose or because he was unwittingly getting senile.

An example: we had talked previously about hiring a clinical psychologist to evaluate me in case we went to trial. He was adamant about not letting Dr. Trontel read the seventy-five page transcript of my call with Tom because Ed Corrigan would use it against us during his cross examination at the trial. But during our meeting on Friday, he had obviously forgotten our strategy when he mentioned that Dr. Trontel was coming to see me that weekend and had already read the transcript.

There was no hiding my frustrations about my imploding cases, but instead of sympathy, Mr. Sherlock had a different response. He looked up from the doodles on his notepad, and with a smug-like smirk said, "I guess nothing is really going your way, is it? Merrill Lynch, this case, the passport charge . . . " It was unexpected and sarcastic coming from the man I had paid to defend me, but I soon realized what this was all about: *The Secret*—a self-help, documentary-like film and book he was going to sell me on.

I never heard of either, and when he explained it, I was more confused than ever, wondering what it had to do with my case. His wife was an avid believer in the film that preached personal improvement through positive thinking and self-control. And now he was going to use it to save me.

"*The Secret* is about people discovering that they can change their destiny simply by the way they think," he evangelized.

Glancing at me with a straight face looking for acceptance, he seemed convinced that *The Secret* was going to be my salvation.

I realized then, that since he had no luck in negotiating with the prosecutor, and I was not cooperating by pleading guilty, his newest tactic was to use *The Secret* to show me it was within my power to end the case.

Like a clever psychologist, he turned to metaphors, and an "open door" analogy, sharing a story about an injured man who was determined to walk out of the hospital by Christmas. All the doctors told him it was impossible, but he was so determined to make it happen that it eventually came true.

"We need to find a way to walk out the door this Christmas too," he asserted. "We need to think about how to find that open door that I can work through."

When I asked about the prosecutor dropping the case, he quickly replied, "That door is closed!" When I mentioned working with the state, federal, and immigration courts to bond out, he countered with a firm, "That door is closed, too!" gesturing in midair with his fingers as if to make a door outline.

He was determined to sell me the idea of saving myself, and when I seemed confused about his new direction, he then turned to brainstorming, encouraging me to find "that open door" he was looking for. It was a strange feeling, sitting with my attorney after three months, trying to come up with a new plan, as if starting from scratch. We sat there for what seemed like eternity, looking for a new angle to his old defense strategy.

Because I was refusing to plead guilty to negligent homicide, he again brought up the idea of *nolo contendere*—or no contest—plea. He had already talked to Ed Corrigan about it and was shot down, but he now seemed invigorated to try again.

In the days that followed, I thought long and hard about our last meeting—the idea behind *The Secret*, my refusal to plead guilty, and his defense strategy. And when we met again on Saturday, I bluntly asked, "Mr. Sherlock, what do you think about me and my case so far?"

"What do you mean?" he replied, as if confused about what I was trying to get at.

I could see that he was reticent and uncomfortable about disclosing which side he stood on, but it was time to clear the air.

I persisted. "Do you think I'm guilty of the negligent homicide charge?"

"I… I have no opinion. I'm just the lawyer."

But that was just pure hogwash! Everyone had an opinion. The judges he talked to had an opinion. The people he discussed the case with at the grocery store had an opinion. The jury at my trial would have an opinion. And *he* had an opinion. In response to vagueness, I smiled, pointed at him, and half-jokingly said, "I'm going to have to call bullshit on that, Patrick!"

He didn't say anything in response, other than to laugh out loud and point his index finger back at me as if to say, "Good one!"

It was frustrating dealing with a man who didn't believe me, or in me, and appeared to be fighting for his own cause. To me, he was like a salesman trying to sell a product, and if he didn't believe in the product, he would never convince anyone—not the prosecutor, not the judge, and especially not the jury.

But instead of dwelling on my stymied case progress, after returning to my cell that evening I decided to focus my energy on something more productive: community work and my cellie. Bill and I had been spending a lot of time talking, and over time I managed to convince him to get his GED. As a result of dyslexia, his reading and writing were at a second-grade level because his teachers—and frankly, the school system in general—opted to advance him each year along with his peers, rather than help him overcome his challenges. With a bit of persuasion, one of the guards got us a few elementary school grammar books to start my tutoring. Hopefully, in the coming months, we'll make enough progress so that I can finally stop reading and writing intimate letters to his girlfriend.

CHAPTER SEVENTEEN

Of All the High Schools in All the Towns . . .

1980 – 1981

IT WAS THE BEGINNING of my junior year at John Oliver High when I first met Dianne Kathryn Babcock, the girl who would change the course of my life forever.

Although on a different floor than mine, Dianne's locker was next to several girls' from the Polish community. During lunch, or between classes, Tom and I would occasionally walk by and strike up a conversation, with Dianne often there, swapping out books for her next class.

A senior like Tom, she wasn't friends with anyone we knew, or a member of the Polish community, but she always had a genuine smile on her face that was pleasant and inviting. At times, Tom and I would tease her about her bouncy sway in her slinky walk, or make a witty comment about her subtle blonde wavy hair that extended to her shoulders, just to get her reaction. But there was always nothing but a welcoming smile in response. Pretty, petite, and fairly thin, she initially came across as reserved, but the more I got to know her, the more I realized she was more than just a pretty face. Her mellifluous, soft-spoken voice and the glowing charisma about her were infectious, so it wasn't long before she began to stand out from the rest of the crowd. It was her innocent, yet noticeably confident and genuine replies during our locker rendezvous that were ultimately responsible for our initial attraction.

Our subtle locker flirting went on for weeks until one day Dianne, for no particular reason, offered to drive Tom and me to his house after school. The first time she simply dropped us off, but next time we all ended up in his bedroom listening to music and talking about our favorite bands and the songs that inspired us.

Dianne was special. She was charming, playful, carefree, and smart—a truly happy person inside—with an endearingly gentle personality that made you feel welcome in any conversation. Never argumentative, she was articulate when it came to getting her point across, but always left room for everyone else's opinion. She was sincere and passionate about nursing and her love for children as much as she was about debating politics. Easygoing, with a quirky sense of humor that blended well with Tom and me, she was no pushover when it came to her views and opinions of our families, her goals, or the world in general, but she always made everyone feel important. She was kind, attentive, and willing to give a hand to anyone who needed her attention. But most importantly, she was fun, affectionate, down-to-earth, and always ready to join in the festivities with her bubbly personality, no matter what the plan was for that evening. In time, I found myself admiring everything she said, did, and stood for.

With several years of friendship behind us, Tom and I shared a rare bond that very few could breach. But because Dianne complemented so much of our views and beliefs, it wasn't long before we welcomed her into our trusted circle. The friendship between the three of us grew throughout the semester, as did the physical attraction between Dianne and me. At first it was just the odd bump on the shoulders or the hipcheck by the school locker, but soon those playful physical encounters evolved into much more.

We never really went out on a formal date. Instead, we slowly found private time for our intimacy. Initially, it was just entertaining conversation during our drives to Dianne's house after we left Tom's place, but eventually those hours of talking turned into physical attraction, beginning innocently enough with a kiss.

I had gotten to first base with other girls before, but with Dianne it was different. It didn't merely feel good—it felt right. Our first romantic encounter wasn't a beach with a sunset backdrop—it was in my car down the street from her house, but we didn't care because it was magic. They say you'll know from the first kiss if someone is "the one" you're going spend the rest of your life with, and that afternoon I think both of us knew. After weeks of talking and feeling the sexual tension between us, we finally crossed that awkward barrier and never looked back. We were two teenagers in high school, but everything seemed to fall in place. It was as if we were pieces of a jigsaw puzzle that finally came together.

As Dianne and I progressed with our intimacy, we kept our growing infatuation private for several reasons. First, there were the kids at school who loved to point fingers and start rumors. Neither of us wanted to be drilled by the gossip spreaders, so we simply chose to keep things casual for the time being. Over time, I think most people figured out we were an item, but we preferred that it stayed speculation.

Secondly, we shielded Tom from our intimacy so as not to make him feel like a "third wheel." The three of us would often hang out together but rarely did we show affection in his presence. Tom and I never really discussed it, probably because it was one of those unwritten high school rules where guys didn't talk to their best friend about falling in love. Obviously, Tom knew about us, and perhaps spoke with Dianne about it, but as open as our friendship was, it was never mentioned during our conversations.

Lastly—and most important—were our families. If the Polish kids at John Oliver knew we were dating, so would their parents. Being a close-knit community, it would be only a matter of time before my parents found out, and a slew of questions were sure to follow.

I was fortunate enough to have a stable home, even though the mood at the house always seemed somber. There were constant issues of trust, and over time I simply learned to avoid arguments through silence. It was easier not to tell my parents my whereabouts, or make up a story, rather than hear a lecture about their disapproval because of where I was going, or what I should be doing.

I had everything I could possibly want—a nice house to live in, three hearty meals cooked by my mother every day, a personal car to use at will, and even my private pilot's license paid for by my parents—but what I was missing was that teenage understanding and freedom that most adolescents need to find themselves.

It seemed that no matter what I did, it was never good enough. When I did something exceptional, there was never any praise for my hard work and effort. The neighbor kids and the Polish community children were always smarter, better, and more obedient. As time went on, I found myself chasing expectations I could never reach.

To add to the pressures of growing up and dating, there was also the expectation that one day I would find that perfect girl whom everyone would approve of. A case in point was a Polish community couple in their mid-twenties where the father would not accept the girl into his family. Opposed to their marriage, the battle raged on as we watched their family life get torn apart. Recognizing their narrow-mindedness, it was clear there was also a dark cloud hanging over our heads. Not only because we were teenagers in high school who couldn't possibly know anything about love, but also because of Dianne's non-Polish bloodline.

Spending hours together in the evenings and on the weekends, Tom, Dianne, and I often contemplated our intricate relationships with our families. Sometimes we talked about Dianne's demanding life, but much more frequently the topic became about Tom and me, the Polish community, our parents, and paternalism. Because of their high expectations, occasional confrontations were inevitable, but all of us understood their motivation for tough love, as they tried their best to improve our lives the only way they knew how.

My immediate family consisted of only my parents, my thirteen-year-old sister, Renata, and myself. Dianne's family, the Babcocks, included her parents, Gerald and Adele, an older brother, Geoff, and three sisters—with Dianne being the middle girl. Throughout the entire length of our courtship, I saw Dianne's parents only a handful of times and spoke with them even less. Dianne's mother offered me lunch only once when I happened to be at their house at noon. Similarly, with her father, we once had a single conversation in their basement game room about getting my license and becoming an airline pilot.

Linda, the eldest daughter, had moved away by the time we were dating. I met her once at Dianne's house and recall very little about her, her character, or what she did for a living.

Geoff, on the other hand, was still living at home while attending Simon Fraser University. According to Dianne, he was a loner and without a girlfriend during the entire time we were together. We occasionally crossed paths at their house, but other than a friendly greeting, we never really talked.

But unlike Geoff and Linda, I remember Dianne's youngest sister, Jodi, very well. Three years younger than Dianne, she was already fully developed and tall for her age. With her peculiar walk and nervous facial tics, she was pleasant enough to be around, often tagging along with us during our bus rides from school, or the occasional weekend tennis match with Tom and me. Compared to Dianne's "cowboy" ex-boyfriend, who had a 4x4 truck and a bad temper, she fully supported our dating. But despite being close to Dianne, her knowledge about our amorous relationship was superficial, and she remained unaware of the details of our intimacy.

Dianne and I kept our relationship relatively secret, avoiding what we believed to be unpleasant and inevitable consequences. It often seemed as if we were leading a double life: during the day we continued our daily routines, but at night it was our private time and that meant no limits.

After Tom and Dianne graduated, Tom joined the reserves and began his first year of undergraduate studies to become a lawyer. Dianne was on a waiting list at British Columbia Institute of Technology (BCIT) trying to get into their nursing program. In the interim, she volunteered at a children's hospital during that fall semester.

Throughout the first few months, Dianne and I saw each other on weekends and the occasional night out. But when Tom went off to SFU, things really heated up. At first, we got together once or twice a week during the midnight hours, but eventually even that wasn't enough. We secretly met after everyone had gone to bed and spend hours huddled in a car until dawn. I would sneak out of my second-storey bedroom by climbing down the balcony, quietly roll my Ford Meteor out of the driveway so as not to wake my parents, and head to Dianne's house before heading to our secret hideout by the river. Other times, Dianne would do the same in the Honda Civic she shared with her brother, and we would head to the BCIT parking lot close to my house for our twilight session of steamed up windows, snuggling, and intimate conversation.

We would discuss anything and everything about each other, about our aspirations for the future, and about our families. Spending each night together naked—reclined in the back of the car, fingers interlocked, with arms wrapped around each other—we never wanted the night to end. There was no need for fancy dates, no expensive restaurants, and no extravagant gifts to show our affection or impress one another. We were perfectly content in our own private bubble, as if we were the last people on Earth. In time, the only thing that mattered was us, and the only important thing was our happiness. As unbelievable as it seemed, even at our age, it felt as if we had found our soulmate, and nothing was as important as each other's wellbeing.

When we were together, the euphoria of being with someone who was up for just about anything and shared the same views, beliefs, and goals was exhilarating. On the outside, Dianne was shy and innocent, but once comfortable, she also had a spontaneous wild streak. It wasn't unusual for us to get "lost" on a hiking trail or pull over on the side of the road and head into the nearby bushes for a quickie. Never complaining or making excuses, she was always ready to initiate or join in the fun with nothing but her radiant smile.

With time, each night became harder to part ways and return to the real world.

It's said you find love when you're not looking and least expect it. That could not be more true in our case, despite the notion that high school was supposed to be about casually dating and never committing to anyone in particular. It wasn't that I was opposed to a serious relationship, but until Dianne, I had never met anyone who made me feel like she was the one I wanted to spend the rest of my life with. When we were together, time seemed to stop.

It may sound unrealistic, and perhaps melodramatic, to think that two teenagers could fall in love so hard at such an early age, but it wasn't long before we both realized we had elevated to the next plateau. It was the most empowering feeling to be with someone who had 99 percent of everything you ever wanted and believed in. To feel like we could take on the world, and no matter what happened, we would always have each other.

CHAPTER EIGHTEEN

A Flathead County Christmas

December 25, 2006 – January 3, 2007
Day 118 – 127

THE MORE TIME I spent in the Flathead County Detention Center, the more I felt like "Brubaker"—a 1980 movie warden who eventually took over a corrupt Southern chain-gang prison, but not until he learned all their dirty secrets by first posing as a prisoner. Throughout the previous few months, like Brubaker, I also heard a few of Kalispell's dirty little secrets from my attorney, the guards, and detainees alike, who were more than happy to share.

There was the prosecutor who was involved with prostitution while the Flathead County authorities turned a blind eye; a judge whose silent partnership in four Kalispell bars posed a possible conflict of interest; a judge who was occasionally spotted behind the Four Corners Bar, partaking in drugs with the local patrons; and others whose actions were questionable. I didn't know how much of it was true, nor did I care about their indiscretions as it was irrelevant to my case. But after hearing the details from what seemed like legitimate sources, it made me wonder about the credibility of all those government officials. As small as Kalispell was, it wouldn't take much for a curious reporter to verify those claims, but it seemed hypocritical that I could be judged by the very same authorities.

As disturbing as that sounded, it seemed unimportant during the holidays, when everything came to a standstill.

I'd had no word from my attorney about Ed Corrigan and the potential new charges. There was no word from the federal government about filing additional social security charges. There was no word from Mr. Cohen after contacting Merrill Lynch to demand the release of my accounts (see Document: 3502 @ www.ambrozuk.com). There was no word from Mr. Bodnar's attorney who rejected our last proposal for the release of my Corvette. And there was no word from Kim and Ken who were still refusing to pay back my $70,000 loan so that I could pay my house bills.

But despite all that, this was still one of the best Christmas holidays I'd had in a long time. It felt good to finally call my family and wish them Merry Christmas. As trivial as that sounds, after twenty-four years, it meant a lot to me.

But the Flathead County Christmas cheer didn't stop there. Starting early in December, the boys and I began to build a Christmas tree using a sharpened pen to score cardboard from the back of a notepad, some coloring pencils, and toothpaste to glue it all together. Eventually, we added colored ornaments and a few tiny presents below the tree to complete the scene. As a side project, one of the guys, who'd picked up a few tricks during his previous visit to the penitentiary, showed us how to cut and fold pieces of toilet paper into an impressive looking rose, complete with stem, petals, and two leaves we shaded with coloring pencils for a more realistic look.

Our craftwork may have been amateur—given the limited tools at our disposal—but it was impressive enough to prompt one of the female officers to issue a "pink slip," preventing other guards from confiscating our hard work during regular inspections because it was considered contraband.

Martha Stewart, eat your heart out!

CHAPTER NINETEEN

Psychoanalysis Mumbo Jumbo

January 4 – 9, 2007
Day 128 – 133

ON THURSDAY, AT 11:00 a.m., I met with Edward H. Trontel, Ph.D., the local clinical psychologist hired by my attorney to do my evaluation. Sitting in the conference room behind a cafeteria foldout table when I walked in, he was an older gentleman, perhaps in his fifties, smaller than I in stature, and looked like a stereotypical doctor. His short, white hair blended into his peppered, full beard that oddly resembled the late Dr. Sigmund Freud. His leg was elevated on the table, he explained, because of a recent operation.

After a brief introduction, he said that the information we discussed would be shared only with my attorney, and pending the outcome, it might or might not be beneficial to my case.

He noted that he had a bad habit of interrupting people while they talked, but it was his way to further explore the current topic rather than waiting until the end. I acknowledged with a nod as he began with the basics: why he was there; what was the reason Dianne and I had eloped? Why did we cut ties with our families and friends? Why didn't I come back? How many people knew about the accident? How was my life growing up? How was I treated by my parents? Was I worried about the federal charges that would follow? And a plethora of other questions I was happy to answer to the best of my ability.

I don't know if he expected to drag things out of me, but after so many years of silence, I was ready to tell all.

We spent several hours discussing many topics, but there were two areas in particular that he focused on: my upbringing, including the reasons why Dianne and I eloped, and the accident itself that ultimately led to the negligent homicide charge.

He was very thorough and spent a considerable amount of time discussing my childhood. Looking to find a reason for our elopement, he focused extensively on my parents and how I had been raised, but there was very little for him to exploit. As with most European Catholics, my parents were more or less normal. We would attend church every Sunday and on special holidays and, in general, their only motivation was the betterment of the children. There was no sexual or physical abuse, and apart from being overbearing at times to make sure we followed their rules, I had a perfectly normal adolescence. But the doctor was not satisfied, looking for a dark secret that was going to explain it all in a neat and tidy package.

During our conversation, I was candid about the reasons behind the need for our freedom, adventure, and a new life, but there was more that Dr. Trontel was after. Like Mr. Sherlock, it became clear that his real mission was to make me understand I should plead guilty to the negligent homicide charge.

Instead of a car crash example, he turned to a closer-to-home analogy about a Lear-jet pilot who ignored instructions from air-traffic control to avoid bad weather by flying over a mountain, and instead flew through a valley, thereby causing the plane to crash. He compared his example to our elopement by adding that the pilot even asked the passengers if everyone agreed with his decision, as if that would negate his responsibility for their safety.

It may have been a noble attempt, but it was not a realistic comparison. When Dianne and I accepted the risk of landing an aircraft on water, it was mutual consent comparable to a weekend racecar enthusiast who signs a release contract exonerating the track facility of any responsibility or liability. That is not the same as a passenger who gets into an aircraft and expects to arrive at their destination in relative safety. Dianne and I planning our dangerous landing for months was not the same as the pilot asking the passengers for their permission in midair.

I could somewhat understand Mr. Sherlock's determination to convince me to plead guilty because of his plea bargain skills and track record, but for a clinical psychologist to follow suit with his own sketchy examples seemed almost unethical.

After four hours of fidgeting in his chair, Dr. Trontel finally ended his clinical interrogation, only to hand me the Minnesota Multiphasic Personality Inventory 2 (MMPI-2) test that he had brought to help him determine my mental state. He said the test consisted of 567 TRUE or FALSE questions and was used to evaluate individuals with mental disorders. After our extensive talk, he was hesitant to give me the test, commenting that he was not expecting to find anything out of the ordinary, but eventually changed his mind and said it should not take more than an hour to complete.

That evening, after dinner, I was escorted to one of the visitor booths downstairs to fill out the lengthy questionnaire. Working systematically, I found some of the questions confusing, but since the instructions explicitly said to answer them all even though some may not seem applicable, I followed the directions in the best way I could.

Here are samples that will explain my confusion:

39) My sleep is fitful and disturbed

71) These days I find it hard not to give up hope of amounting to something

104) Most people are honest chiefly because they are afraid of being caught

110) Most people will use somewhat unfair means to gain profit or an advantage rather than to lose it

143) I am neither gaining nor losing weight

149) The top of my head sometimes feels tender

150) Sometimes I feel as I must injure either myself or someone else

162) Someone has been trying to poison me

187) If I were a reporter I would very much like to report news of the theater

253) I drink an unusually large amount of water everyday

268) I wish I were not bothered by thoughts about sex

327) Bad words, often terrible words, come into my mind and I cannot get rid of them

336) Someone has control over my mind

361) Someone has been trying to influence my mind

371) I have often wished I were a member of the opposite sex

374) Most people will use somewhat unfair means to get ahead in life

418) It is all right to get around the law if you don't actually break it

430) I am often sorry because I am so irritable and grouchy

436) When a man is with a woman he is usually thinking about things related to sex

443) I do not try to cover up my poor opinion or pity of people so that they won't know how I feel

520) Lately I have thought a lot about killing myself

538) Most men are unfaithful to their wives now and then

563) In most marriages one or both partners are unhappy

567) Most married couples don't show much affection for each other

After filling out the questionnaire, I was curious how I ranked on the crazy scale, but that would have to wait until our next meeting.

On Monday, the Super Bowl of college football—Ohio-Florida Fiesta Bowl—was on TV. Instead of attending church, I decided to watch the highly anticipated college matchup. This, of course, meant I was going straight to hell because I picked football over church, but by then my amusement with the never-ending Disciples of God had fizzled out.

Bill, on the other hand, was not discouraged and, after another two-hour church meeting, returned with new faith to overcome his illiteracy. Like the evangelist that night—who himself couldn't read or write at the age of nineteen but miraculously overcame his limitation by the time he turned twenty-four because of his Bible study—Bill was convinced that only the scriptures could save him and improve his vocabulary skills.

As I was not his father, his guardian, or his probation officer, I simply grinned at his decision and considered the matter closed, but it was unfortunate that once again he would be cheated out of a possible brighter future by a wolf in sheep's clothing.

After a seventeen-day absence, Mr. Sherlock showed up on Tuesday with more grim news. In his research, he had discovered it was highly unlikely the seventy-five-page transcript between Tom and me could be suppressed because it had been done by the Canadian authorities, and Tom had agreed to the wiretap. As I was not an avid supporter of his strategy in the first place, that news wasn't bothersome. What was disturbing was the prosecutor following through on his promise to file two more felonies against me: theft and criminal mischief.

Because the airplane was from Canada, because the aircraft rental company was in Canada and no longer in existence, and because Dianne and I were also Canadian citizens, I had a difficult time understanding how a prosecutor in a foreign country could file such charges. But according to my attorney, he could, despite the theft charge being filed and dropped once already twenty-four years ago (see Document: 3001 @ www.ambrozuk.com).

The more I discussed my upcoming trial with Mr. Sherlock—including the omnibus hearing in three weeks that we hadn't talked about or prepared for—the more I felt he was going to drop the ball again, just as he had with the preliminary hearing.

As always, it was difficult to understand and predict his case strategy, including the two new charges, so I eventually gave up and told him about the letter I was planning to send to Dianne's father. My sister and I had previously discussed the best way for me to approach Mr. Babcock after so many years, and in the end, we agreed that an apologetic letter seemed more appropriate now, rather than waiting until my cases were resolved.

When I showed him my handwritten letter (see Document: 7080 @ www.ambrozuk.com), he seemed unmoved but hoped that neither the media nor Ed Corrigan would see it. Twenty-four years was a long time, but I remembered Mr. Babcock as more rational then vindictive, so I explained that I at least needed to let Dianne's father know my thoughts and how I felt.

The letter read:

Dear Mr. Babcock:

I'm writing to you in hope of getting an opportunity to finally explain to you what happened 24 years ago and why Dianne and I made the decision to run away. This has been a long and painful journey for me but I can't imagine the pain and sorrow your family must have felt upon hearing the news of Dianne after the accident.

I would first like to say how truly sorry I am for the loss of your daughter and also for the loss of your wife. They were both very special women and I was saddened to hear about your accident and the tragic death of Mrs. Babcock. My condolences.

But as unbelievable as it all seems, Dianne and I ran away because we were in love and at the time that was the only way we thought we could be happy. There are a lot of crazy things teenagers in love do and this is probably one of the most ridiculous plans we came up with. I know that now and I cannot tell you how sorry I am for the loss of your daughter but there is nothing now nor was there anything 24 years ago that I could have done to undo what happened and bring Dianne back. I spent many, lonely years reasoning out what went wrong, why did Dianne have to die and why would God take her away from me like that. As you can probably imagine, that is not an easy thing to live with for a teenager, especially the first few years.

But when it is all said and done, all I know is that I truly loved Dianne and hurting her or letting anything happen to her was the farthest thing from my mind. And that is why I have pleaded not guilty to the Negligent Homicide charge. I offered to meet with the prosecutor, Mr. Corrigan, and the judge to tell them the details of the accident in hopes of ending this quickly but they all refused. I feel that they are just looking for a scapegoat for Dianne's death and are ignoring all the evidence. Mr. Corrigan told the press that I am not remorseful and that I am not taking responsibility. I feel Mr. Corrigan doesn't know me and doesn't care about the truth and about what happened between Dianne and I in this complicated and highly visible case. I also believe that pleading guilty to the Negligent Homicide charge insinuates that I didn't do everything I possibly could to save Dianne and in fact implies that I am an 'Accused Killer' as America's Most Wanted has already stated in their documentary and on their website.

Therefore, I hope that you can understand why I need to fight this charge. This is very personal to me because I will have to live with it for the rest of my life and because one day I hope to stand in front of you to explain all that transpired. I do not know if you plan to attend the trial but I want to apologize ahead of time for any further pain this might cause you. I'm sure that re-opening old wounds is going to be as painful for you and your family as it will be for me.

What I wish is to finally provide closure for you and your family after so many years and so many unanswered questions. I am not sure even now if I can explain in words why all this happened, why Dianne and I ran away and why I didn't return home 24 years ago but I would like the opportunity to try.

My communication with the outside now is limited to letters and 15 minute collect phone calls but perhaps when this is all over and you wish to meet, I would be more than happy to answer any questions you may have of me.

Once again, I am very sorry for all this and the pain it has caused you and your family for so many years.

Sincerely,

Jerry Ambrozuk

When I returned to my cell, I immediately mailed the letter to the address I found scribbled on one of the evidence documents. I assumed the handwritten address and phone number was recently updated by a local county investigator who had contacted Dianne's father to verify my identity prior to my arrest.

If not, then there was going to be one confused resident in Burnaby, B.C. who would be receiving my letter shortly.

CHAPTER TWENTY

The Id, the Ego, and the Superego

January 10 – 20, 2007
Day 134 – 144

ON WEDNESDAY EVENING, Dr. Trontel showed up again, and this time we met for two hours. "Why did you take such a drastic step to elope?" he asked. "I'm puzzled by your need to eradicate your identity in the process." The clinical psychologist was determined to get answers, even if it meant being overly dramatic.

I explained, once again, our reasons for eloping, but he seemed skeptical. Staging an accident meant minimum suffering and grief for our friends and families. Once declared missing and presumed dead, they would stop looking for us and could get on with their lives. It was as simple as that.

But he seemed unsatisfied, prying deeper for a more profound explanation, even though there was nothing else. Our elopement plan revolved around our disappearance, and getting rid of our identities was simply logical—even for two high school kids.

He didn't appear convinced but nonetheless moved on to his main reason for being there—my refusal to plead guilty and his new remorse tactic.

Not understanding why I would bet my life on a hope that the jury would find me innocent, he began to rationalize "The reason you don't feel guilty is because you do not associate what happened with guilt."

"Typically a person who shoots another human being will be over-whelmed with guilt because they know and feel that they did something wrong. In your case, although you knew that the elopement plan was dangerous, you didn't feel guilt because you tried to save Dianne," he explained.

In some sense he was right. I may have been heartbroken twenty-four years ago, but never have I ever felt guilty. Dianne and I had planned our elopement for months and executed our emergency land-ing on the water as detailed by my ground-school instructor; for me, Dianne's tragic drowning was always a horrific accident.

"Feeling guilty is not the same as feeling remorseful and sorry. But to most people those emotions are intertwined, and that could be dif-ficult for people on a jury panel to reason out," he suggested.

Listening to every word, I could appreciate his warning, but to me, my principle was unshakable. Our elopement may have been irrespon-sible, but it was based on love. I was not about to let a smugly moralistic prosecutor tarnish it because of some erroneous charges.

But my principle was only half the battle—the other half was my conscience. If I pleaded guilty, I would have to live with my decision for the rest of my life. A guilty plea to negligent homicide would mean people like Sheriff Dupont, who went out of his way to make false ac-cusations against me throughout the past twenty-four years, were right. And *that* I had a problem with as much as with *America's Most Wanted* calling me an accused killer—and all the other media sources trying to spin our elopement into something nefarious. If I took their plea deal, it would mean they were right.

Dr. Trontel seemed sympathetic, but he was quick to point out that although *we* could reason out and separate the emotions of remorseful-ness and guilt, would others like the jury be able to do the same?

It was a fair question that I expected to be clarified in court by my expensive attorney and now a clinical psychologist. To that end, I sim-ply said, "I guess I will have to depend on you and Mr. Sherlock to explain it all in laymen terms so that everyone in court, including the media, will understand."

After two sessions with Dr. Trontel, I still couldn't tell if he was on my side and would ultimately write a favorable analysis for the court, or if he was simply there baiting me—trying to convince me to plead guilty as Mr. Sherlock wanted. But the answer to that question would have to wait another day as he packed up to leave.

Curious about the results to my MMPI-2 test, I asked about my score and how I ranked on the 0-to-100 crazy scale. He laughed at my feeble humor attempt and said that the results were "boring," showing only that I had a strong personality. I didn't really know what a "strong personality" suggested, but if he meant I was impervious to coercion, then I wholeheartedly agreed.

Another nine days had passed since I last saw my attorney. I was getting very concerned about the upcoming omnibus hearing less than two weeks away as well as the trial. So far, I had not heard a single word from Mr. Sherlock about our preparation, other than the list of witnesses I prepared, upon his request, after confronting him about it during our last meeting.

When I spoke with Renata on Thursday, she looked up the Sherlock and Nardi corporate website again and noticed that despite mentioning criminal law, Mr. Sherlock's profile stated appellate practice as his strength—specifically DUIs, driver's license petitions, social security, commercial law, personal injury, probate, and real estate. It was his partner, Nardi, who had the bulk of the criminal trial experience, but because he was terminally ill, their receptionist referred us to Mr. Sherlock when Carolyn originally called their office months back. After my arrest, everything seemed chaotic and urgent, so no one took the time to research and verify the attorney's credentials.

Four months before, we based our decision on personality and Mr. Sherlock's tenure in Flathead County. He all but assured us at the time that he had the ear of the presiding judge. But after countless disappointments leading up to the upcoming trial, I realized we were obviously misled. Mr. Sherlock had bungled our chances from the beginning, and now winning at a trial looked more dismal than ever. Even I understood that most cases got plea bargained, but without the realistic threat of losing in a trial, the prosecutor had no incentive to cooperate. Perhaps taking on a negligent homicide case by an appellate attorney just to make $30,000 was not the smartest idea, especially since now his lack of criminal experience put my wellbeing in jeopardy.

But sulking in my cell over past mistakes would not improve my current situation. So after talking with my family and doing some soul searching, I decided to do something positive: revert to my given name. I was born in Poland and officially named Jaroslaw, or Jarek for short. When I moved to Canada, it was loosely translated to Jerry so that people in the Western world could pronounce it.

When I took on my new identity in Texas, I became Michael for twenty-four years. But now that I had come full circle, I was ready to revert to my heritage and return to "Jarek" for the fourth and final time. I know I will spend the rest of my life explaining that the J is pronounced like a Y (as in "Yoda the wise one"), but if people can adapt to Jesus (pronounced "hey-soos" in Spanish), they can also manage Jarek.

CHAPTER TWENTY-ONE

The Master Plan Unfolds

1982

THE MIDNIGHT ESCAPADES between Dianne and me went on for months and no one, not even Tom, was aware how much time we spent together in secret.

I was still going to church every Sunday, keeping up my grades and, in general, doing what was asked. But it was those exciting midnight rendezvous with Dianne that I so looked forward to and could not get enough of. This was the first love for us both, and everything was pure, unblemished, and passionate.

During high school, Tom, Dianne, and I would often hang out on weekends, but once Tom got into university and started part-time with the Canadian Reserves, we saw him much less. When we did find time to get together, many of our conversations revolved around independence and the appeal of simple, idealistic values. Tom's Canadian Reserves boot camp focused on survival skills, and that often became the topic of our many ongoing conversations about living in the wilderness and surviving off the land. Along with his military training, movies like *Apocalypse Now*—with the splendor of its cinematography and a jungle backdrop—also contributed to our talks about how we ourselves could endure living under such harsh and unusual conditions.

But for Dianne and me, it would be the infamous *Tarzan, the Ape Man* movie we saw in the fall of 1981 that would be largely responsible for our change in perception of reality. Starring Bo Derek as Jane and

Miles O'Keeffe as Tarzan, it was a cheesy flick with Jane parading in her skimpy animal skin outfit while Tarzan strutted around her, looking to mate as he staved off "savages." Ridiculous as it was, there was something about the golden beach and blue lagoon that captivated our imagination. Dianne didn't think she was Jane, and I surely didn't believe I was Tarzan, but the wild idea of surviving in the jungle, building a treehouse as our home, and eating what we caught or killed had an alluring appeal.

Living in the wild and fending for ourselves, although initially intimidating, over time became much more appealing. How amazing it would be to make our home in the jungles of Africa as we hunted for food and thwarted off wild animals with our survival skills. There was no question that the challenges would not be easy, but the idea was intoxicating.

Initially half-serious, it was the "what if" and "how amazing it would be" scenarios that preoccupied our many hours together, as we fantasized about our tantalizing adventure across the African continent. The more we revisited our concocted utopia, the more it became a realistic ambition.

If we were to do this, we had to find a way to disappear without making anyone suspicious, or leave any traces of our departure. Neither of us wanted our families to worry about where we were, or if we were in danger. The most obvious and logical solution was to simply fake an accident. Our initial thought was to use the environment to our advantage, and drive our car off some secluded, steep cliff in the Canadian Rockies while on an excursion. Periodically, we would hear about mountain climbers getting lost, never to be found again, so at first our plan seemed credible. Once reported missing, the search-and-rescue authorities would spend a few days scouring the mountains before abandoning their search without success.

But there were obvious problems with that scenario. It would be difficult to make our way on foot across Canada—someone could possibly recognize us along the way—and there was likelihood the vehicle would eventually be found, triggering a full search for survivors. The latter concerned us most. It would be much less traumatizing to our grieving families if they never found the vehicle, we were declared missing, and after an extensive investigation, simply forgotten.

Our other problem revolved around the logistics of getting to Africa. Using an airline or a cruise ship from the East Coast to the African continent would be challenging. It would not only be expensive, but there was also a very good possibility we would be identified. By the time we made our way across Canada, our faces would be on every TV channel during the five o'clock news—making us an easy target to spot in a crowd, or at the check-in counter as we boarded the aircraft or ship.

Therefore, the only practical solution was to cross the Atlantic Ocean as stowaways. But the idea of sneaking onto a cargo ship and spending several weeks among the shipping containers seemed risky and not very appealing to either of us.

We continued to deliberate our plan for months, eventually realizing that it was precarious at best. But as luck would have it, an alternative presented itself from none other than my ground-school instructor at Sol-Air Aviation.

Every Monday night, several other pilot enthusiasts and I met in the south terminal of the Richmond airport to attend ground-school classes. There, we went over the prerequisite material for taking the private pilot's license test. Our instructor, David Firth, an ex-commercial pilot, was responsible for teaching us everything from weather to aircraft mechanics and flight. Outspoken at times, he took his job seriously, but always had room during his lectures to boast about his extensive experience in avionics, whether it had to do with the curriculum at hand or the latest aviation news.

During one of our Monday night classes, one such news story turned into a lengthy discussion about emergency landings. A few days prior, a pilot was forced to land his aircraft on a bridge because he ran out of fuel. The newspapers and the TV media praised him as a hero for safely landing the aircraft, but our instructor had a different opinion.

Outraged, he called the pilot an idiot for not computing his fuel consumption correctly, thereby preventing him from safely returning to the airport.

As his condemnations of the pilot's stunt subsided, the conversation slowly shifted to the possibility of landing a fixed landing-gear aircraft (see Document: 1225 @ www.ambrozuk.com) on an unconventional surface. Taking the lead, one of the more vocal students in class began expanding on the topic, looking for answers to obvious questions if we ever found ourselves in an emergency. The possibility of running out of fuel was remote, as it was the pilot's responsibility to compute the fuel consumption for the flight prior to taking off. But there were always unpredictable circumstances, such as an engine failure, that could force a pilot to make an emergency landing on atypical terrain.

Confident as always, Firth responded to each question without hesitation: What would happen if we had to land in thick bushes or a forested area with no clearing in sight? What would the airplane attitude have to be to land in a wheat field? What should the air speed and flap degree be set to when landing in an Arctic bog? What was the proper procedure to land an aircraft on water, being that Vancouver is a coastal city and there is water everywhere?

Mr. Firth had a viable explanation for every scenario my classmates proposed. Backed by his twenty-year aviation experience, he was confident about his recommendations, making it sound as if there was always a proper configuration for every landing, no matter what the surface.

Of all the hypothetical questions asked in class that night, the idea of safely landing a fixed landing-gear aircraft on water resonated with me the most. The experienced instructor was convinced that keeping the speed to a minimum, flaps fully extended, and adopting a nose-up-tail-down attitude when making contact with the water surface, would yield a successful landing without the aircraft flipping over. Although he had never attempted such a maneuver, the idea that it was possible to do it safely in an emergency was now planted in my mind.

When I got together with Dianne that night, and passed on the details of what my ground-school instructor said, we both knew we had found an alternate plan to our car dilemma. Unlike our previous scenario, landing the aircraft on the surface of the lake would not only cause it to sink—and thus make it nearly impossible to find by the authorities—but it also resolved part of our logistics issue with transportation.

Realizing our farfetched dream of eloping to Africa posed yet another impossible task of crossing the Atlantic Ocean, Dianne and I compromised on South America. It was similar in climate and picturesque scenery, and thus a viable alternative. Using an airplane, we could at least cross the U.S. border without being detected, and then make our way south by hitchhiking, or taking a bus or train without the need for IDs.

It had been over a year since Dianne and I started dating, and although her nursing school was moving along, it no longer carried the same excitement as when she first started. By the same token, my dreams of becoming a pilot also took a back seat to our new and intoxicating plan. After months of methodical reasoning and deliberation, Dianne and I made the decision to follow through with our adventure of a lifetime.

We discussed our elopement at length, and together decided our plan was the best solution for our future. We knew there would be repercussions, but if everything went according to our carefully thought-out agenda, we believed the impact to our families and friends would be minimal. Their anguish of grief would quickly subside once the search for the aircraft ended without result.

Now that we had a purpose, it was time to work out the details. The general plan involved preparing our supplies, renting an airplane that would take us over the U.S. border, ditching the plane in a large lake at dusk to avoid being spotted, and making our way south into the jungles of South America—most likely somewhere in the rainforests of Brazil.

One of the first decisions we had to make was committing to a departure date. The most logical and least conspicuous was August 22,

1982 for several reasons. First, when we made the decision, summer was approaching. I already had my private pilot's license so we could leave anytime, but we needed to save enough money for our trip. To make things worse, our plan called for a casual flight trip where we would encounter an unfortunate accident, and therefore we needed to be discreet with our money collection so as not to attract the attention of investigators after we were gone.

August 22 was also close enough to the start of the fall school semester, and Dianne could ask her parents for the $500 they owed her so she could pay for her tuition and books. The timing seemed reasonable and Dianne's parents would write her a check on August 20, just two days after Tom also repaid the $500 that he had borrowed to cover his previous semester's tuition. Adding her $584.27 bank withdrawal on July 8, that included an income tax refund from April 15 of $450, Dianne contributed close to $1,600.00 to our getaway fund.

Being frugal with my weekly allowance for gas, and periodically helping my father fix cars in the garage behind our house, I also managed to pull together just over $700 for our trip. Collectively, we saved close to $2,300 that would be used to pay for our lodging and supplies along the way (see Document: 3107 @ www.ambrozuk.com).

With our date set, the last critical part of our plan was to work out the logistics of the plane rental and our destination. At the forefront was our concern about my flying experience. Would the airplane rental company allow a novice pilot to fly the aircraft through the mountainous regions of British Columbia? Although I'd had my private pilot's license for several months—and managed to clock in a couple dozen extra hours—was that enough to convince the rental company I was qualified to make a long-distance flight?

Our other criteria required that our destination through the mountains had to be far enough from Vancouver so there would be plenty of terrain to search once our airplane was reported missing. Solving both problems, Dianne and I decided the most logical destination for a day trip would be to Penticton, British Columbia—a city in the Okanagan Valley where I had already traversed the route a few months back.

During the summer of 1981, my flight instructor and two other students flew to Penticton, via Hope and Princeton, to see the Penticton Air Show and log some extra flying hours. Each of the students took turns as we followed the route on the map, observing signs along the way. All of us were learning to fly using Visual Flight Rules (VFR), so being able to identify objects, roads, train tracks, and markers on the ground was essential.

When I contacted the rental company to book the aircraft three weeks prior to our departure, I was pleasantly surprised. I was still considered a novice pilot, but Sol-Air Aviation didn't have a problem letting us rent the Cessna C150 for the one-day trip. As expected, much of their decision was based on my previous mountainous cross-country trip, and my familiarity with the route.

As far as everyone was concerned, we were simply renting the aircraft in the morning, flying to Penticton for the day, and would return to Vancouver before dark. But in reality, once we left Penticton we were going to deviate from our flight plan and head south across the U.S. border (see Document: 7400 @ www.ambrozuk.com). Flying below the radar, the idea was to get as far south as possible, on the available fuel, before landing on a predetermined lake to hide our tracks.

The body of water had to be large enough to land on, without being noticed by the lakeside residents and weekend campers, but small enough that we could easily get to shore. Looking at the regional topology maps I used during my training, we computed the maximum distance we could fly from Penticton and looked for a large lake within the range limit. The only one that appeared large enough on the map to fit our needs was Flathead Lake in Montana, and that became our initial destination.

According to my ground-school instructor, after our landing, we would have between ten and thirty minutes before the plane sank. That would give us plenty of time to inflate the two-man raft and load our bags before paddling to shore as the plane sank to the bottom of the lake. Once on land, we could pass as a couple of hitchhikers heading south. But there was a limit to how many supplies we could carry without looking suspicious. The plan was to start with minimal food and clothing and replenish our provisions as needed along the way.

We also understood that performing an emergency landing on water would be dangerous. We spent dozens of hours discussing the details, and short of practicing our water landing, we went over our exit strategy meticulously, making sure to follow the proper procedures. During my flight training, I had spent months practicing aerial maneuvers and emergency recoveries from possible conditions that could arise during normal flight, including stalls, spirals, and engine failures. I also logged enough hours in the aircraft that I was comfortable with its maneuvering capabilities. So after the assurance of my ground-school instructor that we could safely land on water, we both felt the risks were minimal.

Preparing for our journey, we gathered our supplies and had everything worked out—everything except for our final destination in South America. With no Internet for another decade—and no way to inconspicuously look up maps online or Google directions—our final destination would remain a mystery until the very end. We debated doing some research in the library on South American countries, but soon abandoned that idea for fear of being identified by people who would remember us after we were declared missing and the investigations began.

Counting down the days, we continued with our business-as-usual lifestyle, where everything appeared normal. Dianne went on a vacation with her family weeks before our departure, and I worked on my Canadian citizenship during the summer. After months of preparation, I would finally become a Canadian citizen in July of 1982, one month before we left.[i]

---

i. Although insignificant at the time, that change of citizenship would eventually turn out to be instrumental during my deportation from the United States twenty-four years later.

Keeping a façade for our families and friends wasn't difficult, but the same could not be said about Tom. He was still our best friend and not sharing our plans with him at times became arduous. At one point, Dianne and I contemplated asking him to join in, but we soon abandoned that idea for selfish reasons. Although Tom displayed a passion for the many things we planned, in the end things would have simply been too awkward between us with him there as a "third wheel."

Dianne and I continued to refine our list of supplies. Because we were going to take everything with us on the plane, the idea was to keep things light and compact. Having too much carry-on baggage would look conspicuous if we were just going on a one-day excursion. There would be the dispatcher at the aircraft rental company that morning, and possibly other people who might question the amount of supplies we were bringing with us to Penticton. Our essentials included socks, sweaters, windbreakers, T-shirts, and jeans that were appropriate for that time of the year and would not seem alarming to investigators searching our rooms after we were gone. Everything we took from home had to look like something we would use only during that one day. Things like toothbrushes, and Dianne's retainer for her teeth, we had to leave behind so as not to arouse suspicion.

To make it even more difficult for anyone to recognize us from our photos on TV and in local newspapers, we bought disguises—a hair-dye kit for each of us, and a Toni-perm kit and curlers for Dianne—that we would use once we got to shore (see Document: 3103 @ www. ambrozuk.com).

Everything was progressing smoothly with our plans and our supply gathering until Dianne missed her period and we learned she was pregnant! Whether it was our reuse of the prophylactics—because we couldn't afford to keep buying the ten-dollar boxes every couple of days—or because Dianne miscalculated her monthly cycle, we now had a serious decision to make. We were excited about the pregnancy—both wanting to eventually have children together—but we were realistic, and the timing could not be worse. To undertake such an extreme journey would be challenging under the best of circumstances. Adding this complication to the mix would make it that much more difficult. We talked about it for weeks, discussing its ramifications, but in the end we agreed we had no choice but to abort the pregnancy. It was a difficult decision for both of us, but Dianne handled it with unexpected calm and clarity.

Studying to be a nurse, she was well aware of the entire process. After discussing the options with her doctor, she scheduled the procedure just four days prior to our departure—partly because of her vacation with her family, and partly because of the recommended procedure window. Because Dianne was eighteen, Canadian law did not require her doctor to inform her parents, thus alleviating any complications with her family.

I drove her to the clinic early on Wednesday, August 18. Her stay took several hours, and by the time I came back to take her home, she was already waiting—resting in the recovery room bed in a hospital gown with a gentle smile on her face and a warm hug to greet me. Other than being a little drowsy from the drugs, she assured me she felt fine, got dressed, and we drove back to her house. No one was home that afternoon, so she could sleep for the rest of the day, but if anyone asked, she said she would pretend to have bad cramps.

When I called her the following day, she was back to her bubbly self and excited to resume our journey. We would get together the following two evenings to go over the final details of our plan, making sure we had all our supplies covered and our story straight.

While I was responsible for things like a screwdriver, pliers, and a small crowbar, she took care of the more perishable items. There was orange juice, chocolate milk, peaches, tomatoes, and sandwiches that she secretly gathered. But the roll of toilet paper was unexpected (see Document: 3103 @ www.ambrozuk.com). At first I thought it a bit excessive, but considering we would most likely spend a few days hiking through the woods, her foresight was well appreciated.

On the last day before our trip, we planned to spend the evening with my sister, as if nothing out of the ordinary was about to happen. My parents were heading to the Polish Hall for polka dancing that night, while Dianne, Ranata, and I planned to see a movie.

By the time I picked up Dianne and came back to the house, my parents had already gone. We still had a couple of hours before *Dragonslayer* started, so I got out our sewing machine to do some mending on my pants. The three of us sat around the kitchen table talking—as I carefully threaded the machine needle through the seams of my pants—when my father unexpectedly showed up at the sliding glass back door of our kitchen. This was the second time he and Dianne had met, but now the mood was much less tense. Months back when he had dropped in on us at Tom's place, things were not as cordial between us, but now they both simply exchanged a polite greeting before he got his camera from the living room and left.

That night, in the theater, I asked Dianne one last time how she was feeling and if she was still good to go the next morning. She'd had four days to rest and recover, and she cheerfully confirmed she was back to 100 percent. After so many months of waiting and preparations, we were both eager and excited to get started. We had money, we had a solid plan, we had supplies and disguises, and we were ready for the rest of life to begin.

After the movie, Renata and I dropped Dianne off at her house before we drove home to turn in for the night. With all the plans and possibilities still running through my head, I had a difficult time falling asleep that evening. My mind was racing; full of adrenalin, going through the details of our plan one last time—making sure everything was prepared. I don't remember when I finally fell asleep, but I managed to set my alarm clock for 6:00 a.m. before I dozed off.

CHAPTER TWENTY-TWO

Straight from the Horse's Mouth

January 21 – 25, 2007
Day 145 – 149

MR. SHERLOCK SPOKE with Dianne's father on Sunday morning, and showed up in the afternoon to fill me in on the details. During their hour-and-a-half conversation, Mr. Babcock sounded angry
and told my attorney he hoped I spent the next ten years in prison.
Suspicious about Dianne being a willing participant in our elopement,
he suggested we may have been on a drug run, instead—not unlike
the speculations from the country folks in Kalispell twenty-four years
earlier during their media interviews (see Document: 6803 @ www.
ambrozuk.com).

It was disconcerting to hear about Mr. Babcock's bitterness, especially after Renata's cordial conversation a couple of months before.
But then things got kooky, when he brought up the strangely coincidental date of August 30, and wondered why there were no photographs of Dianne and me.

No photographs was easily explainable. In 1982, there were neither cell phones with built-in digital cameras nor the obsession with
posting them on social media. Pictures were limited to vacations,
graduations, and birthdays, with the majority taken by parents to capture the moment for their photo album.

But his fixation on the date of August 30 was curious. This was the
date in 1982 when they found out the news about Dianne; the same

date when, years later, his wife would sadly die in a car accident on their way to Dianne's grave; and the date on which I was arrested twenty-four years after the accident. Mr. Babcock had been an engineer himself, so it seemed peculiar that he now believed August 30 held some superstitious significance.

Most alarming, though, was a comment he made that explained much of Ed Corrigan's conduct up until then. He said that the prosecutor was intending to postpone my March 12, 2007 trial date, which the entire Babcock family planned to attend. He did not give a reason for the delay, but it seemed undeniable that the prosecutor had been playing games with Mr. Sherlock and me from the beginning. First, Corrigan had threatened to add more charges to my case because I was not willing to plead guilty to negligent homicide; now we discovered he was plotting to prolong my tenure in the Flathead County Detention Center without explanation. In front of the media, he often covered up his intentions with some lame excuse about my not cooperating, but, ultimately, this was about the violation of my Bill of Rights Sixth Amendment—the right to a speedy trial.

The only one who could stop Corrigan was my lawyer, Mr. Sherlock. But now he sounded indifferent, cautioning me about his own list of despairs. He was worried we might not win the trial. He wanted me to understand that the prosecutor was very busy and had not filed the two other charges yet. But when he did, Mr. Sherlock would not be able to help me with my federal charges (which I had already asked him not to involve himself with). And a slew of other discouraging thoughts.

It was unsettling to think he was simply wasting my money—pushing me into a plea bargain that I was against, rather than working on a defense for the upcoming trial. Out of sheer frustration, and recalling his numerous attempts to sway me, I candidly asked, "Mr. Sherlock, are you trying to coerce me into pleading guilty?"

"No. Of course not! I cannot tell you what to do."

Between him and Dr. Trontel, I was fighting on two battlefronts against the very people who were supposed to support and defend me. For some reason, they had already deemed me guilty and were using every trick in the book to convince me of their idealistic point of view. I'm sure to them it was a simple solution to a complicated dilemma: plead guilty and end the state case. But to me, things were not as straightforward. In addition to being morally opposed to pleading guilty to an unfortunate accident, I also had to consider what Ed Corrigan and Judge Stadler would do if I did plead *nolo contendere*. Corrigan was known for pulling out of plea bargains in court. And when Judge Stadler, over a drink in a bar, told a *48 Hours Mystery* reporter that he was considering giving me two years in prison because I was writing a book[ii], my plea no longer seemed that simple.

But when it rains, it pours in Flathead County. Adding to my disappointments, Monday, Carolyn got an email containing two attachment letters from my two best friends, Kim and Ken—one to Carolyn and one to me—regarding their loan repayments. Both letters were written by Ken and stated that although I had their complete support, they did not want further contact with Carolyn, except in case of emergency. Further, they had decided to stop making loan payments on their outstanding $70,000 balance that Carolyn was using to pay my house bills.

In 2001, I had loaned Kim $17,000 for a new Jeep Cherokee, then another $18,500 in 2002 to pay off her high-interest second mortgage on her new house. When Ken came into the picture and couldn't secure a bank loan to close on his condo in Virginia, I loaned him $40,000, just a few months before my arrest. And all that I did without ever asking for a single IOU.

Dealing with my state case, my attorney, Merrill Lynch, and the release of my Corvette were frustrating enough, but this, coming from

---

ii. To pass the time in detention centers, I kept a detailed journal of my experiences and wrote about the accident—the genesis of this book. Everyone was aware of my activity at the time.

my best friends, was tough. I could deal with Ed Corrigan and his games, and I could even put up with Mr. Sherlock's badgering, but this was regrettably a hard lesson to learn about my two best friends and what our friendship really meant.

To pile on the gloom, on Tuesday, I got the letter back I had tried to send to Mr. Babcock. Every other letter mailed to Canada was delivered without delay, but this particular one—the one I showed Mr. Sherlock on January 10—was returned after thirteen days because of insufficient postage (see Document: 4105 @ www.ambrozuk.com). I had a strong suspicion that my attorney had somehow delayed the delivery. Tampering with the mail was a federal offense—even in a detention center—but instead of confronting him, I simply re-mailed the letter and hoped it would reach its destination the second time around.

On Wednesday, Mr. Sherlock showed up with a new attitude and a voluntary summary letter (see Document: 5105 @ www.ambrozuk. com), apprising me of my current position in the state case. We met for over two and a half hours and covered numerous topics ranging from his talk with Mr. Babcock to Genea. In general, the letter outlined our current stalemate. The purpose of it was clearly CYA (Cover Your Ass), and its import was twofold: not only exonerating him from any wrongdoing in case things didn't work out in my favor, but also a not-so-subtle warning about my grave future if I didn't cooperate with him and the state prosecutor.

But to me, pleading guilty was more than just a violation of my principles. I would have to live with that declaration of guilt for the rest of my life. It also meant that what Dianne and I shared was a lie.

And that I could not compromise on.

CHAPTER TWENTY-THREE

Help Me Doc, But No More Coercion

January 26 – 29, 2007
Day 150 – 153

FRIDAY EVENING WAS my third and final talk with Dr. Trontel. He continued with our previous topics and threw in a few new ones, including my life in Texas after the accident and my relationships with Carolyn and Genea.

During our conversation, he made several observations regarding why, in general, relationships eventually fail. Criticism, contempt (superiority), defensiveness, and cutting the other person off were the four main reasons, he said, that accounted for all the failed relationships and marriages. His definitions may have been sound, but they were not all-encompassing as was demonstrated by what I went through with Genea. Our whirlwind relationship was not rooted in his scholastic truisms, but rather her mental state based on past trauma and abuse and, hence, why things were not as clear to me as they appeared to him. Looking for the cause rather than the effect, I would have been more interested in hearing the reasons why criticism or defensiveness came about in the first place.

But that was not the topic of the day—love was. He sounded cynical and jaded as he tried to explain the love I had experienced with Dianne.

"Infatuation only happens when one is an adolescent," he said, "and eventually most people settle for security and companionship rather than love."

That may be true for most, but this was not about some middle-aged couple who were settling—this was about two nineteen-year-olds in 1982. Listening to his interpretation, I quickly realized that he himself had never experienced such passionate intimacy and love. This was not something one learned from books or could base on a lifetime of pessimistic experience. How do you explain what the color red looks like to a blind man? They can imagine, but until they actually see it for themselves, they can neither understand nor appreciate it.

Aside from our divergent points of view on relationships and love, there was still the relentless underlying echo of coercion. Like Mr. Sherlock, he had also adopted the mindset that I was the only participant in our elopement. Dianne was assigned no agency—no role in our getaway plan, despite both of us concocting, committing, and executing it together, while knowing perfectly well the danger involved. I may have been the pilot, but it had been a joint venture, and I found their erasure of Dianne and the part she played in our elopement disturbing.

For the most part, our two and a half hours of exploratory analysis went as expected, except for the end, when he asked to see the notes I had been scribbling throughout our meetings. I was surprised by his forwardness but freely offered my notepad for his review. The top of the page contained several questions that quickly put him on the defensive:

- *Mr. Sherlock said this will help me to better analyze myself and help me, how? What exactly does he think is wrong with me? Because I'm not pleading guilty?*
- *If we eloped in a car and Dianne died, would they also charge me?*
- *If I came back twenty-four years ago, would they charge me? Mr. Sherlock says NO!*
- *What about me and my feelings in all this? Everyone is just looking for a conviction. Isn't the shrink supposed to help me better cope with the tragedy twenty-four years ago instead of trying to coerce me into pleading guilty?*
- *Aren't you supposed to rehabilitate people instead of trying to break them down and guilt trip them?*

As soon as he read my notes, he seemed flustered and began reassuring me that he was not trying to change my mind about anything. His job was only to listen and question so that he could better evaluate my condition, both now and twenty-four years ago.

I found it odd that he said nothing about rehabilitation, or my well-being, after the accident. Neither he nor Mr. Sherlock had ever mentioned it, or asked how I managed to get over my grief and trauma over the years. These days, when someone gets shot in high school, there are counselors and psychologists everywhere helping students cope with their loss. I realized it was twenty-four years ago when I faced that nightmare by myself, but how about a little sympathy and compassion if only for diplomacy sake?

When Dr. Trontel left, I was more confused than ever about his conduct, and more important, his evaluation to come. But all that would soon be put into perspective when I saw the result. Perhaps peeved after reading my notes about his coercion and lack of empathy, he produced two interesting reports for the purposes of a possible trial. The original, unfiltered report was included in the bulk of the state evidence from Mr. Watson after my return to Canada (see Document: 5650 @ www.ambrozuk.com). There was also an alternate version I received from Mr. Sherlock during my restitution hearing (see Document: 5651 @ www.ambrozuk.com). At an additional cost of $2,000 for his evaluation, I was not only curiously surprised about the contents of the reports, but also very impressed that he could create two different versions of the same clinical analysis at Mr. Sherlock's behest. The revised letter was much more tamed and less colorful, so perhaps on his third pass—with let's say another $1,000 for his efforts—I might have gotten a favorable review without prejudice.

CHAPTER TWENTY-FOUR

Nolo Contendere: The Plea Bargain Compromise

January 30 – February 8, 2007
Day 154 – 163

MR. SHERLOCK SHOWED UP Wednesday to go over the acknowledgement of rights and plea disposition agreement. During our review, he said the prosecutor could legally extend my trial for up to 431 days by asking for more time to prepare, gather more evidence, and locate additional witnesses, among other stall tactics.

The court system was clear about the negligent homicide definition, but there was enough ambiguity built into the law that the prosecutor could exploit. With no one to stop him, he was free to manipulate the case at will. And so he did: with his games at my bond hearing, his comment to Mr. Babcock about postponing the trial date, and, more recently, his threat to file two new charges. Those were unmistakable red flags of a district attorney fixated on dragging my case out for as long as possible.

I had been determined to stand my ground on some principles, but even I have a breaking point. After months of pressure from Mr. Sherlock, Dr. Trontel—and even my sister who was nudged by my attorney to sway me—I started to see justice through a new pair of eyes. Like the Flathead County justice system, I had become cynical—realizing my case was more about what the public and the court wanted to hear, rather than evidence or what I believed. As much as I loathed the way things were going, my options were limited. With great reluctance, umbrage, and a heavy heart, I changed my plea to *nolo contendere*. According to Mr. Sherlock, the loose definition of *nolo contendere* meant that "you have read and understand the evidence but you are not pleading guilty." And that I could live with.

Mr. Sherlock noticed my somber attitude and managed to move up my court appearance an entire week—perhaps out of fear that I would change my mind. On Thursday, he showed up an hour before my court hearing to finalize the plea bargain agreement (see Document: 3217 @ www.ambrozuk.com), and go over the court procedure I would be expected to follow. I was not in a talkative mood, so we quickly went over the paperwork to make sure he had changed all guilty references to *nolo contendere*. I was then escorted to a holding tank on the bottom floor where I was allowed to change into my street clothes prior to my hearing.

The room was barely full when I walked into the main courtroom on the third floor where Judge Stadler was finishing a divorce case. By the time my case began, half the guest seats were filled. There were two video cameras set up in the jury box, and I noticed a photographer sitting in one of the bench seats, clicking away, capturing every detail on his large digital camera.

Gathering his composure, the judge began his official change of plea introductory statement as soon as my attorney and I took our seats at the defendant's table. Turning to Mr. Sherlock and me, the judge asked what my plea was.

My attorney stood and quickly responded, "Nolo contendere, Your Honor," as if to make sure I would not contest our agreement.

I was sworn in and took the stand. Judge Stadler began a rundown of the stipulations found in the acknowledgement of rights document, pausing periodically for my confirmation.

When he finished, Mr. Sherlock asked several questions of his own from the document, including, "Are you aware you could be found guilty if this case goes to trial?"

It was a question more suited for a prosecutor than my attorney, but I confirmed that I understood the possible consequences with a simple, "Yes, I do."

When Ed Corrigan took over, he said something surprising rather than launching into another interrogation as Mr. Sherlock had speculated.

"Do you understand that the state is not going to file the theft and criminal mischief charges against you?"

Up until then, every statement that Judge Stadler and my attorney had paraphrased during the hearing was found in either the acknowledgement of rights, or the plea disposition agreement. But this was not in either document. It was the first time these possible new charges were mentioned in court—perhaps a subtle way for the prosecutor to introduce them to the media.

It didn't take long for my suspicions to be confirmed about Ed Corrigan, who once again appeared to be planning more games of deceit. When Judge Stadler commented I would have the right to back out of the plea agreement and change my plea if the sentence was not what we agreed to, Corrigan quickly stood up and said, "That clause was removed from our binding document."

But Judge Stadler apparently smelled a rat, too. They exchanged several heated words before the judge finally put his foot down. He told Corrigan that he didn't care what our agreement was because he was going to allow us to pull out of our plea agreement during sentencing if we so chose.

This was the first time I saw the prosecutor aggressively contest the judge—confirming what Mr. Sherlock told me just before the hearing. Over the last few years, Ed Corrigan had become ornery, choosing to go on his own, rather than side with the judges.

"He's treading on thin ice with all the judges. They're going to do something about it soon," he forewarned.

I didn't care much about the internal courtroom politics of Flathead County, but I could see that after his exasperated confrontation with the judge, Ed Corrigan was a man on a mission who had his sights firmly fixed on my case.

With the change of plea complete, the next step was my sentencing. Before we could get to that hearing, I needed to quickly fill out the DEPARTMENT OF CORRECTIONS PRE-SENTENCE INVESTIGATION QUESTIONNAIRE and give the probation officer ample time to do his research if we were to make our March 8 sentencing date.

CHAPTER TWENTY-FIVE

0 to 180 in the Blink of an Eye

August 22 – 29, 1982

MY MOM WAS working a half-day on the morning of August 22, and had already left for work when I got up. Just after 6:00 a.m. I slipped into the bathroom to wash up before getting dressed and gathering my supplies for the trip. For months, Dianne and I had collected provisions that were hidden in our bedroom closets and under our beds. The yellow two-man raft for getting to shore from the aircraft was stowed beneath a carpet in the trunk of my Ford Meteor.

Although we had told everyone we were flying to Penticton, British Columbia for the day, in reality we were leaving for the rest of our lives, and that made it the last time I would see my family. Realizing the gravity of the situation, I quietly opened each of their bedroom doors, and in a non-ceremonial fashion whispered goodbye under my breath before returning to my bedroom to finish packing.

When I arrived at Dianne's house, her parents were already up. She came out to greet me and brought out one of her packed bags. She went back inside and used the excuse that she forgot our lunch to bring her second bag out to the car. Minutes later, we were on our way to the South Terminal of the Vancouver International Airport in Richmond, B.C.

When we pulled into the Sol-Air Aviation parking lot just before 8:00 a.m., the rental company was still closed. It seemed prudent to consolidate the contents of our bags while we waited for the doors to open. We each had several bags containing our clothes and perishables, and none were completely full. To remain inconspicuous to the aircraft attendant, the fewer bags we had, the better.

When the rental office finally opened, Dianne and I made our way to the lounge with only a couple of bags in hand. Waiting for the airplane to be re-fueled and prepped for flight, we discussed our route to Penticton and back, making sure that nothing looked out of the ordinary. When eventually we were reported missing, there would be many questions. It was imperative that potential witnesses like Howard Thiessen, the dispatcher on duty that morning, could definitively vouch for our predetermined route and verify to the authorities that nothing had seemed out of place when we boarded the aircraft.

Before taking off on any flight, especially a long-distance trip, it was the pilot's responsibility to plot the course and calculate the trip legs based on the current weather conditions. Once the flight plan was established, it was typically filed with the Air Traffic Control (ATC) of the departure airport. Although Dianne and I discussed our route from Vancouver to Penticton in the lobby, we followed through with the charade only for the benefit of the dispatcher. We had no intention of filing our flight plan with ATC, if for nothing more than authenticity. Looking inexperienced and careless would only help explain our disappearance in front of the RCMP, who were sure to look at every detail during their investigation.

Once the airplane was ready and the appropriate paperwork filled out, the dispatcher gave us the keys and aircraft log book. We grabbed our bags and flight maps and headed outside to the Cessna C150 two-man aircraft with call letters C-GICK. It was parked a few hundred feet from the rental company's back door, making it difficult to sneak out all our supplies at once. Instead, we opted to get the rest of our things after the aircraft inspection.

It was customary before each flight for the pilot to inspect the plane and verify that all controls were in proper working condition to make the plane airworthy—a procedure I was very familiar with by now, as

I had done the same walk-through before each flight during my training. When the inspection was done, I ran back to the car to get our last bag. Carrying the rest of our provisions past the counter where the dispatcher was standing, I enthusiastically remarked, "I can't forget this. It's very important." Darting out the backdoor, I placed the blue duffel bag in the storage area behind the two seats.

It was around 9:10 a.m. when Dianne and I finally buckled in, closed the aircraft doors and, after a short engine warm-up, began our slow ride toward the airport runways. Although taking off in between the large 747 airplanes at the Vancouver International Airport was no trivial matter, I was well familiar with the taxiing routine performed many times during my training. I waited to get the clearance from Air Traffic Control before we began our full throttle take-off to Penticton.

The weather that day was exceptional for a flight through the mountainous regions of British Columbia. There were a few cirrus clouds, but in general the skies were clear. It was pleasantly warm with visibility at 100 percent. Once again luck was on our side, and there would be no trip cancellations because of bad weather that day. Steadily climbing to our cruising altitude, I tapered off the ascent and trimmed the elevator on the aircraft to maintain optimal flight performance.

During long cross-country flights, particularly over winding terrains, it was customary for the pilot to call in periodically and identify the aircraft position over specifically marked checkpoints. Implemented as an additional safety measure to track the aircraft, it was a voluntary procedure entirely at the discretion of the pilot—and Dianne and I agreed it would be best not to leave any unnecessary breadcrumbs. Calling in checkpoints to Penticton, but not on the way back, might look suspicious, so we avoided the procedure altogether.

Our 160-mile flight took just under two hours. We filled the time with small talk and the occasional wink and a kiss to confirm our excitement and exhilaration, before arriving at the Penticton Airport during the late morning hours.

Penticton was a small airport in comparison to Vancouver. The Air Traffic Control tower gave us a direct landing trajectory without any delays, and within minutes we were on the ground, taxiing towards a clearing to park the aircraft. During my first flight to Penticton to see the air show, the airport had been busy with hundreds of people walking around, and dozens of planes scattered about. Today, the airport looked deserted, with only a few planes docked along the designated gravel parking strip.

The plan was to relax for several hours, lounging around near the airport, before beginning our final leg in the early evening. Dianne and I grabbed a few items from the back of the plane—clothes to sit on, our lunch, and our navigation maps—before we made our way to the outskirts of the airport. Avoiding unnecessary contact with people, we found a grass patch just outside the airport. Propped up against the chain-link fence directly in front of the runway, we spent the better part of that afternoon watching the planes take off and land, and gazing at the people playing on the Skaha Lake beach in front of us (see Document: 7431 @ www.ambrozuk.com).

We lay on the grass until approximately 4:30 p.m. before walking back to the aircraft to prepare for departure.

One of the most critical factors to our plan's success was the timing of when we would reach our destination lake in Montana. Arriving at the lake too early would mean we would be in plain sight during our descent and therefore risk the possibility of being spotted. Arriving too late meant that I would have to fly IFR (Instrument Flight Rules) at least part of the way. Flying in the dark also meant we couldn't see much of the terrain below, making it difficult to navigate through the Montana mountain regions where landmarks were scarce and likely barely visible at night.

By then, Dianne and I had spent hours looking at my navigational maps and calculating the distance the aircraft could fly on a single tank of gas. Our timing was crucial, and our fuel consumption and distance calculations needed to be precise if we were to arrive at the lake just after nightfall. The Cessna C150 cruise speed was defined as 109 mph, with the average fuel consumption of six gallons per hour, and a maximum range of 421 miles on a single tank of gas. Dividing the range by the cruise speed gave us approximately 3.9 hours of flight time. Multiplying the fuel-burn rate by the number of flight hours also gave us 23.2 gallons that would be used to traverse the maximum distance.

Knowing the maximum flight range from Penticton, the most logical lake to land on was Flathead Lake in Montana—the largest body of water depicted on our navigational maps. With less than four hours of flight time, we needed to leave Penticton at 6:00 p.m. if we were to arrive at our destination at approximately 9:30 p.m.—the time of sunset.

To remain inconspicuous and divert any search and rescue operations away from our actual destination, we filed a detailed flight plan from Penticton to Vancouver, before starting preparations for our final flight leg. After changing into our bathing suits, we reorganized our supplies and perishables into two large green garbage bags that we doubled-up to make waterproof. We unscrewed the back panel between the storage compartment and the tail-end of the fuselage, thereby removing the air cavity that would prevent the aircraft from sinking once we landed and were safely in our yellow raft paddling to shore. One of the bags we sealed and stored deep inside the aircraft's hollow tail-end along with the yellow raft (see Document: 7148 @ www.ambrozuk.com). The other bag we left open until we were ready to land and could put away our navigational maps.

With everything prepared and organized, we got clearance from the Air Traffic Control (ATC) tower and took off for Vancouver heading westbound. Once clear of the ATC tower visual tracking, we deviated south and dropped our altitude from 3,500 feet to below 2,000 feet to remain invisible to radar. Turning southeast, we crossed the U.S. border and worked our way through the mountainous valleys of Washington and Idaho before reaching Montana.

Without a cloud in the sky the entire day, at dusk we eventually spotted the reflective moonlight of Flathead Lake in the distance. The lake looked much larger than what Dianne and I envisioned. Densely populated lights were scattered around the shoreline, indicating local residents and campers who could spot our landing. Instead of taking a chance, we scrapped Flathead Lake and headed for Little Bitterroot Lake, where only a few flickers of light were glimmering.

With the sky now practically pitch black, we put away our navigational maps, sealed the garbage bag in the storage compartment behind our seats, and began preparations for our landing. To allow greater water inflow into the cabin once we were floating on water, we opened both door windows before changing our seatbelt configurations. As an extra safety precaution, Dianne used the optional shoulder harness and attached it to her waist seatbelt. I, on the other hand, removed my waist seatbelt altogether because we believed the aircraft's flight controls would provide me with adequate stability and safety during the landing.

With everything accounted for and prepared, we began our landing approach. Turning off the engine and outside marker lights, we placed the aircraft into a glide by fully lowering the flaps to decrease airspeed to approximately 45 mph, and trimming the elevators.

Little Bitterroot Lake was 3.3 miles in length. Because of our shallow angle of descent to clear the trees and avoid being spotted by local campers, we were still several hundred feet above the water surface when we reached the middle of the lake. With the nose of the aircraft elevated, and the stall speed indicator steadily buzzing in our ears, I began a shallow left turn using the rudder to change direction. Within seconds we were oriented toward the north, and by then the water reflection below us was clearly visible.

This was a typical landing procedure I performed dozens of times during training, with the only difference being the landing surface. According to my ground-school instructor, David Firth, the landing would be impactful, but as long as the nose was elevated to allow the tail to drag along the water surface, the aircraft would not flip over.

But that was not what happened.

As soon as the undercarriage wheels jackknifed into the water, the aircraft came to an abrupt stop with the forward momentum rotating the aircraft up and over itself. The nose lunged down and forward into the water, damaging the engine cowl (see Document: 7164 @ www.ambrozuk.com); the violent rotation of the aircraft around its lateral axis caused the right wing to penetrate the water first, crushing the leading edge (see Document: 7166 @ www.ambrozuk.com); and the instantaneous 180-degree up-and-over rotation of the fuselage caused the damage to the tail-fin (see Document: 7167 @ www.ambrozuk.com).

During the tumultuous impact, Dianne was secured by her waist seatbelt and shoulder harness. I was not wearing any restraints, and was catapulted forward, breaking a rib on the steering control handle, knocking off the padding from the steering column with my knee (see Document: 7152 @ www.ambrozuk.com), and completely shattering the front plastic, flexible windshield with my body (see Document: 7156 @ www.ambrozuk.com).

When I finally got my bearing in the icy cold water and came up to the surface seconds later, I was at the back-left side of the aircraft, facing the tail end of the plane. With the left wing completely submerged and the right-side airfoil extruding at a shallow angle above the water surface, I spit out blood mixed with icy water, and yelled, "Dianne! Where are you? Are you OK?"

From inside the cabin Dianne called out, "Jarek, I can't get my seatbelt off!"

I immediately started to make my way to the passenger door by jumping on the left elevator to get over the tail portion of the fuselage. Seconds later, I reached the right wing, pushed the flap down flush with the airfoil surface, and lunged onto the wing to reach the door latch.

With the windows open and the front windshield completely gone, the aircraft was filling with water at an accelerated rate. By the time I got to the door, part of the right wing was already submerged. I yanked at the door latch multiple times before the pressure differential between the cabin air and the water outside gave way.

Flowing forcefully around the door into the cabin, the water splashed into my eyes and mouth, preventing me from seeing or reaching Dianne. During my disorientation, and based on the topological view of the aircraft, I assumed Dianne would be on the right hand side. But because the plane had flipped over, she was now upside-down on the left side of the aircraft, farthest from the door I just opened.

It took no more than fifteen to twenty seconds from the time I was catapulted through the windshield to the moment I reached and opened the door, but that was enough for the aircraft to completely submerge below the surface.

In frantic disbelief, I watched helplessly as the plane disappeared in front of my eyes. The girl I vowed to love, start a family and spend the rest of my life with, went down with the plane and there was nothing I could do to stop it.

We had great plans for our future, and now everything was shattered. She was my world. She was my life. But now, in the blink of an eye, all that was gone.

I treaded water in a circle, muttering, "Dianne! Oh God! Oh my God!..." over and over again. My mind was filled with rage and disbelief that the plane had sunk within seconds. It was not what the instructor assured us would happen.

It was unfathomable that Dianne was gone because of a device whose sole purpose was to save and protect her in case of an accident. Unclasping a seatbelt was a trivial task even a child could manage. I refused to accept that she could not unbuckle the seatbelt herself. My head boiled over with ferocity and exasperation as I scanned the water around me, hoping she would miraculously emerge above the surface.

I don't remember how long I treaded water, but it seemed like an eternity. Adrenalin rushed through me, with my body eventually responding to the numbing cold. My legs were frigid, and I could no longer feel my toes. The small treading circles I made with my arms and legs were no longer sufficient to circulate my blood, and I began to experience leg cramps. My face ached from the impact with the airplane dashboard and the windshield, and there was a strong taste of blood from my nose. I was in shock and confused about what to do next.

Only with numbing reluctance did I eventually concede I had to start for the shore if I was to survive the long swim. Looking around, I could see only a couple of distant small lights glittering on the coastline. I picked the shortest distance to swim that also appeared unoccupied. Bobbing a few feet in front of me in the dim moonlight, I noticed a garbage bag that had floated out of the aircraft. I grabbed it and started my long and grueling crawl to shore.

I don't know what the distance to the land was, but it felt as if I swam for over half an hour, switching between a side crawl and a dog paddle. With the garbage bag in tow adding to my fatigue, I tried to process what just happened—mumbling phrases of disbelief under my breath. The coldness was excruciating, and at times I felt like stopping and letting fate take its course. It would have been so easy to give up, but somehow I reluctantly continued.

By the time I reached the shore wearing only swim shorts and a T-shirt, I was exhausted, shivering, and numb. The cold breeze blew over my wet body as I stumbled over the baseball-size rocks, looking to find a place to lie down for the night. The beach was empty, with only a faint light in the distance as I made my way inland. The bag I dragged behind me was torn and everything inside was completely wet. I had nothing dry to change into, and sleeping in wet clothes seemed suicidal in the cold, Montana night.

Not far in from the water, there was a sparingly wooded area, with trees scattered between the leaf and needle-covered forest bed. Walking blindly forward, I stumbled across a small ditch partially covered by a large fallen tree trunk. There I left the soaking garbage bag while continuing toward the distant light of a small cabin, hoping to find some relief from the freezing cold.

On the porch, I noticed a piece of carpet acting as a door mat, and something that looked like a cloth neatly folded on the railing. Shivering, teeth clattering, I quietly grabbed them both and headed back to the trench in the woods. I remembered how people on TV always took off their wet clothes and used body heat to keep warm. I had nothing to dry myself with, and no one to share body heat, but I shed all my wet, skimpy clothes anyway before covering up with the small piece of carpet and what turned out to be the net of a hammock.

I lay there for hours, curled up in the ditch in a fetal position to minimize heat loss, shaking uncontrollably. Adrenalin from the shock and my rushing thoughts kept me awake. I would not allow myself to believe that Dianne was actually gone, and kept hoping she would emerge from the darkness at any moment—ready to spoon on the cold ground to share our warmth. I tossed, turned, and shivered in the frosty air but couldn't fall asleep the entire night.

When morning came, I crawled out from under the log and put on my wet clothes to search for a patch of sun. Everything in the garbage bag was completely soaked, and I peeled off the layers one at a time before spreading each piece on the forest floor to dry. I sat on the cold ground for hours, my chin resting on my curled up knees, staring blindly into the distance.

There was no mirror to look at my face, but I could see the deep scratches all over the front of my body, legs, and arms. The sharp ends of the airfoil ridges had etched long, parallel streaks of blood as they scarred into my skin while I crawled over the underbelly of the aircraft to reach Dianne. The scratches looked horrid, but they were negligible compared to my broken rib that hurt every time I moved.

Despite the harrowing accident and the many emotions racing inside me, I was determined to continue with what Dianne and I started. The only thing that made sense was my instinct to carry on. Contacting authorities or my parents was the furthest thing from my mind. We had a goal and I was determined to execute it. If I fulfilled our plan, somehow it felt like I would not let Dianne down.

Because of the weak August sunlight poking through the trees, the clothes I spread out on the ground for several hours never dried.

Discouraged, I packed them into a small, blue, tubular nylon duffel bag and went to the cabin to seek help.

An older man answered the door. When I asked if I could build a fire on his property, he seemed reluctant. Instead, he directed me to the other side of the dam to build a fire on the river's edge. Because of my appearance, that was probably the best response I was going to get from the local residents.

Crossing the bridge—along the shoreline in a public area—I found the remains of an old campfire on the rocks, and tried to use the wet matches we had brought to start a fire. Unsuccessful but undeterred, I tried rubbing a couple of pieces of wood together, hoping for a sign of smoke or a spark. But neither that, nor twirling a stick between the palms of my hands on a dry wooden plank produced results, and I eventually gave up on my Boy Scout skills.

Although I wasn't dressed properly or in the right frame of mind to talk to anyone, solving my fire problem and drying out my clothes were my only immediate priority. Reluctantly, I approached a couple of teenage boys who were passing by on the bridge. Dressed only in wet shorts and a T-shirt in a forest, with scratches all over my body, my appearance must have looked curious, but they said nothing, handed me their matches, and walked away.

Returning to the campfire, I used small sticks and old paper scattered along the shore to start a fire within minutes. First warming my hands and body, I waited until there were no onlookers passing by before I unraveled my wet clothes from the duffel bag and spread them on the rocks around the fire. With smoke blowing in my eyes from the damp wood, the clothes slowly dried, taking on the distinct stench of campfire. But it didn't matter because all I cared about at that moment was to have something dry for the night. In time, I changed into a pair of dry jeans and a T-shirt, before turning my attention to the wet money.

Back at the Penticton Airport, Dianne and I had randomly packed the two garbage bags with our belongings. It was pure luck the bag that floated out of the aircraft contained not only money, but also some of my clothes. If by some chance the other bag lodged deep in the fuselage had floated out instead, I would have nothing but Dianne's jeans and a blouse to change into.

Focusing on the lump of cash stuck together, I peeled off each bill, one at a time, and placed it around the fire to dry. I shaved off my mustache using the yellow BIC razor we'd brought, and began to systematically incinerate any flammable items that were still in my duffel bag—our navigational maps, our IDs, and the microphone chord we removed from the aircraft's glove-compartment box. That was the plan Dianne and I had laid out, and that was what I still instinctively intended to carry out.

I sat on the beach rocks most of that day—keeping warm by the fire, staring aimlessly into the distance with tears pouring down my face—as I tried to come to grips with the nightmare from the night before. My thoughts were anything but rational, and I would continuously go back to those twenty seconds as the plane sank, questioning what went wrong and what I could have done differently. I was angry at myself, at God, and at anything that might have caused this accident. But no matter how I rationalized the landing, I kept returning to why Dianne couldn't unbuckle the seatbelt herself.

I wanted nothing to do with the authorities, the people back home, or the world for that matter, but even after that horrendous night, there was still a piece of me left inside that could not leave Dianne at the bottom of the lake. I was brought up Roman Catholic with strong values and morals, and in conscience could not walk away without giving her a proper burial. I had incinerated all the maps we brought with us, except for one—the one that showed where the plane and Dianne were located. I was alone, confused, and incoherent with rage, but in the back of my mind I knew I would eventually have to let someone know where to find her. I tucked the map in my bag and waited for the rest of my clothes and the money to dry.

It was early in the evening when I finally left the campsite and started walking deeper into the woods. I didn't know where I was going, or why, but I needed to keep moving. Making my way in search of the next place to rest for the night, I stayed close to the lake so as not to stray too far from Dianne. I was enraged and in a melancholy mood, grieving over the one person I had vowed to spend the rest of my life with as the tears kept on coming.

Wandering aimlessly for several days, I eventually came across a wooded pasture inhabited by a large, black bull. When I saw him moving in my direction, I quickly changed course and headed for a meter-high pile of ten-foot-long logs scattered underneath a tall tree. I wasn't about to go head-to-head with a bull—as did the Archangel in the film *Michael*—but being King of the Hill gave me a superior advantage. As I stood on top of the pile, taunting him to charge me, the more I shouted, the more I felt the rage and bitterness of the last few days pour out of me. It felt good to let some of it out, even at an innocent animal.

Snorting and angrily pawing the ground with his forefoot, the bull circled the pile of wood several times during his fifteen minutes of superiority, before getting discouraged and moving on. There would be no clear winner in that confrontation, but when it was over, a tiny bit of my anger and hostility left with it.

The next few days provided little solace as I wondered from one area to another in search of a new place to sleep. Nothing seemed important, nothing was urgent, and the excitement of our elopement was now nonexistent. I spent most days sitting on a hill or a mound, huddled with my chin resting on my knees, rocking back and forth in mindless despair.

The few cans of food and perishables that Dianne and I brought with us I used sparingly, but when my resources were depleted, it became a necessity to take leave of the lake. It had been a week since the accident, and although everything still seemed chaotic, I had but one purpose—to contact Tom and tell him where the aircraft and Dianne were located.

CHAPTER TWENTY-SIX

Flathead County Sheriff's Office Investigative Reports

February 9 – 20, 2007
Day 164 – 175

FRIDAY, DURING MAIL call, I got the last of the outstanding investigative reports related to my case.

When I first arrived in Kalispell, Mr. Sherlock gave me the bulk of the original report from 1982 that contained the narrative of the case, as well as attachments A through M, including the seventy-five page transcript of the call between Tom and me (see List: 9580 @ www. ambrozuk.com). These were the follow-up reports the county sheriff's office was now diligently working on to fill in the missing details.

Follow-Up #1, dated 08/30/2006, contained a narrative outlining the evidence of my identity (see Document: 3114 @ www.ambrozuk.com). The first line read "On August 28, 2006, Sheriff Jim Dupont received an anonymous phone call from a person who knew the current identity of Jerry Ambrozuk." That anonymous caller was my ex-girlfriend, Genea (see Document: 8620 @ www.ambrozuk.com). The report contained Attachments N through S, including my Yahoo Personals profile she had forwarded to Sheriff Dupont (see Document: 3115 @ www. ambrozuk.com).

Follow-Up #2, with Attachment T included the email correspondence between Detective Sergeant Pat Walsh and Dianne's father,

Gerald Babcock, to establish my identity (see Document: 3118 @ www.ambrozuk.com).

Follow-Up #3, with Attachment U was my booking photo from Texas on 08/30/2006 (see Document: 3120 @ www.ambrozuk.com).

Follow-Up #4, created a week later, contained Attachment V and included the coroner's report on Dianne, a list of names of the personnel who helped in the recovery of the plane on Bitterroot Lake, and a newspaper article from *The Missoulian* (see Document: 3122 @ www.ambrozuk.com).

But last, and most interesting, was Follow-up #5, a short narrative outlining the process taken to recover, examine, and test the Cessna C150 after it was pulled out of the lake in 1982 (see Document: 3124 @ www.ambrozuk.com).

At first glance, nothing seemed unusual about the report, but upon closer inspection, I noticed there were a couple of new entries. Listed at the top, below the negligent homicide charge, were *Theft, All Others*, and *Criminal Mischief/Vandalism*, with the *Total Value of ALL Properties* summed up at *$24,175.00*.

Although the case status for all three charges was set to "Completed," this was the first time the two additional charges officially appeared on paper. Until then, Corrigan had expressed his intentions only verbally to my attorney and had cleverly brought up the possibility of new charges before the judge during my *nolo contendere* change of plea hearing.

During our *nolo contendere* plea agreement review, I specifically remember Mr. Sherlock adding a clause on Page 5 that read: *2a. The state agrees to not file any other charges in this case* (see Document: 3216 @ www.ambrozuk.com). Out of curiosity, I checked to see if that hand-written stipulation was still in the final copy of the plea document (see Document: 3217 @ www.ambrozuk.com). It was no longer there. Mr. Sherlock had once again undermined me by quietly removing it from the final plea document—playing directly into the prosecutor's hand.

But the part that struck me as most unusual was the triplicate valuation of the aircraft for cost and repairs. There had been no mention of properties or their values in any of the previous evidence or follow-up reports, but now there were three entries totaling $24,175.00:

1) *Stolen/Bribed/Defrauded for $8,000.00*
2) *Recovered for $8,500.00, and*
3) *Damaged for $7,175.00*

First of all, the aircraft was not stolen—it had been rented. Hence, the first property value damage of $8,000 did not apply. Even so, why were there two additional charges that served the same purpose? The Blue Book value of the aircraft in 1982 was $8,500, and the repairs were estimated at $7,614.00, so why were there three amounts listed? Shouldn't there only be one—either the Blue Book value or the repair costs?

But the more obvious question was: Why were there any amounts listed in the first place?

Like any responsible business owner, David Oliver, the co-owner of the now-defunct rental company, Sol-Air Aviation, must have had insurance on the aircraft, and the insurance company would have already paid him for any damages.

When Renata checked into the *Johnson and Higgins Willis Faber Ltd* aircraft insurance company in Vancouver, responsible for insuring the aircraft, she discovered they were no longer in business. Who, then, would collect the restitution money? Would it be Mr. Oliver again?

When I asked Mr. Sherlock during our Sunday meeting about the aircraft repair costs, and why he omitted the clause in the plea agreement that would prevent the prosecutor from charging me with additional felonies, he had no rebuttals to either, other than to say he was confident that Corrigan would not file any further charges. In our previous conversations, he had told me the district attorney had been reprimanded by the Montana Supreme Court for unethical conduct on several occasions, and had a propensity for backing out of plea agreements, yet here he was suggesting that the prosecutor was a changed man. I could not be more frustrated dealing with an attorney obviously out of his league, and when faced with controversy, repeatedly back peddling as if nothing were wrong.

But getting upset about things I had no control over would serve no purpose, so I shook my head and moved on to the pre-sentence investigation questionnaire I had filled out Saturday. The fifteen-page document included: Identification, Emergency Information, Offense Information (including history), Health, Chemical Dependency, Mental Health, Family and Social History, Marital History, Educational and Vocational History, Employment History, Financial Status, Military History, and Future Plans and General Health Questions—Medical Screening.

And if that weren't enough, there was also an AUTHORIZATION FOR THE RELEASE OF CONFIDENTIAL INFORMATION form that required my signature. It would be used not only for the release of my criminal history records, but also to give the probation officer access to my complete financial history, including personal and corporate statements and credit reports. Essentially, everything a probation officer would want to know if he were to invade my privacy and not worry about my constitutional rights. I debated about refusing to sign the consent, but as that would surely cast a shadow over my case in the eyes of the presiding judge when it came to sentencing, I had no choice but to comply.

Detention center or not, Wednesday was Valentine's Day, and the perfect opportunity to express my gratitude to the women in my life. Following tradition, I had Renata send Carolyn three dozen roses and some chocolates to her workplace, along with a single gold rose that I gave her each birthday and Valentine's Day to add to her five-year collection.

For my reunited family, I asked Carolyn to order my mom and Renata several dozen roses a piece. And to further commemorate the occasion, I also sent a personalized Valentine's Day card to Renata complete with a heartfelt poem I wrote:

Roses are Red,
Violets are Blue,
I'm Sitting in Jail,
Thinking of You...☺

After twenty-four years, I finally had something to be exceptionally grateful for—my family. Carolyn, Renata, and my mother had been supporting me unconditionally for the past five months; sending them flowers and a cheerful Valentine's card was the least I could do to show my appreciation.

CHAPTER TWENTY-SEVEN

Pre-Sentence Investigation Questionnaire and the Hinzman

February 21 – March 2, 2007
Day 176 – 185

IN PREPARATION FOR my sentencing that had been rescheduled for March 8, I met with Kyle Hinzman, the probation officer who would interview me before submitting his recommendation to court prior to my hearing.

It was three o'clock in the afternoon when he and my attorney finally showed up in the full-contact visitor's booth to go over my case and the pre-sentencing questionnaire I had filled out days before.

In his late twenties, with no law degree and only a few criminal courses under his belt, Kyle was essentially considered a neophyte probation officer. "He makes less money than my secretary," Mr. Sherlock tittered, during one of our conversations before the meeting.

"My job is not that important," Kyle had initially professed. But he was quite serious as he worked through the questionnaire one page at a time, pausing periodically only to ask for brief explanations. That is, until we got to the three questions Mr. Sherlock had taken the liberty to fill in on my behalf:

1) In your own words, what did you do to get arrested on this charge?

2) What reason do you have for your involvement in this offense?

> 3) *Give your recommendation as to what you think the court should do in your case?*

He paused at each section and asked me to explain it in laymen terms. Mr. Sherlock had coached me about being straightforward and brief with my answers—without sounding as if I were avoiding the questions—and that is exactly what I did. But Kyle wasn't satisfied with my replies. He began questioning me extensively about our elopement, the details of landing the aircraft on water, and why we used a plane instead of a car as our getaway vehicle.

Before I could finish my explanation, he jumped in with a clarification, "I don't care how you tried to save Dianne! I'm more interested in how you flew the plane and if you used proper judgment during the landing." His remark was curious, but not as enigmatic as when he brought up Carolyn and Genea—my two recent ex-girlfriends who had nothing to do with the accident. Perhaps this was his way of fishing for some dirt I would inadvertently divulge and that he could use in his report. His curiosity seemed out of place, but eventually he returned to the topic at hand.

"Why didn't you stay after the accident?" he asked.

Mr. Sherlock finally jumped in. "If he'd called the authorities twenty-four years ago, there probably would not have been any charges filed."

With a nod, Kyle acknowledged the remark and appeared satisfied with his interrogation. He said he was going to talk to Carolyn, Renata, and Dianne's brother before he would be ready to make his recommendation to the court.

All in all, Mr. Sherlock and I both thought the interview went well, but the real litmus test would be Kyle's final pre-sentence investigation (PSI) report that would ultimately reflect his opinions about our elopement, the accident, and my future.

Early on Tuesday afternoon, after six months in the Flathead County Detention Center, my cellies and I went out to REC, and for the first time since I had arrived, I got to feel the sun on my face. That elusive phenomenon depended on several factors: the courtyard layout, when our REC time occurred, and most importantly, what time of the year it was. It was a rare moment, but it was greatly appreciated after all those months.

When I got back from REC, Kyle showed up again in the pass-through visitor's booth to ask a few more follow-up questions. This time, he came only with his cell phone (no pen or paper) and looked confused, as if no longer remembering why he came by, with his eyes nervously bouncing around the walls. Unprepared and fidgety, he eventually gathered his thoughts and asked just two questions: "When did you get your Canadian Citizenship?" and "How did you get your identity in the United States?"

Although they were the exact same questions Mr. Sherlock was interested in after he spoke with Dianne's father, I tried not to read into his curiosity and simply elaborated on each to his satisfaction. This time our meeting took less than twenty minutes. On his exit, Kyle once again clarified that because he was trying to wrap up his recommendation by that Friday, he might be back again in the next few days if he had any more questions.

And come back he did on Wednesday with the exact same questions we went over during our first meeting. Perhaps he was distracted and wasn't paying attention—or perhaps he was trying to catch me in a lie—but that night felt like déjà vu as we hashed out the same details about the accident.

Not to be outdone, when Kyle finished his questions, I had a few of my own. Mr. Sherlock told me the PSI report would not only contain my sentencing recommendation, but also the potential fines and restitution. Sitting in front of Kyle seemed like an opportune time to discuss the Follow-Up #5 report that included a combined total amount of $24,175.00 for the aircraft repairs—an obvious triple charge on the value of the plane. Kyle acknowledged the error and said the actual amount would only be $7,175.00 for the repairs. But when I asked who was going to be the recipient of the money—given that neither the insurance company nor the airplane rental company were still in business—he seemed puzzled by the dilemma and simply smirked, offering no explanation.

He ended our meeting by describing how he was going to create the PSI report using multiple sources, including the follow-up reports, my answers from the questionnaire and, of course, the conversations he had with individuals relevant to the case, before he would submit his report to "Stew."

"Stew?" Who the hell was "Stew?"

It dawned on me that he was referring to Judge *Stew*art Stadler, who was apparently on a first name basis with Kyle. It seemed insolent to hear a new probation officer refer to his superior as if he was a drinking buddy, but perhaps that was common in a quaint little town like Kalispell.

Aside from the ongoing drama in Flathead County, on Friday morning my nutty sister, Renata, once again managed to surprise me. She called to tell me she was leaving Vancouver at noon by bus to Seattle, would catch the Amtrak train to Whitefish, Montana, and after a short twenty-minute bus ride to Kalispell, would be here tomorrow morning for a visit.

Excited about another opportunity to see each other, this was also going to be a work weekend for her. She was planning to meet with my attorney to not only go over the details of my upcoming sentencing but also prep for her court appearance. She was nervous about testifying on the stand, and Mr. Sherlock was going to coach her about the dos and don'ts in case the prosecutor interrogated her—just as he did with me during my bond hearing.

Since my arrest, she had been working non-stop—dealing with my attorneys and all my court cases—so hopefully a train ride through the scenic countryside was at least going to put her in a more relaxed mood at my sentencing.

CHAPTER TWENTY-EIGHT

Pre-Sentence Investigation Report

March 3 – 6, 2007

Day 186 – 189

I WAS STUNNED when I received the copy of the probation officer's PRE-SENTENCE INVESTIGATION REPORT (see Document: 3220 @ www.ambrozuk.com). Kyle Hinzman's report contained many of the facts I provided in my questionnaire and during our interviews, but instead of being an unbiased recommendation based on previous court cases, he put his own spin on it—challenging even what the prosecutor and Judge Stadler recommended.

Instead of probation, his recommendation was ten years in the Montana State Prison—with four of those years suspended—resulting in a net incarceration of six years. He also calculated my restitution, fines, and surcharges as follows:

- *Restitution of $13,840.25*
- *Net fine of $10,000.00 (after $9,500.00 credit for 190 days' time served was conveniently subtracted from the original fine of $19,500.00), and*
- *Additional total surcharges of $1,060.00.*

I was expecting him to at least be professional enough to include my twenty-five character reference letters submitted to court by my immediate family, my close friends and, of course, Tom (see List: 9560 @ www.ambrozuk.com). But Kyle had other ideas. Instead, he omitted them all from the PSI report and included only the victim impact statements from the Babcock family (see List: 9570 @ www.ambrozuk.com).

This was the first time I had seen their letters to court, but there was no question about their intentions. Reading through each statement, one could only conclude from their comments and dissection of the twenty-four-year-old transcript quotes between Tom and me (see Document: 3111 @ www.ambrozuk.com), that they believed our planning and elopement was completely *my* idea, and that Dianne had just been an innocent bystander.

Dianne's father, for example, used a quote from the transcript that read:

JA: WH-, what would I have to do wrong, if I, I didn't do anything wrong either, I didn't kill her or nothing.

Interpreting it literally, Gerald Babcock explained it as:

"His talking about murder made me suspicious that he may have done her in."

Using another transcript excerpt:

Page 47 JA: I'm not Tom, I'm not much different than you, you know, and especially, I've been there, I seen her, I, you know, I, I been there, and she's crying for hel-, ...says I can't take my seat-belt off, and she's going down with the plane. And I'm just sitting there, and I, what am I gonna do, I, like I jumped and I opened the door, I told you before right.

Dianne's father, once again, falsely assumed that I was in the air-craft. My conversation with Tom took place days after the accident, and I was still in shock when I tried to explain how I opened the door from the outside to get to Dianne after being catapulted through the front windshield. But instead of appreciating my mental state, Mr. Babcock interpreted my ramblings otherwise:

This statement angered me. Jerry is sitting beside Dianne, she's telling him she can't get her seat belt undone and he opens the door and jumps without helping her. And he grabs a bag with his belongings and money (IN THE DARK). I can't imagine the terror my daughter had when she saw him jump without helping her. If there is anything that has impacted me, it is this.

Both of Dianne's sisters also had their own interpretations and theories about our elopement and the accident, but Geoff Babcock, Dianne's only brother, went a step further:

> ... *the biggest fear I have is that Jerry ends up in the same town as my kids. From the transcript of a previous phone call and some things I have heard from the letter he wrote my father I feel that Jerry is the type of person that will blame others for his actions or his misfortunes. Because of this I worry that he will try to take it out on members of my family. I don't want this man anywhere near any member of my family. He has already taken my sister away from us; I don't want him to have any chance to do the same with the rest of my family.*

It was clear that their intention was vindictive; looking to smear and pretend that there was no love between Dianne and me, and that she had nothing to do with our elopement planning. But as sad as their comments read, what I found most disturbing was an excerpt from Dianne's younger sister's victim impact statement. Jodi wrote:

> *Ed Corrigan has told me that there was a possibility that Jerry could have gotten off of the negligent homicide charge should it have gone to trial and it been shown that Dianne was a willing accomplis [sic] in the event. He agreed to the probation sentence so that he could get the conviction.*

And there it was.

Looking at the overwhelming evidence—from Dianne's hair dye and curlers found in the recovered evidence, to the money she withdrew from the bank before we left, to not paying for her school books and tuition—Corrigan knew that Dianne was a voluntary participant, and this was nothing more than an unfortunate accident. And yet, he chose to pursue the negligent homicide charge nonetheless.

As slanderous and premeditated as the Babcock family's victim impact statements may have been, what mattered most was the PSI report that my attorney brought on Sunday evening to go over. Like me, he appeared startled at the recommendations and made several derogatory comments, trying to grasp why the report grossly deviated from the plea bargain agreement that he had worked so hard to solidify with the prosecutor. How ridiculous was the PSI report? Bad enough that even Kyle's boss saw the absurdity. He would eventually send Kyle to Mr. Sherlock's office to sheepishly apologize, but by then the damage was done.

Although Carolyn and Renata were both distraught about Hinzman's report, Mr. Sherlock reassured us that there was nothing to worry about. Everything was moving forward according to our original plea agreement. "The Babcock family are just venting," he said. He pledged to file a sentencing memorandum first thing Monday morning to rebut the inordinate PSI report, along with the omitted twenty-five character reference letters.

Going through the report with Mr. Sherlock, I again pointed out the three hand-written statements he took the liberty to fill out for me that still contained "I" (i.e.: "I planned the route") instead of "we" (i.e.: "We planned the route") throughout. The last time we'd met, we agreed and manually changed them all from "I" to "we." But since then, Mr. Sherlock had obviously submitted the *original* paragraphs to the probation officer.

It was unbelievably taxing dealing with an attorney who continuously undermined me, and the case, at every turn. Thankfully, there were just a few days left before my court appearance and what now seemed like an inevitable departure from Flathead County.

In addition to his evaluation and recommendations, Kyle Hinzman also included some questionable probation conditions in his report that made very little sense. Out of the twenty-seven he listed, one in particular was confusing:

> If the defendant is sentenced to a probationary sentence, he will be extradited to Canada for his immigration offenses where he will not be under the jurisdiction of the United States.

If that were the case, why even list the probation conditions?

Since the day I agreed to sign the *nolo contendere* plea, Mr. Sherlock had been reassuring both my sister and me that everything was moving according to plan. But I could plainly see things were not as he was asserting. In addition to the prosecutor's track record of pulling out of plea agreements during sentencing, there was now the stigma surrounding the probation officer's PSI report. In its present state, it would not look favorable to the judge at my sentencing.

To that extent, my suspicions would further be reinforced after I met with the detention center's Chief Hutton on Tuesday—the day before my hearing—for a pep talk and to go over courtroom etiquette. He approved my wearing a suit in court because that was my right. But he asked that I not hug any family members no matter what the outcome. I could understand the no hugging, but the "no matter what the outcome" sounded ominous.

And if that weren't suspicious enough, he offered a visit with my family not only that night but also after my sentencing, which seemed unorthodox. Why would Chief Hutton go out of his way to grant me these special privileges if I was done with my state case tomorrow and would be leaving Flathead County in the next day or two? My concerns were real, but I was not about to *look a gift horse in the mouth*. With enthusiasm I accepted his offer to visit with my parents and sister.

They had driven down to Kalispell for my hearing and were all in a festive mood, looking forward to putting the state case behind us. We spent over an hour talking about what was next on the agenda—what my federal case would entail and how Renata's cross-examination by the prosecutor would go when she took the stand.

Right after my visit with my family, Mr. Sherlock showed up with a copy of the Defendant's Sentencing Memorandum he had just submitted to Judge Stadler (see Document: 3221 @ www.ambrozuk.com). At first, his rebuttal to the probation officer's recommendation for a prison sentence appeared admirable. The memorandum was extensive—thirty-seven pages in total—and included not only my attorney's reasoning for a deferred sentence with unsupervised probation, but also several exhibits containing legal documents that supported his arguments, photographs of the aircraft during recovery, and several character reference letters omitted in the PSI report. Mr. Sherlock said he had spent the better part of the weekend researching and digging up cases Hinzman overlooked in order to strengthen his argument.

But why? Why would my attorney need to do all this research, waste his time—and my money—to file a memorandum if the probation officer's recommendation accounted for very little, and he was confident that Judge Stadler was still on board with my plea and probation? The more I thought about it, the more it felt like things were not adding up. From Chief Hutton's pep talk and his unusual visitation offers to the elaborate memorandum, I was getting a bad feeling in my gut that the hearing tomorrow would not go well.

CHAPTER TWENTY-NINE

Heading to Nowhere

August – September, 1982

THERE I WAS in the United States, and I knew no one. Continuously bombarded with unbearable thoughts of the accident days before, I was rational enough to seek out the only person I knew of in America—Tom's mother who lived in New York. Throughout our friendship, Tom had often talked fondly about her, and that perhaps explained my desire to head for the Big Apple. I knew very little about her—had never spoken with her and didn't know her name or address—but contacting her became my new objective. Once in New York, I could also call Tom after August 29—the day he returned home from his maneuver exercises in Washington State with the BC Reserves—to tell him what had happened and where to find the plane.

It was late morning on the seventh day after the accident when I packed everything I owned into the duffel bag and headed out in search of civilization. Hungry and without direction, I started walking through the woods until I came across a paved road that appeared devoid of traffic.

Walking along the side of the rural road, my duffel bag in one hand and my thumb out in the other, I eventually hitched a ride with an older man who was heading to the town of Whitefish. There, I made my way to the train station and bought a one-way ticket to New York. I bought some food at the station for my journey east, and spent the better part of the day gazing mindlessly at the passing scenery through the railcar window.

I was in physical and mental anguish but determined to continue with the elopement dream that Dianne and I started. In the small lavatory, I used the men's hair dye kit we bought in Vancouver to change my hair color. The process was messy, but after twenty minutes I emerged a new man: my mustache was gone, and my hair had changed from light blonde to a shade shy of black.

Arriving in New York, I purchased a street map and began walking randomly throughout the city, stopping occasionally only to eat a hotdog or a hoagie from a street vendor. Using telephone booth phonebooks, I spent hours systematically calling people with the unique last name of "Pawlowski." More times than not, I got an answering machine. But occasionally someone would pick up the phone, and I pretended to look for Tom, hoping they would identify themselves as his mother. I spent days trying to call every Pawlowski in the phonebook—retrying the answering-machine numbers the next day—before getting discouraged and giving up. It was a clever plan but futile right from the beginning. Still in shock and not thinking clearly, I never realized that Tom and his mother *didn't share the same last name.*

I wandered the streets aimlessly during the day; nights I spent either on a bench in Central Park, or in a seat at the train station where the police would prod me to wake up and move on. I had $2,300 Canadian dollars in the bag, but I didn't care about hotels or a comfortable night of rest. That money was for Dianne's and my journey, and I was not going to spend it frivolously until absolutely necessary. I no longer had a home, friends, or a family that I could call for support. I felt alone, and it made no difference if I slept on the streets like a vagrant. I would respond when spoken to, but for the most part, my mind was continuously preoccupied with the night of the accident.

After spending days on the streets feeling dejected, I walked past an old theater showing the movie *Pink Floyd: The Wall.* I had no desire to go anywhere or do anything, but the familiarity of the music

Tom and I had often shared drew me in. I spent the entire day sitting in the second row of an empty theater watching the film over and over again. With the music as background noise, I could not stop replaying that dreadful scene from Little Bitterroot Lake. Tears kept pouring down my face as I relived that unrelenting nightmare.

It was approximately 10:00 a.m. on Monday morning August 30, when Tom picked up his phone and accepted the collect-call charges. He was back from his maneuver exercises, and all I wanted was to tell him about the accident, where Dianne was, and to find out why she couldn't get her seatbelt off. Once they found the aircraft, I was sure the answer to that perplexing question would emerge. During that first call, I recalled very little about our conversation[iii]. By chance, my father was at Tom's house and briefly got on the phone to plead that I return home. I was cooperative in the moment, but I had no intention of complying.

As promised, I called Tom again the next day at around 5:00 p.m. and spoke with him for another fourteen minutes (see Document: 3108 @ www.ambrozuk.com). As before, I was frantic and barely understandable, but this time I conveyed a couple of important facts, including the approximate location of the aircraft in Little Bitterroot Lake. The call was eventually traced to the Port Authority Bus Depot in New York, but I told him I was still in Whitefish, hoping to throw him and the authorities off track.

Spending days on the streets, it slowly became clear I would not find solitude in the north. The weather was starting to turn for the worse, and with winter approaching, things only appeared more grim. As I wasn't fond of cold weather, I instinctively headed south to Texas. There was no rhyme or reason for my impetuous decision, other than my always having preferred a warmer climate, and from what I had seen on TV, Texas was the place I needed to be.

iii. Tom's handwritten transcript that he eventually submitted to the Vancouver City Police summarized our conversation and the state of my mind at the time of the call (see Document: 3110 @ www.ambrozuk.com).

Moving from place to place provided comfort because it gave me purpose. There was a never-ending battle raging inside that I would fight in silence for years to come, and the only thing I could hold on to that made sense was to continue with what Dianne and I started.

CHAPTER THIRTY

The Botched First State Sentencing

March 7 – 26, 2007
Day 190 – 209

WEDNESDAY WAS GOING to be the day I finished my state case and got the hell out of Dodge, leaving Flathead County behind for good. The plan was to appear at my sentencing, let the Babcock family speak their mind, and after it was all over, the judge would give me probation—just as it was agreed to by the prosecutor in our plea agreement.

Unfortunately, that's not what happened.

Shortly after lunch, I met with Mr. Sherlock in the full-contact visitor's booth to go over court formalities prior to the hearing, and his defendant's sentencing memorandum. "It's about positive attitude, Jerry!" he said exultantly. He was in a festive mood, telling me how good he felt about the sentencing, and even recounted a long-forgotten anecdote about Judge Stadler to brighten up the mood. While attending Stanford University, Stadler one day decided to take a hiatus from school himself—and disappeared for *months* on a motorcycle trip to Mexico. Mr. Sherlock felt it was a comparable story to our elopement. He seemed confident that the similarity to both of our youthful ventures, coupled with sympathy, would play a large part when it came to Judge Stadler ruling in favor of probation. We were still talking when a guard knocked on the Plexiglas window and took me to a temporary cell in the booking area to change. Because all my clothes were still in Texas, my sister brought her eldest son's tight-fitting, high-school graduation suit for me to wear as an alternative.

Properly dressed, I was escorted to the third floor by two guards who wished me luck before I walked into the small Number Three Courtroom outfitted with only a few benches for audience seating. The first row was reserved for family only, with the Babcocks directly behind the prosecutor's desk, and my family behind Mr. Sherlock and me.

Mrs. Sherlock—a recently retired school teacher and an avid evangelist of *The Secret*—sat between my mom and sister, holding their hands in support and to console them if need be.

Waiting for the hearing to begin, I was initially instructed to sit in the jury box for close to ten minutes as my attorney worked the room with small talk. When Judge Stadler appeared in his black robe and took his place behind the bench to begin my sentencing, I was moved to the defendant's table with Mr. Sherlock taking his place alongside me.

Following a short, introductory speech, the judge turned control over to the prosecutor and his first witness, Linda Babcock. Ed Corrigan's plan was to call four members of the Babcock family to the stand, beginning with Dianne's eldest sister. I had briefly met Linda once, so there was very little she could say about our crossing paths. Using her victim impact statement as a guide (see Document: 7072 @ www.ambrozuk.com), the prosecutor began with simple questions about her relationship with Dianne, whether we were acquainted, and how the loss had impacted her family.

They brought up Dianne's non-existent missing purse that Sheriff Dupont often alluded to in his media interviews (see Document: 6802 @ www.ambrozuk.com), and the coincidental date of August 30—the same date on which her mother had died and I was arrested. Linda even praised my ex-girlfriend, Genea, for her bravery in turning me in. But the bulk of her testimony echoed her victim impact statement innuendos—comparing our elopement to a hit-and-run accident, the consequences for which I was solely responsible.

Corrigan then called Gerald Babcock to the stand. Dianne's father was in his mid-seventies. He spoke in a soft voice and frequently took long pauses after each question from the prosecutor, as if to gather his thoughts. Like his daughter before him, he started with an introduction of Dianne, including her accomplishments, her traits, and how they all missed her dearly. But within minutes the focus shifted to the accident, the taped phone conversation between Tom and me, and why he didn't believe Dianne was a willing participant in our plan.

Out of all the family members testifying, he seemed the most composed, prepared, and determined to dispute her participation. With a stack of reference papers one inch thick at his fingertips, he systematically worked through his own four-page victim impact statement (see Document: 7070 @ www.ambrozuk.com), looking to not only explain but, more importantly, discredit the idea of Dianne's voluntary involvement and indirectly, the accident.

Following his lengthy dissection of the phone call between Tom and me (see Document: 3111 @ www.ambrozuk.com), he postulated on my every line before introducing–several new observations that were puzzling to him. "Even minor things don't make any sense," he said. "Dianne never went anywhere without her teeth retainer. She would never have left the retainer at home if she was eloping. And why are there no pictures of them together? If he was the love of her life, shouldn't there be pictures?" he asked, as if looking for understanding and confirmation. Even Dianne's choice of bathing suit was scrutinized. He argued she would have never put on that particular one if she intended to swim to shore. There were obvious, simple answers to everything he questioned, but he remained vigilant and in complete denial of the facts. When Mr. Sherlock began his cross-examination, he pointed out the woman's hair-color dye and curling kit found in the green garbage bag recovered from the aircraft. The key words there were "woman" and "curling kit," as I had my own *men's* hair dye kit that I used on my way to New York after the accident.

But Mr. Babcock insisted, "They were for *his* disguise!"

"What about the two-man yellow raft? That would seem to indicate they planned to leave the aircraft together," Mr. Sherlock suggested.

"They were probably going river rafting in the Penticton area," Dianne's father speculated.

Despite Mr. Babcock's persistence to present his own version of the facts, there was evidence to rebut his every argument. In 1982, the Royal Canadian Mounted Police spent months logging details surrounding the accident—including interviewing both families, the aircraft rental owners and their employees, my private pilot school instructors, and Tom—to compile an extensive list of testimonies and affidavits that were irrefutable (see Document: 3107 @ www.ambrozuk.com).

Among the evidence were also details about the money Dianne and I had saved over a period of months. For Dianne it was close to $1,600.00. Mr. Babcock told the court he believed Dianne hadn't paid for her tuition and books because she was intending to pay for my half of our trip. Even if true, at $38 per hour for aircraft rental—multiplied by approximately four hours of flight to Penticton and back—that only added up to $152, and therefore made no sense.

When asked about the unusual list of items found in the green garbage bag recovered from the aircraft, he had no explanation as to why we had packed so many things for a day trip, or why most were Dianne's personal items (see Document: 3103 @ www.ambrozuk. com):

- *a roll of toilet paper*
- *a woman's Toni Perm Kit and Curlers*
- *a woman's Nice & Easy Hair Dye*
- *a green sweater*
- *a pair of Levi's*
- *a white and red pullover shirt*

- *a white blouse*
- *a blue and white pullover shirt*
- *a gray sweatshirt*
- *a pair of blue cords*
- *two pairs of panties*
- *one pair of green socks*
- *one pair of white socks*
- *various uneaten perishable food items including sandwiches, fruit yogurt, peaches and tomatoes*
- *a liter of orange juice, and*
- *a liter of chocolate milk*

Why would anyone bring so many clothes, including a roll of toilet paper, for a one-day excursion to Penticton and back? Those were questions in need of an explanation, but Mr. Babcock could provide none, other than his suspicions.

His slow testimony seemed to drag on for the better part of the hour as everyone patiently listened in silence. He clearly felt this was his chance to finally put his opinions and theories forward and be heard, remaining undeterred to the very end.

Jodi, Dianne's younger sister, took the stand next. She was a lot older than the last time I had seen her, and although her quirky walk and the facial tics were gone, she appeared emotionally distraught when she sat down in the witness chair next to Judge Stadler. Her face was flushed, as she tried to refrain from sobbing, periodically brushing off the occasional tear running down her cheek with the tissue she grasped tightly in her hand.

Like the others, she started her presentation with praise and fond remembrances of Dianne. Then the prosecutor turned to her victim impact statement (see Document: 7073 @ www.ambrozuk.com) that contained many unsubstantiated interpretations about Dianne, me, and our relationship. Twenty-four years ago, she had told me I was better looking and nicer than Dianne's ex-boyfriend, but now there was only animosity and bitterness toward me. In between her sobs, it was often difficult to understand her not only verbally, but also what her point was. She jumped between topics as fast as she changed sentences, making it impossible to focus on her message. But despite her scattered dialogue, there was no doubt to her purpose.

Referring to my success over the years, you could hear the hatred in her voice. "He drives a *Viper*! He lives in an expensive house! And she's dead! It makes me *sick*!" she punctuated her emotions by emphasizing the words *Viper* and *sick*.

Later, I would find out from Renata that just before the hearing began, she saw Ed Corrigan meet with the Babcock family in a private room. When they emerged a half hour later, Jodi appeared to be in emotional turmoil. I didn't know what the prosecutor's motivational talk was about, but it was obviously enough to set Jodi off on the witness stand.

Dianne's brother, Geoff, was the last to be called to testify. Of all the Babcock family members, he seemed the most nervous and timid. It took him a good two minutes to settle down and collect his composure before he could respond. Noticing his trepidation and flustered demeanor, one of the guards brought him a tall glass of water to help him relax as he nervously followed the prosecutor's lead.

Referring to excerpts from Geoff's victim impact statement (see Document: 7071 @ www.ambrozuk.com), Corrigan coaxed him about his fear for his family's safety if I were given probation and returned to Canada. The prosecutor spent much of his time gently prodding statements out of the jittery witness, before asking the same final question he had finished each of the Babcock's testimony with: "Is there anything you want to say to Mr. Ambrozuk?"

Just as the rest of them did, Geoff turned to face me with a somber look and said, "Why would you do such a thing?"

It was a rhetorical question that none of the Babcock family members wanted to hear the answer to. But I wished that the judge had allowed me to reply. I wanted to stand up and finally explain everything that each of them got wrong about my relationship with Dianne, with our elopement, and with the accident itself.

Listening to them come together in myopic hatred, I could not help but wonder what Dianne would have thought of her family now. I knew her better than anyone through our countless intimate moments, and I could honestly say she not only would have been saddened by their behavior, but also ashamed. Those were not the same kind and gentle people I remembered. And if Corrigan was responsible for their inflamed absurdities at their own emotional expense, then shame on him, too.

When the prosecution rested, it was our turn. According to Mr. Sherlock, the only witness needed to speak on my behalf was my sister, Renata. He had already submitted all the character reference letters from my family and friends to the court (see List: 9560 @ www. ambrozuk.com), so there was no need to prolong the hearing if probation was inevitable, based on his understanding from Judge Stadler.

Taking the stand after being apart for twenty-four years was an emotional moment for my sister. It wasn't long before tears began streaming down her face, but unlike Jodi, these were the tears of joy and anxiousness. Mr. Sherlock began with a few simple questions before getting to more complex issues such as my past and present relationship with my family. Between her sobs, it was sometimes difficult to hear her response, but the sentiment was that everyone was ready to put all this behind and move on with rekindling our family bonds.

Because of my sister's emotional state, even Ed Corrigan refrained from pressing her too hard during his cross-examination. But he did ask a few questions, including a curious one about whether it was my intention to continue with my software development when I returned to Canada. Although no one knew exactly what the prosecutor was after at that moment, he seemed satisfied enough with her confirmation to excuse her from the stand.

Judge Stadler then turned to me and asked if I had anything to say.

During the last couple of days, Mr. Sherlock hinted about making an apologetic plea to the court before the judge decided my sentence. To that extent, I stood up and read:

Yes, your honor, I would like to make a short statement if I may.

I now know the hurt and the pain that I have caused my family, my mother, my father, my sister, and the Babcock family with my foolish ideas that resulted in the loss of Dianne Babcock twenty-four years ago. There is no apology sufficient enough to erase the pain and the suffering of all those involved. But I would also like to say that the one and the most important reason why I could not come forward earlier is because of the pain and the sorrow I had in my own heart due to the loss of Dianne, whom I still cherish and hold dear to this day.

I am hopeful that someday the Babcock family will be able to find peace. I am very sorry for all I did and did not do in their eyes. I ask God to help us all and that He may someday allow them to forgive me.

Thank you.

The statement may have been tailored by Mr. Sherlock to his liking, but my reverence was unquestionable—my apologies to the Babcock family for their loss were just as sincere as the painful grieving I endured for so many years after the tragedy.

It was then that Corrigan called Kyle Hinzman to the witness stand. Calling a probation officer to testify at a sentencing was unorthodox, but Corrigan had a plan. With a pompous look on his face, Hinzman explained that after consulting with an immigration officer, he was told there was a 95 percent probability I would be deported to Canada after I was done with my federal case. In fact, that piece of information was no secret at all. He made that same argument in the PSI report he had submitted to Judge Stadler and Ed Corrigan days before.

When he returned to his seat at the prosecutor's table, Judge Stadler began his closing remarks. He believed that, despite what the Babcock family stated in their victim impact statements and during their testimony, Dianne and I were eloping and she was a willing participant in our plan.

But that was when he deviated from what he had all but assured my attorney.

He said that since he had learned I would eventually be deported to Canada where the probation conditions could not be enforced, he could no longer give me probation.

Taking the queue, Corrigan then stood up and expressed his own concern about the plea agreement he had signed (see Document: 3217 @ www.ambrozuk.com). He asked for a private conference with my attorney and the judge to resolve this new dilemma.

"The court will take a ten minute recess!" Judge Stadler announced, before the three men—he, the prosecutor, and my attorney—hastily left the courtroom, gathering in the hallway outside the back doors.

The guards took me to a small holding cell in the back of the courthouse while the three men deliberated. I sat quietly for what seemed like close to ten minutes before Mr. Sherlock emerged and shut the door behind him. "The judge wants to give you a two-year sentence, or we can withdraw our *nolo contendere* plea and go back to trial." Looking to sweeten the deal, he went on to suggest "Judge Stadler might be persuaded to drop the sentence to eighteen months, and with good behavior and time served, you'll be out in less than six." He waited for my reaction, but his courtroom enthusiasm was now absent.

He had spent months working on me, coercing me, and making sure that when the time came I was ready to plead *nolo contendere*. But now all that was for naught because the prosecutor and the judge had yanked the carpet from under his feet using a technicality. I didn't know who to feel worse for—him or me. Out of curiosity, I calmly asked, "So what do you think we should do, Patrick?"

Realizing that I was not going to bite at the rock-bottom offer of six months in the penitentiary, he looked disappointed. But after a long pause and some thoughtful soul-searching, he reluctantly said, "Let's go to trial!"

When we returned to the courtroom, there was still the matter of public perception and the media. With someone in need to initialize the first move, Ed Corrigan stood up and said, "Judge, I'm probably going to lose my job over this, but I cannot go along with the plea bargain because none of the probation conditions will be enforceable in Canada, and Mr. Ambrozuk will be free to go about his business without supervision."

Whether today, tomorrow, or months from now at my next sentencing, the same rules would apply—I would still be exempt from any probation conditions they imposed once I left the country. But that was not the point. Prolonging my stay was—either in the detention center or a penitentiary—just as they had tried to do minutes earlier.

After noting the prosecutor's withdrawal from our plea agreement, Judge Stadler asked Mr. Sherlock what our decision was. My attorney stood up and announced that we were changing our plea to not guilty. "We request a trial," he said. I imagine there were many confused people in court at that moment who had not been privy to our backroom closed-door drama.

After accepting our change of plea—and considering I had already spent six months in the detention center—Judge Stadler and the prosecutor agreed to reset the trial date eighty days from that day to expedite the process. It almost seemed human of Corrigan to be so accommodating, yet I could not forget what he told Gerald Babcock over two months earlier about postponing my upcoming trial date.

Leaving the courtroom, I glanced back at my family and could see the disappointment in their eyes. It had been a long six months for them, too, and much like the guards I passed in the hallways on my way back to my cell, they also appeared disconcerted and confused.

But I was not going to let Mr. Sherlock, Ed Corrigan, or Judge Stadler rain on my parade. The botched sentencing was no doubt an unfortunate setback, but somehow, deep down inside, I felt it was a blessing in disguise. I never wanted to plead guilty or *nolo contendere* to negligent homicide in the first place! Now that I would have my day in court, the mystery surrounding the accident could finally be cleared up.

When I watched the news later that night, the headlines read, "Strange Twist In Ambrozuk Case" and "Ambrozuk Changes His Mind With Plea Bargain." It was disheartening to see how easily Corrigan and Judge Stadler could sell to the media the idea that I changed my mind and pulled out of the plea agreement, where in fact the opposite was true.

On Friday, Mr. Sherlock finally showed up with renewed optimism. Gone was his anemic outlook, because the federal prosecutor apparently had had a change of heart. He was not only contemplating replacing the passport charge with a lesser offense, but was willing to move the case from Texas to Montana after hearing what happened during my state sentencing.

"This way, Jerry, we might be able to resolve the federal charge before the state case," he professed with an ardent voice. "I feel good about this!" he repeated throughout our conversation, as if to negate his faux pas still clearly on my mind.

But after six months of dealing with him and his pointless positivism, I had lost all confidence in anything he was still trying to sell. If he couldn't close a simple state plea deal, what were the chances he could actually succeed in federal court?

I had disclosed every detail about myself and the case since the first day I arrived in Flathead County, and in return all I got back from him was skepticism, suspicion, and coercion. It was time to get to the bottom of what actually happened at my sentencing. Pressing him for specifics without causing confrontation, he eventually admitted that when he spoke with Judge Stadler several days before the hearing, the judge was already wavering about my probation.

And that just pissed me off.

He'd known the judge had already backed out and kept lying to me and my family, stringing us along with his deceptive motivational speeches as if nothing was wrong. He'd spent the entire weekend putting together the thirty-seven-page defendant's sentencing memorandum to save face; got his wife to hold my mother's and my sister's hands at my sentencing; kept inviting my family to his home for dinners—reassuring them there was nothing to worry about, and that by Wednesday this would all be over—while all along knowing everything was about to spin out of control.

All these pieces were falling into place, and I could now finally understand how and why things went south.

During our full disclosure conversation, Mr. Sherlock said that it would take another $10,000 to $50,000 if we went to trial, because his $30,000 retainer was almost exhausted. But after six months of disappointments—and now back to what seemed like square one—this was the case of "Fool me once, shame on you! Fool me twice, shame on me!" It was time to move on and find his successor.

With full support from my family, Renata and I decided to look for another state criminal-defense attorney. This time, though, she would make an exhaustive Internet search, verify their credentials, and hopefully find someone who would be a worthy adversary for the prosecutor when we got to trial.

While my sister was diligently scouring the Internet for a new lawyer, I decided to splurge on a pair of new tennis shoes if I was to remain in Flathead County for another three months. My old ones had developed holes in the bottom, and a new pair of Bob Barker[iv] specials was just what I needed to keep my socks dry and prevent blisters while I walked the court in circles and played basketball with my cellies during REC.

My faith in my attorney may have been shattered, but I still had not lost hope in my fellow detainees, who needed nothing more than

---

iv. Yes, the same Bob Barker from *The Price Is Right*—as the label on the bottom attested (along with the Made in China stamp).

a gentle push in the right direction to become productive citizens in their own right.

Case in point was my latest project—a Native American cellie named Adam. There were constant conflicts and taunting between him and Nick, but when Nick got transferred, Adam's attitude changed completely. With a bit of encouragement, he seemed motivated to finish his GED certificate. He was going to use the *free* Indian Reservation money he was entitled to, he said, to eventually go back to school to learn a good trade. I was more than happy to help with his GED vocabulary and math tests, but at times I felt like the Tony Robbins of FCDC and probably should have collected some sort of motivational consulting fee for my efforts.

Thank You, Sir! May I Have Another!

March 27 – April 3, 2007

Day 210 – 217

AFTER REPEATED THREATS about filing additional charges if I didn't cooperate and plead guilty to the negligent homicide charge, Ed Corrigan finally delivered on his promise. Mr. Sherlock showed up Tuesday with the bad news and a copy of the two additional charges filed in court by the state prosecutor on March 26, 2007: theft and criminal mischief.

Each additional felony carried a maximum sentence of ten years in a state penitentiary and/or a maximum fine of $50,000 each. The prosecutor's court filings included several documents: AFFIDAVIT IN SUPPORT OF MOTION FOR LEAVE TO FILE AN AMENDED INFORMATION (see Document: 3223 @ www.ambrozuk.com); Amended Information (see Document: 3224 @ www.ambrozuk. com); and MOTION FOR LEAVE TO FILE AN AMENDED INFORMATION (see Document: 3225 @ www.ambrozuk.com). Although Corrigan would be absent from my arraignment because of his timely vacation plans, the NOTICE OF ARRAIGNMENT ON AMENDED INFORMATION (see Document: 3226 @ www.ambrozuk.com) stated it would take place on March 29, 2007 at 8:30 a.m.

But the obvious question was why Corrigan would go to the trouble of filing two additional charges? Was it because I had bruised his ego in the letter I sent to Mr. Babcock explaining why I was fighting the negligent homicide charge, and within it stating I thought the prosecutor was simply looking for a scapegoat? That was undoubtedly part of it, but Corrigan also knew he would lose in court with only the negligent homicide charge. He bluntly confessed this to the Babcock family—as Jodi had written in her victim impact statement—and hence why he eventually agreed to a probation sentence because it guaranteed a conviction. He was afraid if we went to trial, the evidence would show Dianne as a voluntary participant, and our elopement and the resulting crash, although irresponsible, would be deemed as nothing more than a tragic accident.

The two new charges were his side bet—he was sure to lose on negligent homicide, but perhaps he could get lucky with a theft or criminal mischief charge. With no one to question his conduct in a small town like Kalispell where collusion runs deep, even Judge Stadler seemed reluctant to defy the prosecutor's motive when he approved the two new charges (see Document: 3228 @ www.ambrozuk.com).

When Mr. Sherlock showed up at my arraignment on Thursday, he appeared melancholy—as if he had lost all enthusiasm for my case. The courtroom was practically empty this time, with only a couple of well-dressed reporters sitting in the audience. As soon as I sat down next to my attorney, Judge Stadler began by asking if we needed to go over the acknowledgement of rights I had reviewed with Mr. Sherlock and signed a couple of days before (see Document: 3227 @ www.ambrozuk.com). Without a reason to prolong the hearing more than necessary, I waived my right.

"How do you plead?" Judge Stadler asked.

Mr. Sherlock and I stood up and I confidently answered, "I plead not guilty, Your Honor!"

He then warned me that the sentences for the three felonies would run consecutively and, if convicted, I could be sentenced to a maximum of thirty years in the state penitentiary and pay a maximum of $150,000. "Do you still plead not guilty?"

"Yes, Your Honor."

The judge scribbled down my reply and reiterated the upcoming court dates for my trial on May 21, 2007 before standing up and walking out of the courtroom to conclude the hearing.

As the entire arraignment took less than ten minutes, I asked Mr. Sherlock if we could meet and go over some outstanding issues, including the $30,000 retainer and the breakdown of his professional service fees he offered to disclose in our last meeting (see Document: 5110 @ www.ambrozuk.com). His itemized list showed an outstanding balance of $3,262.58 on the last page, meaning he had exhausted the $30,000 retainer and was looking for more—$10,000 more—to resolve the case as a plea bargain, and $50,000 if we decided to go to trial (see Document: 5109 @ www.ambrozuk.com).

It was no secret I was disappointed with his representation, and that is perhaps why he called for a change. He looked me directly in the eye, and with a morose look on his face, humbly said, "This might be a good time for you to look for another attorney." He had hinted at this a couple of days before, but I could see he now meant it. He tried his best with the plea agreement, but after the fiasco at my sentencing, he seemed frustrated not only with the case, but also with himself.

Fortunately, Renata and I had thought ahead and were already working on a contingency plan. After several days and an exhaustive Internet search, my sister found Chuck "Herman" Watson, a trial lawyer with thirty years' experience, who seemed like a formidable adversary for the prosecutor. During our phone conference the previous day, Mr. Watson came across as calm and confident when we briefly discussed my case and the possibility of retaining his services. He had a monotone way of speaking—with long pauses between sentences—but his presentation, at least over the phone, sounded encouraging.

Watson also said he wanted to bring on board his colleague, Larry Jent, who was a two-time Montana senator and would be a valuable asset with both the state and federal charges. Based on their tentative schedule, we planned to meet the following week. But before we disconnected, I candidly asked about his fee structure, looking for a ball-park figure in comparison to what Mr. Sherlock quoted.

"Until I know more about the case details I can't commit to an exact number," he replied, "but it should be somewhere between $50,000 and $100,000." It was obviously more than what Mr. Sherlock quoted and we expected, but since we were getting two attorneys for the price of one, it seemed justifiable.

If you're still keeping score, we're up to eight attorneys: Clancy (dismissed), Davis (Texas), Sherlock (Montana), Palmer (Corvette release), Cohen (Merrill Lynch), still to be determined lawyer to deal with the passport charges, and now Watson and Jent.

And so when Mr. Sherlock brought up the notion of finding another attorney, I told him the bad news. He appeared surprised but retained his composure and offered a word of caution with a hint of sarcasm, "They are good lawyers, but they're expensive."

"I know, but I no longer have a choice," I politely replied, wondering what to do about his services. Firing him would not only look bad for him, but also reflect poorly on the case. Instead, I offered to let him stay on board as counsel with the understanding that it was strictly *pro bono*.

But that didn't go over well.

"I have enough business and I'm not worried about my reputation!" he retorted. Somewhat agitated, he went on to defend his character before incongruously attacking me and my unwillingness to play into his hand. "You've got mental issues!" he lashed out. "Dr. Trontel thinks you're still living in 1982."

This was the first time I had seen him in such disarray. But rather than getting sucked into his emotional outburst, I calmly reiterated my offer and asked that he at least think about it. I knew he would interpret it as a slap in the face—taking a backseat after seven months and having to explain the demotion to everyone in Kalispell—but I'd had enough of his coercion and his representation.

One would think this news would be discouraging enough to leave our meeting hastily, but for some inexplicable reason, he stayed for another hour. Revisiting the accident, he once again disputed the aircraft flipping over and my being catapulted through the front windshield. Still insistent we had landed in an upright position, he now believed that the damaged tail fin seen in the recovery photos (see Document: 7167 @ www.ambrozuk.com) was caused by rocks as the plane descended to the bottom of the lake. But unless there were rocks falling from the sky in Montana, that obviously made no sense from a physics perspective.

Coming from an aerospace engineering background, I even tried using viscous fluid principals to explain that the aircraft design was primarily responsible for its natural tendency to correct its attitude whenever it was moving through a fluid. Whether it be air or water, the plane was designed to reorient itself, and that is why it was found in an upright position at the bottom of the lake after its 240-foot descent. But he was stubborn and single-minded and refused to let go of Sheriff Dupont's theories.

When he showed up again on Monday, he initially came in with a form to sign— authorizing the release of my case information to my new attorneys. But soon that turned into a lengthy discussion about my case, my sentencing, and the new charges. Trying to justify why the hearing went belly-up, he proposed a new theory that implicated Judge Ted O. Lympus—the Flathead County District Attorney in 1982, who originally filed the negligent homicide charge. "It was he who spoke with Judge Stadler and got him to back out of our plea agreement," he speculated.

I had no doubt collusion was involved, but when I asked if he could back up his accusations with any facts or details, he offered none.

Switching topics, he then said Judge Stadler was only trying to intimidate me during the last arraignment when he warned that the sentences for my three felonies would run consecutively. After some research, he had discovered that because they all occurred at the same time, they would run concurrently, and therefore the maximum sentence I could receive was ten years and $50,000 in fines.

But most curious was his final attempt to get me to reconsider the last plea bargain offer. He pulled out a local newspaper that he'd brought and ran through the numbers that the prosecutor and the judge had offered three weeks earlier behind closed doors. Using the newspaper's empty margins, he recalculated my time already served and suggested that if I took the twenty-four month sentence, I would most likely be out in six months with time served and good behavior. He was sure the sentence could be further reduced to eighteen months if he had the go-ahead to plead with the judge, thereby decreasing my incarceration to just three months.

I don't know what his motivation was, but it sounded impetuous. We were in the process of hiring new attorneys, yet he was still hanging on to the hope I would change my mind and take their offer.

That would not be the end of his persistence, because on Friday things got even more ridiculous. During mail call, I got a letter from him that contained an email his daughter, Elizabeth, had forwarded to him with a list of the "100 quotes from *The Secret*" (see Document: 5115 @ www.ambrozuk.com). At the top of the first page, he had scribbled "Jerry – Read this! Pat."

The list of quotes was extracted from *The Secret* documentary video, and contained profound food for thought:

> *#2. The Secret is the Law of Attraction.*
> *#14. EVERYTHING in your life you have attracted... accept that fact... it's true.*
> *#62. Create a Vision Board . . . pictures of what you want to attract . . . everyday look at it and get into the feeling state of already having acquired these wants.*

There were quotes from Winston Churchill, Albert Einstein, and Buddha sprinkled throughout the axioms supporting the idea that, by creating a "vision board" to help overcome problems and obstacles, everyone had the power to change their surroundings and their destiny.

But there was one item in particular that he highly regarded above all, and he had placed an asterisk next to it:

> #82. *No one else can think or feel for you... it's YOU... ONLY YOU.*

In other words, if I would only believe in *The Secret*, I had the power to change my current circumstances. Somehow it was my belief—rather than his council—that was responsible for me still being in Flathead County. Well, shit, if I'd known all I had to do was create a vision board and believe in order to make the prosecutor drop the negligent homicide charge, I'd have done so in a heartbeat the day I arrived in Kalispell, saving myself not only $30,000 but also a lot of aggravation.

Embarrassing as it was, I showed the four-page list to my cellies who erupted with laughter, each in disbelief about what my case defense had turned into.

But there would be a silver lining to the madness. Renata found out from Mr. Watson that Sherlock changed his mind about remaining on the case as an advisor. To bring my potential new attorneys up to speed on case details, he would meet with them on Wednesday, following their visit to the detention center.

While I looked forward to their fresh set of eyes on the case strategy, I could only hope they would not be easily scared off when Mr. Sherlock mentioned *The Secret* as his secret weapon.

CHAPTER THIRTY-TWO

State Case Defense Counsel—Take Two!

April 4 – 10, 2007

Day 218 – 224

I MET WITH Mr. Watson and his private investigator of fifteen years, Ron Maki, on Wednesday. They stayed for almost three hours, and after our brief case overview, I once again felt encouraged about my chances in court.

With his molasses-like discourse, Mr. Watson introduced himself as cautious but driven, and made it clear he was up for the challenge of dealing with Ed Corrigan, despite the prosecutor's unethical court-room reputation and the ACLU investigations into his conduct.

He was also adamant about taking control of all my cases—state, federal, and immigration—and I wholeheartedly agreed. They were indirectly interwoven and required a single helmsman to navigate through the obstacles still ahead. But unlike Mr. Sherlock, who felt that "the longer you spend time in jail, the better it will look," Mr. Watson was ready to do battle—at least in spirit. He was surprised I was still in the detention center and suggested I would have been al-lowed to post bond months ago if he were in charge. It was refreshing to hear the possibilities as he breathed new life into the case, but I was acutely aware that the difference between his promises and his future accomplishments was our unsigned contract.

Our meeting flowed smoothly right up until the very end when he surprised me with a six-page agreement that he had already taken the initiative to prepare. He pulled out the document from his briefcase and handed me a copy to read while he excused himself to go to the bathroom—leaving me with the private investigator sitting quietly across the table. Most of the paragraphs were standard attorney gibberish protecting both the attorney and the client, with only the retainer fees drawing attention. When we had conferenced the previous week on the phone, he quoted us a range between $50,000 and $100,000 for his services. But what the contract stated was *$250,000*, plus expenses—and he wanted the money upfront. The fees were appropriated accordingly: $150,000 would go to him, while the rest was intended for hiring a federal attorney in Texas. The fine-print detailed the additional expenses I would be responsible for, including, but not limited to, all their travel costs, lodging, hiring of private investigators, and even legal research that I had assumed would automatically be part of the attorney fee.

On his website, I recalled he proudly listed one of his defenses as *Pro Bono*—making him look like a compassionate and reasonable attorney. But since our telephone conference, I speculated that he'd done a quick Google search—discovering mentions of my house, lake property, and Viper—and opportunistically decided to revise his conservative estimate. Unfortunately, the reality was that such an amount was impossible for me to raise in the next few weeks let alone the next several days.

We adjourned for lunch so I could discuss the contract and his fee with my family—while he consulted with Mr. Sherlock about the case details—before we reconvened in late afternoon to complete our interview.

He seemed in good spirits after meeting with my ex-attorney but quickly lost his enthusiasm when we got back to the retainer fees. I explained that although my financial situation might not be his problem, it was my reality, and that it was impossible for me to get my hands on $250,000 because I was still dealing with Merrill Lynch, who were playing games and unwilling to release my money. He seemed to take that personally. Suddenly, he was no longer the understanding attorney who'd walked into our meeting with an open mind and a professional attitude. Appearing resentful, he offered to re-write our agreement, grabbed it out of my hands, and darted out the door.

Two hundred fifty thousand dollars was a lot of money, and I would have a difficult time justifying it even if I had access to my accounts. I hoped that by contesting his retainer—rather than tarnish our relationship—he would eventually come around and compromise to something more reasonable.

On Thursday, Carolyn and I conferenced with Mr. Cohen to discuss the latest updates with my frozen Merrill Lynch accounts. It had been several weeks since we'd last spoken with the attorney, and I was curious about the progress. Using Pig Latin-like legal jargon, Mr. Cohen explained that although he received a reply from Merrill Lynch, their rebuttal said nothing, and therefore he was in the process of filing a Request for Disclosure, Request for Production, and a First Set of Interrogatories (see Document: 3506 @ www.ambrozuk. com). Merrill Lynch's attorneys had twenty days to reply with the Answers to Discovery, after which we would proceed with a Motion for Summary Judgment in the next thirty days. If we still had no satisfactory answers, we would go before a judge to get them to capitulate.

After seeing what a state prosecutor was capable of, and now being forced to deal with Merrill Lynch's attorneys, it sometimes felt as if the law was put in place more to be manipulated than to solve a problem or serve justice. I was not a national threat, and Merrill Lynch was nothing more than a bank, yet they could legally withhold my money indefinitely as if they were a judicial system. It seemed crazy, but there was nothing we could do about it. They had my money locked up, and the only way I could force their hand was to take them to court. How bizarre and flat-out wrong was that?

April 8 was Easter Sunday, and although it often felt as if I were staying at the Flathead County Resort and Spa—with all the built-in luxuries of free food, daily laundry services, and television—I found the holidays especially tough now that my family was back in my life again.

When I made my morning phone rounds to wish everyone Happy Easter, they were all cooking up a storm. Carolyn's family was coming over to her new place for the first time, and she was busy making everything from corn dip to chicken enchiladas.

At my parent's house, they were expecting twelve people and putting together a feast worthy of a king. It had been twenty-four years, but I still remembered the taste of the Polish delicacies my mother used to cook: *pierogi, gołąbki* (stuffed cabbage rolls), *placki kartoflane* (potato pancakes), *kotlety mielone* (schnitzels), *barszcz* (beet soup), *flaczki* (tripe soup), and countless other dishes I couldn't wait to sample again. Throughout the years, I would venture out with friends to restaurants and try a variety of European foods, but it never tasted as good as my mother's.

I might have missed out on Easter with my family, but there would be good news on Monday morning to compensate. One of the guards brought me a large sealed envelope with the appended attorney-client fixed fee contract from Mr. Watson (see Document: 5250 @ www. ambrozuk.com). The modified agreement contained much of the content found in his original draft with a few distinctive exceptions. For starters, the initial fixed fee was reduced to $150,000, due immediately. There were also several other stipulations, including an additional fee of $25,000 if there were a mistrial. The contract encompassed both the state and federal charges, with an understanding that any immigration charges were also covered under the federal umbrella.

But the most interesting part was the fine print that offset the decrease in his retainer fee. Additional costs and expenses—process servers' fees, fees fixed by law or assessed by courts or other agencies, court reporters' fees, investigation expenses, consultants' fees, expert witness fees, and other similar items—were now defined as my sole responsibility.

Mr. Watson played his card, I called his bluff, and now that he came back with what appeared to be a $100,000 discount on paper, I had a decision to make—ask my parents to front the money for the new attorneys, or keep searching for someone who was more financially reasonable.

CHAPTER THIRTY-THREE

On with the Mission

1982 – 1983

AFTER ABANDONING THE idea of staying in New York through winter, I bought a U.S. map and decided to head to Dallas, Texas before the weather turned for the worse. To save money, I hitchhiked daily, getting rides that varied from a few miles to hundreds, with a few exceptions spanning multiple states.

Every morning, I went to a truck stop or gas station to shave, wash up, and grab some food for the road. Hygiene was not a priority, and I made do with whatever was available. During the day, I would get on the highway with my thumb out and head south. But the lonely, quiet nights were agonizing. I had incinerated all my identification back in Montana, so I couldn't check into a hotel. Instead, I lived like a hobo, curled up in a ball under the flat crawlspace of a bridge overpass. I rarely slept, partly because of the bright car lights and the noise from the passing cars, but mostly because of the scenes from the accident that flashed over and over in my mind.

I was numb, not thinking, and not engaged in anything I was doing. The world, once in color, had now become black and white.

After days of hitchhiking, my final ride was with Tyrone—a short, stocky African-American man with dark skin and a buzz haircut, who was heading to Dallas to find work in his faded green Pontiac Parisienne with no air conditioning. The temperature that day was typical for Texas—sunny and hot—and the warm air breeze from the open windows felt soothing on the back of my neck as we continued south-bound on the highway.

After driving for hours in the smoldering heat, we eventually pulled over into a campground off the highway for the night. Neither one of us had a tent, so we used his blankets on the ground and lay there talking until we fell asleep. My money was hidden between the clothes in my duffel bag, and since I always kept it within an arm's reach, I felt comfortable enough not to worry about getting robbed by my newly acquired friend.

When morning came, we freshened up in the camp restroom and drove to the nearest unemployment office in McKinney—a small town outside of Dallas suburbs—to apply for a job. But there would be no work for either of us that day. Instead, we got back in the car and headed south to downtown Dallas, a much bigger city with many more opportunities.

With the scorching sun overhead, we pulled over at a gas station in the afternoon to quench our thirst. I went inside to use the bathroom and buy a couple of Cokes, but when I came out a few minutes later, Tyrone's car was speeding off onto the highway service road with my blue duffel bag still in the back seat. Until then I had always kept an eye on the bag, but this time I left it in the car and learned a valuable $2,300 lesson.

Just a week before, the girl I loved and eloped with, drowned in front of me. I lost my family and friends because of it, and now the only possessions I had were just stolen—leaving me with only the clothes on my back, and a few dollars in my pocket. If you've ever felt alone, lonely, and without a place to call home, you would still not come close to what it was like for me at that moment.

Angry and frantic, I stood in the middle of the gas station parking lot, yelling at the car as it sped away. I couldn't chase the vehicle on foot, so I ran back inside the store and asked the attendant to call the police. But when the cops showed up a few minutes later, they were reluctant to help. On their tiny pad, they took down the description of the car and the guy responsible for the theft but appeared hesitant to track him down. When asked what I was supposed to do now, they shrugged their shoulders and replied, "We don't know," before driving away.

It was demoralizing to watch the police car leave, but I was now on my own—in the middle of nowhere—and the only thing that made sense was to continue south to Dallas. Hitching a ride, I made it to downtown and found myself once again without direction. It was late in the afternoon and I was finally here, but I had no idea how I would eat or where I would sleep.

I stood on the corner of South Griffin and Commerce Streets, next to the McDonalds facing the Federal Immigration Building, for a couple of hours before I noticed a car circling the block several times. There were lots of cars passing the busy intersection, but this one stood out. It was an old Volkswagen Beetle with dark blue, faded paint and blotches of colors seeping through. The muffler was worn out and loud, and as the car accelerated to change gears, it often backfired. Eventually, it pulled up along the sidewalk where I stood. The man inside leaned over, rolled down the passenger window, and asked if I needed a ride. As I was hungry and had no other place to go at that moment, I reluctantly accepted his offer and got in.

If the outside of the car looked atrocious, the interior was even worse. The side panels were torn, the overhead ceiling material was ripped and drooping, there was no carpet other than a rubber mat, and a couple of straw seat covers hid the coil springs that protruded through the ripped upholstery.

With his soft voice, the laid-back, large man occasionally asked a question, but for the most part kept both eyes on the road ahead and his hands on the upper part of the steering wheel during the entire drive. He was around six foot five, 270 pounds, probably in his early fifties, and had a large potbelly that almost touched the bottom of the steering wheel. His disheveled silver, thinning hair was brushed over the front to cover his receding hairline, and his arched upper back posture reminded me of the hunchback of Notre Dame. He looked more like a gentle giant than a predator, and I felt no cause for alarm.

With a Kool menthol cigarette loosely hanging from his lips, and ashes occasionally dropping onto his belly, he asked what I was doing in Dallas. When I told him I had just arrived, got robbed, and had no plans, he offered to take me to his favorite dive café in East Dallas.

As I was new to Texas, he recommended I try the popular Chicken Fried Steak special with mashed potatoes and gravy to start. We continued our conversation about food, the Texas weather, and ourselves. The large, quirky man sitting opposite me came across as very shy and timid. After introducing himself as Lee—a veteran of the Vietnam War—he asked for my name in kind. Caught off guard, but realizing I needed an alias, I quickly improvised with the most common name I could think of—John. I said I was from Pittsburg, Pennsylvania—a town I had passed through on my way to Texas. Curious why I decided to leave, I confessed that there was nothing left for me back home after the girl whom I loved had died in an airplane accident[v].

Leaving the restaurant, he sounded sympathetic to my current circumstances and offered to let me stay at his house until I got back on my feet. Although I didn't know much about Lee at that point, I did feel comfortable enough to accept his offer, especially since my options were somewhat limited.

His home was a tiny three-bedroom shack located in an East Dallas Mexican neighborhood (see Document: 7503 @ www.ambrozuk.com). The front porch had two large columns supporting the roof, and a rotting wooden floor in the entryway. Most of the grass in the front yard was nonexistent, and overgrown bushes, tall grass, and weeds were scattered along the fence. In the back, there was a wooden garage full of magazines and rusting equipment, largely because of the collapsed roof and the large hole that let the rain in. The small backyard was covered

---

v. Over the years, I kept my answers about my past to a minimum, and other than adding the bad economy up north as an excuse, in general, I changed only what was needed to remain anonymous.

in waist-high weeds that he cut only once a year—in the spring—because of tickets issued by the City of Dallas.

But if the house on the outside looked abhorrent, the inside was even more repulsive. All the rooms were filled with three-foot-high piles of magazines among the plethora of boxes full of collector items he treasured. The only walkway was from the front door of the living room into the bedroom on the right, where he spent most of his leisure time reclining on the bed, flipping through the latest magazines and watching TV.

There was a small bathroom and a kitchen in the back, along with two medium-size bedrooms in the middle—one of which eventually became my safe haven. It was the complete opposite of what I had grown up in, with my mother constantly cleaning the house, but all I cared about at that moment was a roof over my head and a bed to sleep on.

Beginning that first night, Lee and I established a regimental daily routine we followed for weeks to come: Up at 6:00 a.m., we headed off to work—Lee to his records-and-maps job with the City of Dallas, and me to look for work at employment agencies like Manpower. He dropped me off in the morning and picked me up after work; we came home to clean up before heading out to dinner; and after we returned to his house, we spent the rest of our evening watching TV and talking— me reclining in the large, brown leather chair, and he in his weight-sunken bed with his head propped up by several pillows.

He was a quiet, lonely man who appreciated my company, just as I didn't mind the free meals that accompanied our conversations while I continued to struggle with my bereavement. To make room for my sleeping quarters, I cleared out a small area in one of the spare bedrooms. Lying on the metal spring bed that stood six inches off the floor, I spent the next several months crying myself to sleep every night, unable to focus on anything but the insufferable accident. Random thoughts of Dianne suddenly appearing to lie down next to me each night continued relentlessly, and all I wanted was to have her back. I missed her so much, and although I kept my emotions private—rarely letting Lee see the tears—he knew I was emotionally distressed by something that lay heavily on my heart.

In the weeks that followed, I would occasionally find a five-to-ten-dollar per hour labor-intensive job for half a day, but most of my time was spent either looking for employment or waiting downtown for Lee after work. The few dollars I made wasn't much, but I was frugal and saved every penny, determined to eventually buy the survival equipment needed to continue with my mission to South America.

Two weeks had passed since the accident, and even though my mind was still in a rage, I desperately needed to find out why Dianne could not get her seatbelt off. I had called Tom twice before, on August 30 and 31, to tell him where the plane was located, but when the Flathead County authorities were unable to find the aircraft, I called again a week after I got to Dallas. On the morning of September 7, Tom's father answered the phone. When the operator asked if he would accept a collect call from "Louis Gomez[vi]," I hung up. In my current mental state I wasn't ready to speak to anyone but Tom, so I waited another couple of days before trying again. On September 9, 1982 at 8:36 p.m. I called from a public telephone booth at a nearby Schepp's Food Store in East Dallas (see Document: 7500 @ www.ambrozuk.com). This time Tom answered, and we spoke for over an hour[vii].

During our conversation, Tom used his best psychology to persuade me to return home, but there was too much anger, frustration, disappointment, confusion, and feelings of desolation bottled up inside me

---

vi. I had spent several days in East Dallas, a predominantly Mexican neighborhood, so it seemed only natural to use a random local name to preserve my anonymity. That carless fib would eventually become one of my aliases (see Document: 4104 @ www.ambrozuk.com), after my extradition.

vii. Aware I had previously called Tom at his residence, the RCMP placed a phone tap on his home telephone, allowing the Canadian authorities to record our entire conversation. The recording was later transcribed into a seventy-five-page document. Despite some omitted Polish dialogue, the transcript clearly underscored my emotional state at the time (see Document: 3111 @ www.ambrozuk.com).

to be responsive. I incoherently rambled on about the many thoughts still running through my head—from how we were heading to live in the jungle to hunt leopards, to how Dianne was the love of my life, and when she died, half of me had died with her. I was still in shock, and could not be reasoned with. In a sense, I was literally out of my mind. All I could fathom was the completion of our plan, convinced it would eventually bring me peace. Despite our intense talk, no questions would be answered that day. Tom and I ended with the understanding that I would need to call again to get the answers I was still searching for.

Working the odd manual labor jobs for the next several weeks, it soon became obvious I needed a legitimate ID and a social security number if I was to pursue any meaningful employment in the interim. Even my quest to South America—requiring crossing the U.S.-Mexico border—would be difficult if not impossible without proper documentation.

I consulted Lee about the dilemma, and he came up with a viable solution. To apply for a valid driver's license, one only had to show proof of birth. To get a birth certificate, Lee suggested I borrow the identity of a deceased male from a cemetery grave. Walking through hundreds of gravestones at the nearest cemetery the next day, I stumbled across "Michael Lee Smith," who had passed away in his infancy. Not only would his financial, medical, and dental history records be unblemished, but our birth dates were also less than a year apart. To boot, the name was as generic as one could hope for. Once I had a legitimate name and birth date, the process was simple: I filled out a form at the Dallas records building to get his birth certificate as one of his relatives, and minutes later the clerk came back with a certified copy, no questions asked.

With the birth certificate in hand, I applied for a social security number, and within a week, went to a Dallas Motor Vehicle branch with one of Lee's friends to pass the exams and get my Texas driver's license. Backed by my three pieces of ID, I was now a bona fide U.S. citizen who could begin a new life as Michael Lee Smith.

Lee also suggested I keep my background story plausible, and use Hartland, Maine as my home town. Although my place of birth on the certificate was Dallas, he knew of someone from that small city who, along with his many relatives with the same surname, were still current residents there. Trivial at the time, this little detail came in handy over the years, as I would often refer to Hartland as the place where I grew up and went to high school.

Armed with my new identification, in late September I got my first official job at the State Fair of Texas as a security guard. I sat in the blistering sun for twelve hours a day on the edge of a parking lot guarding cars, but it was steady work and it paid $5.50 an hour. It was a mundane job, but I was content to return to my post each morning to make the few dollars I needed for the trip.

With cash in my pocket, I went to the Army-Navy Surplus store—blocks away from Lee's house—weekly. There I purchased survival gear for my upcoming trip: a backpack, a canteen, a machete, a collapsible army shovel, a hunting knife with a compass ball on the end, a sleeping bag, a small one-man tent, and some camouflage clothes, including a jacket and a pair of army-issue boots.

Working odd jobs here and there, to others I appeared whole, but on the inside I felt alienated from the world. During the day, I spent time downtown around people who provided a distraction, but in the evenings, when things got quiet, my mind filled with sadness and despair. If only for a few minutes at a time, I looked for diversions that provided temporary relief from the constant battle in my head. Whether working out with dumbbells at Lee's house, or venturing out to an all-day outdoor concert, the preoccupation was always temporary, and I would be back to the familiar, painful melancholy every night.

As agreed, I called Tom again on November 16, 1982 at around 10:00 p.m. (see Document: 3112 @ www.ambrozuk.com). After several hang-ups throughout the day because his parents answered, we eventually connected and talked for almost an hour.

Tom said the Flathead County authorities had since recovered the plane. When it was lifted out of the water, Dianne was still strapped inside her seat, with the seatbelt around her waist twisted inside-out, and the shoulder harness disconnected. There was no sign of injury, other than a broken clavicle (collarbone), most likely caused by the shoulder harness during the aircraft's fierce impact with the water.

I had been looking for answers for months, mulling over and over in my head why a nineteen-year-old girl drowned because of a seatbelt, but nothing would be resolved that night. Why couldn't she unbuckle the seatbelt? Why was the waist-belt buckle flipped inside out? How could she unclasp the shoulder harness but not the belt around her waist? Was it a bad seatbelt design? Were there manufacturers who made better, single-release mechanisms? Why didn't the aircraft have more dependable equipment installed? Why didn't the owner of the plane, David Oliver, upgrade to a single-release seatbelt easier to operate, and one that might have saved Dianne's life? I had struggled with these questions on a daily basis, but now that Tom had filled in many of the details, I was more confused than ever. A seatbelt, whose sole purpose was to save lives, was responsible for Dianne's drowning, and no one could explain why. When we hung up[viii], I was just as baffled about the reasons behind the tragic fatality as when it happened.

That year I spent Christmas and New Year's with Lee, but during the first week in January of 1983, I told him I was going on a "walk-about"—heading to Houston to do some traveling and sightseeing. He seemed disappointed I was leaving but graciously offered me a place to stay if I ever decided to come back.

With all my clothes and camping equipment neatly packed into my orange backpack, I went to the bus station and bought a one-way ticket to San Antonio. From there, I took a second bus to the small town of

---

viii. When Tom and I ended the call that night, it would be the last time I spoke to anyone in Canada for the next twenty-four years. On December 16, 1982, I sent my parents a Christmas card to let them know I was doing fine and not to worry (see Document: 1500 @ www.ambrozuk.com), but after that, I permanently severed ties with my best friend and family as I prepared for my departure to South America.

Nuevo Laredo, and with my new ID crossed the border, heading for Mexico City via Monterrey. The bus ride was hot and muggy, with periodic stops along the way for bathroom breaks, or to purchase a refreshing beverage, before I arrived in the capital of Mexico.

I had a large map of the country and a detailed map of Mexico City, but I had no idea where I was going next. During the previous months, I was confident that when I got to Mexico, the adventure that Dianne and I started would, once again, make sense. But now, standing alone in the middle of the downtown central plaza, watching and listening to the vendors and the hustlers working their deals, that feeling of direction was nonexistent.

Nonetheless, I was there, and I was determined to follow through. I looked on the map and arbitrarily picked the coastal town of Veracruz as my next destination. The tropical city located on the Gulf of Mexico was over 200 miles away, but at least it would bring me closer to the water. I didn't know what to expect, but the plan was to make my way to the beach, walk along the shoreline, and eventually reach some distant, secluded area to set up camp.

Unfortunately, when I finally got to the sandy gulf beach at dusk, I found civilization as far as the eye could see in all directions. Exhausted from travel, I checked into a shady hotel off the coast, and spent the night in a small, cabana-like room with only a ceiling fan to stir the hot air—tearfully reminiscing about Dianne.

The next morning, as I looked along the shoreline, there were resorts everywhere, and I was not going to find my tropical paradise no matter how far I walked along the beach. Discouraged, I packed my belongings and headed for the opposite coast, the Pacific Ocean, hoping it would be more accommodating.

Staying away from known tourist traps like Acapulco and Puerto Vallarta, I found a small town on the map near the coast where the Greyhound-type bus lines terminated. From there, I took a yellow school bus crowded with dozens of locals that brought me within a half hour's taxi ride to a small village near the ocean.

When the cab stopped, it was already dark, and I stood at a dead-end street that terminated at the beach. I could barely see in front of me, but I could hear the sound of waves gently washing onto the sand. With no map to guide me, I started walking along the shore, passing several isolated homes in the distance, before reaching an area that seemed remote enough to settle down for the night.

The sand was still warm from earlier in the day, so I lay down beneath a palm tree, cocooned in my sleeping bag. Without a single cloud in the sky, the moon shimmered over the water and the stars sparkled above as the cool breeze from the ocean gently blew over my body. Making my way from the Gulf of Mexico to the Pacific Ocean in one day was exhausting, and it felt good to rest on the shore without a soul in sight.

When I woke the next morning, the beach was as desolate as I remembered from the night before. There were a few scattered palm trees, and in the distance I could see the odd shack house, but for all intents and purposes, I was alone. The zigzagging shoreline made it difficult to see around the next curve, but I was sure if I continued, I would eventually find what I was looking for. Before venturing deeper into the unknown, I made my camp there for the next several days, acclimating myself to the surroundings.

This was not the jungle Dianne and I had seen in the movies, but at least I was roughing it. My plan was still to head deep into the forests of South America, but in the back of my mind I was already wavering, beginning to realize this was not the paradise we had imagined and left our homes for.

Having all day to do nothing, I tried putting my survival skills to the test. Rubbing wood together to start a fire proved pointless—just as it had at Little Bitterroot Lake. When I tried to climb the forty-foot-tall palm tree to get the green coconuts bunched at the top, I managed to get only a few feet off the ground before realizing it was much more difficult than seen on TV. Even my attempts at cracking open the browning coconuts lying underneath the trees were disappointing. Using my machete, I eventually split the outer shell, but the taste of the coconut water inside—along with the white flesh of the drupe—made me nauseas. Discouraged, it wasn't long before I realized that living off coconuts was not in my future.

With nothing to build a shelter, no tackle to fish with, no animals in sight to hunt, and my food supply running out, I slowly began to see things in a new perspective. Despite my will to continue, the reality was that this was never going to be the adventure Dianne and I had envisioned. If I searched long enough, I might find an amicable place to live and survive. But it would never be the same. Sitting on the beach alone and feeling abandoned, gazing at the water that was more green than paradise-blue, my mind slowly gave way to clarity.

Without Dianne, nothing seemed the same, and now I simply felt out of place. After staring into nothingness for days, mulling over the reality of spending a lifetime alone in the jungle without her, it was then that I had an epiphany moment: the day Dianne died was the day our life in paradise also ended.

All the plans we had shared, and all the adventures we had imagined meant nothing without her. As much as I refused to give up, I finally realized that spending the rest of my life in isolation because of a dream that no longer existed was futile.

With my food supply depleted, I packed my survival gear and began my journey back to Texas and civilization. Every night I still relived the painful night of the accident, but I no longer needed to fulfill our mission. The cloud of unrelenting commitment to our adventure that once hung over my head was gone—and I was free to return to society.

CHAPTER THIRTY-FOUR

The Retirement of a Birthday

April 11 – 13, 2007
Day 225 – 227

AFTER SPENDING NEARLY a quarter century as Michael Lee Smith, I still found my head turning every time I heard someone call out, "Michael!" Sorting out my legal issues had brought me back to the name I was born with, but retraining my mind to ignore "Michael," and respond only to "Jarek," was another matter. Along with the name, there was also my birthday to consider. For the past twenty-four years, I had celebrated on April 11, but that was to be no more. This year it would be on July 22—the birthday of "Jarek." With my family back in my life, things were looking up, but considering the circumstances, what I really needed was time and temporary immunity to adjust—at least until my mental metamorphosis was complete.

On Wednesday morning, Mr. Watson, Renata, and I conferenced to go over the details of his latest contract revisions. Before either of us could ask a question, the attorney jumped in to clarify his $100,000 fixed-fee retainer discount. His decision was based on multiple factors, including my current financial situation and his better understanding of the case. Unwilling to speculate about additional expenses in the upcoming months, the only dollar amount he was willing to commit to was that of the jury consultant, estimating the cost at around $50,000 if we went to trial.

Renata and I penned questions to ask, including:

- What were the ramifications associated with a mistrial?

- Why would a second trial cost an additional $25,000?

- What would the cost of appeals be if we lost the trial?

But we decided to forgo the inquiries due to time constraints and Mr. Watson's vagueness with his cost estimates.

Once Mr. Jent's senate session concluded in two weeks, he explained, they intended to fly down to Texas and speak face-to-face with the assistant U.S. district attorney regarding my federal charges. They were also looking into dismissing at least the theft and criminal mischief charges in the state case.

Although Mr. Watson was eager to begin, his work pended on the signing of our contract and, indirectly, on the understanding that unless $150,000 was deposited into his business account immediately, I would remain in limbo indefinitely in Flathead County. It took several days of deliberation with Carolyn and my family, but on Thursday I signed the attorney contract and sent it back to Mr. Watson. It was not an easy decision, considering I had to ask my parents for the loan, but everyone agreed we could no longer continue with Mr. Sherlock. My parents were still upset about his lying and covering-up the fact that, days before the hearing, he had known Judge Stadler would not go along with probation at my sentencing. Renata too had lost respect for the man after realizing he had coerced her into convincing me to plead *nolo contendere*.

Reflecting on what I had endured for the past eight months, I only hoped that Mr. Watson could deliver on the promises his website so boldly stated: "A quick resolution of the case with a favorable outcome for the defendant."

CHAPTER THIRTY-FIVE

The Surprise Visit, the Omnibus Hearing, and the Absurd Plea Offer

April 14 – May 3, 2007
Day 228 – 247

UNANNOUNCED, RENATA SHOWED UP with her three kids for a surprise visit on Saturday morning at the Flathead County Detention Center's front door. The day before, she picked up Daniel and Matthew after school and drove 1,100 kilometers in thirteen hours just to see me twice for forty-five minutes during weekend visitations. It sounded nuts thinking about it, but there she was with her three awesome kids, putting a smile on my face as everyone took turns on the phone. Everyone, except for my shy two-year-old niece, Angelina, who played peek-a-boo every time I looked at her and waved.

Between these excursion expenses and our phone bills, my family was spending an ungodly amount of money, but it all seemed justified and insignificant whenever I heard Renata's voice or saw her infectious smile.

But like a typical family, not everything was always grand—including that Sunday morning, just prior to my visit—when a major crisis erupted: they couldn't find Angelina's flip-flops in their hotel room and all hell broke loose. Apparently that little fashionista loves her shoes, and if she wasn't happy, no one was happy (see Document: 7308 @ www.ambrozuk.com).

The following Friday, during a brief conference call with Renata and my attorney, we learned that Mr. Watson was contemplating postponement of my trial date until October. He was planning to visit his son in Italy in May, and hence the change of itinerary. We were prepared for Ed Corrigan to reschedule the date again—after learning he was pestering Tom about the taped transcript intended to be used at the trial—but we didn't expect the same from my own attorney. I was not about to spend another five months in the detention center just because of Mr. Watson's pending vacation! As soon as Renata and I voiced our concerns, he quickly changed his mind and said he would be "100 percent" ready to proceed on May 21.

Unlike Mr. Sherlock, who had shunned the seventy-five page phone transcript, he embraced the idea of submitting it to court, saying it would help explain much of my behavior and state-of-mind at the time of the accident.

Before we disconnected, he also recommended I get familiar with a well-known book about grieving in preparation for the upcoming trial. *On Grief and Grieving* by Elisabeth Kübler-Ross defined the five stages of loss: denial, anger, bargaining, depression, and acceptance. It would help me understand not only what I went through after the loss of Dianne, but also explain my comments in the taped phone call with Tom two weeks later. He further suggested that a grief counselor would be helpful, especially from a medical point of view during court testimony, but for now the book would suffice.

On Tuesday morning, Mr. Watson showed up again with the private investigator to go over more case details—the specifics of the accident, my relationship with my parents and Dianne and, of course, the reasons why we eloped. I answered their questions to the best of my recollection based on the events of the past and the present. The verdict was still out on Watson and Jent and whether they were really worth the money, but it was encouraging to have an intelligent conversation without manipulation, coercion, or judgment. I never looked for sympathy or compassion from Mr. Sherlock or Dr. Trontel, but I appreciated Watson's diametric point of view to that of my previous counsel.

He was heading to Vancouver on Thursday to meet with Renata, my parents, and Tom to get their input and perspective. Mr. Jent, who was wrapping up his senate session that week, planned to devote his attention to my case by filing motions to dismiss one, if not all, of my state charges.

Watson said he was in regular contact with the prosecutor, who was apparently worried about the amount of time left before the trial began. Seizing the opportunity to strike a plea bargain, he offered to move the trial to October if Corrigan was willing to drop the two new charges, but as expected, the district attorney declined.

It was a game of legal hardball that would no doubt continue until the trial on May 21. But at least my attorney was engaged in direct negotiations with the prosecutor. It finally felt like progress after so many months of impediments, disappointments, and frustration.

After our meeting, I returned to my cell and got a letter from Sean Donnelly (see Document: 7060 @ www.ambrozuk.com), a fellow pilot student from 1982 who had been following my story in the news. The letter was not only a pleasant surprise, but also a well-timed coincidence. An hour ago, Mr. Watson and I had been discussing my adolescence, how I got my pilot's license, and the elopement details, and here was a letter from the one person who could verify how it all began. Sean could confirm how the instructor, David Firth, had inadvertently planted in our heads the idea of safely landing the fixed-gear aircraft on water.

The timing couldn't have been better or more advantageous, especially if he was willing to speak to my attorney during his trip to Vancouver, or, appear as my witness at the trial.

But as much as things seemed to be moving in the right direction with Watson and Jent, I was still being haunted by the *curse of Sherlock*. I had specifically asked Mr. Sherlock to include me when he attended the omnibus hearing—as it was my right. But on

Wednesday he showed up with a copy of the completed four-page *Action Taken at Omnibus Hearing* document from the meeting, which he attended with the prosecutor and Judge Stadler earlier in the day (see Document: 3235 @ www.ambrozuk.com). The omnibus hearing determined the admissibility of evidence, including testimony and evidence that would be used during the trial. Being new to the whole court process, I was curious about the details. Once again, he ignored my multiple requests and did it his own way.

During our talk about continuing with the state case, Mr. Sherlock seemed bitter as he explained he was not a public defender and wouldn't work for free. Mr. Watson had mentioned he was looking for another $25,000 to stay on as the local Kalispell counsel, thereby making it easier to file paperwork, motions, and make local court appearances, if need be. He eventually accepted the per-hour offer, but perhaps that was the source of his discontent.

Although no longer my lead attorney, he told me he was still being approached by Ed Corrigan in the halls, and that just the other day the prosecutor tried again with a new offer. "He is now willing to send you to the Department of Corrections (or DOC) where he thinks you will then be picked up by the federal government. It's not prison, but you will still be locked up."

The DOC was where half the FCDC detainees ended up for rehabilitation, but to me the offer felt more like adding salt to injury, rather than justice. I was not sure if that was the prosecutor's idea of a joke, or if he seriously thought I would consider his proposition; in any case, I simply grinned and replied, "No deal!"

My new attorneys appeared to be formidable opponents for Corrigan, and I felt much more confident to let the prosecutor prove my negligent homicide charge at a trial. After all, it was not we who had to show I was innocent but rather he who had to convince the jury beyond a reasonable doubt that I was guilty—and that would be difficult once all the facts and evidence were revealed, showing Dianne as a willing participant in our elopement. Corrigan knew that, and that was why he filed the new theft and criminal mischief charges, partly to strengthen his case for the trial, and partly because it would affect my sentencing when I got to federal court if I was convicted on multiple state felonies.

But as ridiculous as the new charges were—given that the plane was rented and not stolen, and the aircraft rental company, Dianne, and I were all from Canada—I looked forward to his challenge of proving it all in court.

On Friday, Mr. Watson met with Tom in Canada, and they had an interesting conversation about the twenty-four-year old phone transcript (see Document: 3111 @ www.ambrozuk.com), Tom's subpoena, and possible deposition.

If Tom decided not to attend the hearing, it could take at least six months for the prosecutor to either subpoena Tom—or to get his deposition—according to the Canadian-U.S. jurisdiction law on the official Canadian government website. That would again delay the trial date, which Judge Stadler already had frowned upon. And even if the prosecutor managed to get Tom to testify, there were strict rules he would have to follow to lay the foundation for presenting his evidence. Corrigan would not only have to produce the transcriptionist and the translator of the Polish-to-English dialogue, but also the individuals responsible for the actual tape recording. After twenty-four years, it was highly unlikely any of these people were still around, let alone located in the three weeks before the trial.

For arguments sake, let's assume Corrigan was somehow successful in using the transcript as evidence. During his meeting with Mr. Watson, Tom brought up several valid points that could render the taped phone call irrelevant.

First, there was the matter of our English vocabulary. Twenty-four years ago, Tom had been in Canada for less than four years and I for just eight. We were both considered newly landed immigrants with limited English vocabulary and thick accents, making it difficult for the transcriptionist and translator to accurately interpret the dialogue.

Second, part of our conversation was in Polish, calling for an interpreter to accurately decipher and translate the *context* into English. As the transcript stood, much of that was either completely omitted or only a vague interpretation was recorded.

But most importantly, our conversation overlapped, was jumbled, and at times must have seemed like indecipherable gibberish, making it difficult for accurate interpretation when followed chronologically on paper.

A case in point was something Mr. Babcock brought to Mr. Sherlock's attention during their phone conversation, and months later Kyle Hinzman brought it up again during my PSI report interview. Page fifty of the transcript contained a muddled line in the middle of the page that read:

No, she wa-, well I mean, she was calling, auh a cop, she was calling out.

After careful review, both Mr. Babcock and the probation officer interpreted this to be Dianne calling out for a police officer while the plane was sinking; in fact, it was nothing of the kind.

To better understand my dialogue at that moment, one only needs to glance at the bottom of the page where I said:

. . . oh shit, the cop's turning, I hope he's not gonna come here...

where I was referring to a police car that had just arrived at the scene of a car accident half a block away from the telephone booth where I had made the call from in East Dallas. Although the "cop" had nothing to do with Dianne or the accident itself, it was enough for her father and the probation officer to misinterpret the words of someone still in shock—twisting them out of context.

In addition to the transcript ambiguity, there were several other defense strategies to explore. One of the options involved Ed Corrigan and unethical conduct. According to Mr. Watson, there was a law in Montana that prohibited a prosecutor from provoking the victim's friends and relatives—in this case the Babcock family—by aggravating their emotions at my sentencing. It was a long shot, but if my attorneys could prove it, the judge could throw the entire case out.

A more realistic scenario, though, was to win the case at a trial using witnesses like Tom, Sean, and a seasoned pilot. The private investigator had found a pilot with over thirty years of flight experience who once had witnessed a fixed-wheel aircraft landing on water. His testimony would confirm that Dianne and I were prepared—at least as much as one could be when landing on water—and despite the aircraft flipping over, we properly executed the landing maneuver as instructed by David Firth.

Many options were still possible before the trial began, but no matter the outcome, we finally seemed to be moving in the right direction—and that motivated me to fight even more against the baseless state charges.

CHAPTER THIRTY-SIX

Will Work for Food

May 4 – 6, 2007
Day 248 – 250

ON FRIDAY AFTERNOON, I had an unexpected meeting with
Commander Cathy Frame, head of the Flathead County Detention
Center, who took me into a conference room for a private talk. Out of
the blue, she offered me an Inmate Worker job. Detention centers often used non-violent detainees for grunt labor like cleaning the halls,
laundry service, and kitchen help, but those positions were not for
people with high classifications—especially not ones with a negligent
homicide charge pending.

Although I appreciated her initiative, my decision was simple—
keeping busy doing odd jobs at the FCDC would only distract me
from my preparations for the upcoming trial, and therefore I politely
declined.

She didn't seem very surprised, but quickly followed up with another offer. "Then, do you see any reason why you should not be in
general population?" she asked. When I first arrived in Kalispell, I
was automatically housed in the detention center's "Max" section to
minimize the gossip in the general population area because of the case
publicity. Why the change now? Why would the commander offer me
such privileges after eight months and with only a couple of weeks
left before my trial? Were they just being nice or was there something
sinister behind their kindness?

Although most detainees would jump at the chance to move into a larger area with more social interaction, I was perfectly content to spend my remaining days in Flathead County in quiet isolation—just as I had done from the beginning. The commander seemed disappointed with my decision, but accepted my reasoning before walking me back to my cell.

When I got back to my "house," as some detainees affectionately called their cells, the guards had already brought my lunch, complete with a fresh cup of coffee. Except for the coffee—which I didn't drink and used to barter with others for milk or juice—this was as good as could be expected from a small-town detention center.

I made fifty dollars per day just for occupying space. But the services and amenities that each of us received on a weekly basis, at no cost—via the well-trained professional staff, mind you—were impeccable. Here's what I mean:

Monday: *Clothing change (fresh shirt, pants and socks); custom fit XL pants and shirt for me.*

Tuesday: *Razor, towel change.*

Wednesday: *Sweatshirt change; freshly washed and tailored to body size; XL for me.*

Thursday: *Clothing change again (as before, freshly washed shirt, pants, and socks), razor.*

Friday: *Towel and linen change (fresh smelling mattress sheet "sock," albeit with a disappointing thread count of 20; perhaps a bit rough, but doable).*

Saturday: *New razor.*

Sunday: *Coffee cup exchange; nail clippers upon request.*

And, of course, there were three meals a day, REC with optional sports equipment, access to reading material on alternating book carts, and regular disinfecting supplies to clean your sink, toilet, and sweep and/or mop the floor as necessary.

There wasn't much to complain about, and if it weren't for my family, whom I was desperately looking forward to spending time with, I might never want to leave.

When I called Renata to share the exciting news about my employ-ment opportunity with the FCDC, she mentioned two emails she had received: one from Mr. Watson, and the other from the jury consultant he recommended for the upcoming trial.

Mr. Watson's email was actually a forward from Mr. Sherlock, who had reversed himself on what he told me about Judge Stadler—and my three felonies—during my arraignment. A month ago, he be-lieved the judge was only trying to intimidate me when he said my three felonies would run consecutively. After some research, he dis-covered that they would run concurrently. But now the email to Mr. Watson stated otherwise, suggesting they would run consecutively again, and I could face up to thirty years in prison, rather than ten. I was no attorney, but weren't there some Montana law books that would quickly resolve this once and for all? This was not some ob-scure ambiguity based on unverifiable evidence—this was about three presumed felonies that occurred at the same time. It was a simple question that called for a simple answer. Surely someone out there could get to the bottom of it because Mr. Sherlock's research into the matter meant diddlysquat.

The second email was from Stacy M. Schreiber, M.A., a jury con-sultant from Texas, who was going to screen the possible jury mem-bers in preparation for the trial. Her services were for approximately three days—two days prior to the trial for research and preparations with Mr. Watson, and the third day to hand-pick the jury for a favor-able trial outcome.

Her grand-total estimate for three days of work was $26,300, with an expectation that there would be more charges to follow. At $400 an hour, I was obviously in the wrong line of work; but with that sticker price she had better walk on water.

CHAPTER THIRTY-SEVEN

[CTRL] [ALT] [DELETE]—Life Reboot

1983 – 1984

LEAVING BEHIND THE jungle fantasy adventure life Dianne and I had dreamed of, I crossed the U.S.-Mexico border and made my way back to Dallas. I had been gone for just a couple of weeks, but Lee welcomed me back with open arms. We had already established a solid rapport— beneficially mutual to both—so it was reassuring to know I had a place to stay when I returned.

Although I was well aware of Lee's sexual preference the first day I got to Dallas, I kept my distance, and over time our relationship matured into mutual respect and friendship. Lee would often joke over dinner how he was "putting lead in my pencil for some girl," but in the end, it was just a verbal game from a lonely man who was more interested in companionship than sexual favors.

During the first few months after my return, we spent a lot of time together at dinners and watching TV—as I needed and wanted nothing and cared about no one. I was still torn inside, withdrawn from the world, and in constant turmoil about the accident and Dianne's passing. My outlook on life was dismal, but I appreciated Lee's dry sense of humor, and his company, as I continued to struggle with my emotions and sanity each and every night.

Keeping my end of the bargain, I slowly began to organize and clean the rooms in his home, one at a time. I used the attic as storage for the hundreds of magazines he refused to part with that were scattered around the house. Before long, we not only had a path to the kitchen and access to the refrigerator, stove, and microwave, but I also had my own bedroom in the back that wasn't used as a walkway to the kitchen. Buried under boxes and magazines, I found a twin-size wooden frame with a mattress that became my new bed for many years to come. Slowly making progress, the cleanup took months to complete, but it was therapeutic and a welcome distraction from my nightly nightmares.

In need of money, I turned to the *Dallas Morning News* Classified Ads to find a full-time job that would give me a steady paycheck. In the middle of the classified pages, in bold letters, I found a listing that promised thousands of dollars per month to motivated individuals who were driven, hardworking, self-starters, and had a car. As the job provided onsite training and required no experience, I jumped on the opportunity and borrowed an old clunker from one of Lee's friends to begin my new career in sales.

The company was located on the other side of Dallas, and occupied a suite in a business park that seemed legitimate enough from the outside. Along with a dozen other new recruits, I sat in a barren conference room for close to two hours listening to a lengthy motivational speech by the branch manager, who explained how each of us could make lots of money. When his sales pitch was over, the majority of the room cleared, with only a few of us willing to try our luck at selling music to pre-qualified customers.

The product was a yearly subscription, with monthly installments, to buy cassette tapes from artists that spanned various decades and genres. From Benny Goodman to Johnny Cash to the Beatles—the library had it all. Although it was a high-pressure sales job that I was not fond of, I was determined to give it a legitimate chance. I spent the first few days memorizing scripts and listening to experienced sales reps explain how

I should respond to questions so that at the end of my pitch, even the most skeptical customers would beg to sign on the dotted line.

All the potential clients were already pre-screened by a separate cold-call team, so all we had to do was "close the deal," as everyone kept reminding us throughout the day. When the manager first explained it, it sounded like a dream job with unlimited possibilities. But when I pitched my presentation to live customers, I felt like a snake-oil salesman, and things never went smoothly.

The company closed its doors within a month, and although I did make a few hundred dollars, more valuable were the lessons: 1) sales was not my forte, and 2) people are willing to do just about anything to make money.

Putting that eye-opening experience behind me, I returned to the unemployment line, and applied for a job at a small manufacturing plant in Mesquite, Texas. The electronics company designed and built their own brand of home-stereo speakers, and I was hired to work on the assembly line—bringing their creations to life. Once the speaker panels were cut and routed, several workers, including myself, would assemble the entire speaker—starting with gluing the wooden box, to covering the speaker grills with cloth—before boxing it for shipment. It was not a glorious job by any means, but it did pay $5.00 an hour, forty hours per week, and I was finally making steady money.

The job wasn't difficult but it was monotonous, and having a good sense of humor throughout the day made it bearable, especially with people like Wes around—the class clown of the bunch. He was in his late twenties, always ready to tell a joke or a funny story, and before long, we became good friends. On weekends, we would hang out in his white Ford pickup truck, driving around town drinking cold "roadies" and listening to music in the hot Texas sun. I had spent many months in isolation, sober, and refusing to use drugs to ease the pain as I dealt with my emotional state, but after so much sadness, it felt good to have someone like Wes around to cheer me up with his happy-go-lucky free spirit.

Three months after I started at the factory, Wes quit and moved on to construction. He walked onto a construction site on Monday, got a job as a roofer, and showed up in the parking lot of the electronics factory that Friday afternoon—telling everyone that the construction foremen were paying $7.00 an hour to anyone who could swing a hammer. This was the time before the Texas oil collapse, and everyone was moving south to find work and join in the prosperity. There was such a high demand for apartments and condominiums in the Dallas area that the construction companies couldn't find enough carpenters to complete the residential complexes popping up everywhere.

I was always mechanically inclined, and already had some construction experience under my belt—as a teenager I had helped my father finish out a rental basement unit. The downside of working construction in Texas during the summer was the hot weather, but getting a $2.00 an hour raise more than compensated for the inconvenience and discomfort. I was young and preferred hot weather over cold, so first thing Monday morning I went to the construction site, got hired, and returned to the factory that afternoon to give my notice.

When I arrived at the construction site, there were two superintendents running the entire project—and they were overwhelmed. There were plenty of workers, but what they lacked were self-sufficient leaders who could manage small crews, thereby giving the superintendents more time to oversee the entire construction project. I didn't have any leadership or management skills at the time, but what I did have was patience and work ethics. I always had been a perfectionist, and when the superintendents saw my work, they offered me a crew lead position two weeks into my new career.

Their concept was simple: at the end of the week, we would walk through the site, along with other crew leads, and bid on unfinished housing units. There were different crews doing different construction—from framing to roofing to finishing the outside—so there was plenty of work to go around for everyone.

My three-man crew and I were in charge of finishing the apartment-building cornice, including siding, rafters, and framing in the windows and doors. Most of the buildings were eight-unit apartments, which a crew of four could complete in less than a week. The work was project-based—at an average pay of $4,500 per building—and I was responsible for my crew's payroll. That meant after the job was complete and everyone was paid, any leftover money was mine to keep. Doing the math, that usually left me with close to $2,000 per week as my take-home pay. The previous month I was making $5.00 an hour. The week before I moved up to $7.00 just for swinging a hammer, and within a week I was making $2,000 per week—running a construction crew with carpenters who ranged in age from their mid-twenties to over forty-five. Not a bad gig for a young, inexperienced teenager straight out of high school.

Despite the money, I took my new-found success in stride, knowing I had no intention of spending the rest of my life working in the construction business. Imagine nailing a piece of siding, two stories high in 100 degrees Fahrenheit temperatures. You're standing on a ladder and holding the siding in one hand, the hammer in the other, and nails in your mouth for convenience. The sweat pours down your face as you're trying to balance yourself on the ladder while aligning the board with a guy sixteen feet away holding the other end. That's fun work when you're nineteen, but not a future I looked to embrace.

Education and a good career were always at the top of my family's priority list. Now more than ever, that gave me strength and purpose, despite my continued battle with grief every night. With the money I was making, I could afford to go to college and get a degree even my parents would be proud of.

Although I could afford a new car, I opted to buy an old 1968 MGB convertible with a locked-up engine for $500. I turned it into a project car that would keep me busy for months in the backyard of Lee's house. Working construction during the day, and being a hardcore grease monkey in the evenings and on weekends, I tore down the engine, guided only by a Chilton automotive book as my reference. Rebuilding the engine block, I meticulously cleaned and repainted every part. The rebuild cost less than $220, but my thirst for designing and customizing the car eventually turned it into an evolving project I would continue for the next several years. From a hidden ten-speaker stereo system with ten-inch woofers and multiple amplifiers, to the custom wheel flares and polished aluminum INKI mags, the British car became my labor of love and, for the most part, kept me focused and out of trouble.

I was working and making good money, yet something inside was eating away at me. Much time had passed since the accident, but my emotions were still running rampant. One minute I would yearn for Dianne, and the next my stomach was in turmoil, as I felt contempt for everyone who let us down. I was angry at the authorities for their thoughtless handling of the case, at David Firth for telling us it was safe to land the aircraft on water, at David Oliver for not having better seatbelts in the plane, and even at God for taking Dianne away from me. Every night I walked through the details of the accident— trying to find another angle I missed so that it would once and for all put my mind at ease—but my unrest only spilled over from one night to the next, resulting in nothing but frustration and animosity.

It was during those resentful and bitter nights that I would sometimes walk the dark streets and neighborhoods of East Dallas to vent. I never had been a violent person, but I was slowly losing the battle to control my inner anger. With my project car occupying half my time, and my mind not right, I turned to what seemed like the only logical action to get back at the authorities—I decided to steal a car battery.

I tried this for the first time on November 6, 1983, and again on February 16, 1984, three months later. The first time I got arrested I was cocky and full of cynicism, but the second time, I calmly accepted my fate and the consequences of my actions. I had money in the bank and $300 in my pocket when I was taken into custody, but all that didn't matter because I was frustrated at the world.

Appearing in court with my attorney, my attitude was still rebellious, even toward the judge, who recognized my mental state. He ordered that I spend a day at the Texas State Penitentiary as part of my probation terms so I could experience what was waiting for me if I continued on the present path. The prison visit was nothing more than a tour with a sampling of the daily meals, but it was enough for me to finally come to my senses and begin a less calamitous and more productive life.

While all this was going on, I was still working on the construction site, running a crew, and saving money for school. I had no complaints working during the hot summer and fall days, but when winter arrived that year, with the cold northern wind blanketing the state, I saw an opportunity to change gears and throw in the white construction towel.

It was one of those freezing Monday mornings in early December when two other crewmen and myself were determined to tough it out and hang sheetrock. I had on two pairs of socks, two pairs of pants, a T-shirt, two long-sleeve shirts, a winter jacket, gloves, and a balaclava to shield my face from the wind. With all that protection from the cold, we could barely hold a hammer in our hands because of the crisp, dry arctic air that pierced through the gloves. The three of us spent over half an hour trying to nail one piece of sheetrock, at which point we all decided to hang up our hammers until the weather mellowed.

Evaluating my options after the forecast called for freezing temperatures for the rest of the month, I made the decision to quit construction and begin preparing for my return to school. Although I had a free place to stay and my only expenses would be tuition, books, and gas, I still needed a part-time job to carry me over for the next several years as I worked toward a degree.

Watching TV one day, I was drawn in by an infomercial that promised a job where you could make thousands of dollars, meet great people, and work in a fun environment—so I signed up. After a week of memorizing drink recipes, practicing the art of pouring, and learning all about the etiquette of a bartender, I graduated from the American Bartenders School as a Qualified Mixologist, complete with a diploma that no one in the real world seemed to care about. Optimistic about the possibilities, I started looking for part-time bartender work I could do on the side when I returned to school.

I began filling out applications at exclusive hotel restaurants in the Dallas Metroplex area, but without experience, the managers wouldn't give me the time of day. Instead, I downgraded my search to more realistic expectations—Bennigan's and TGI Fridays included. Keeping busy working banquet events, it took several weeks before I finally got a steady part-time job at Steak and Ale, from February to October of 1984.

My initial shifts were on Monday and Tuesday nights, the slowest days of the week. I wasn't going to get rich on $2.01 an hour plus tips, but the staff was fun to work with, so I stuck it out. Slowly working my way up the corporate ladder, I eventually advanced to the primetime slots on Friday and Saturday nights, when the pace was fast and the rewards at the end of the six-hour shifts were quite respectable.

Working at a restaurant, constantly surrounded by people, also went a long way toward my mental recovery. I was interacting with young, energetic wait staff, who were not only a pleasure to work with, but also fun to hang with after hours. In the evenings after our shifts, many of us would meet at a pub around the corner to socialize over a few beers. There was always laughter throughout our conversations as everyone told jokes or shared their highlights of the day. After spending so long isolated from the world, I began to appreciate their kindness and friendship.

My tenure at Steak and Ale also marked my return to the dating scene. It was over two years since I had lost Dianne, and with the healing of time and the camaraderie of my coworkers, I finally felt comfortable enough to begin dating again. In late September, a hostess named PJ joined the wait staff and would often accompany us after hours for a social evening out. She was a few years older, but always smiling and fun, and before long we were involved in a casual relationship that would last through the better part of my college years.

CHAPTER THIRTY-EIGHT

The Second Theft Felony Arraignment—A Clever Word Game

May 7 – 10, 2007
Day 251 – 254

ON MONDAY AFTERNOON, Mr. Sherlock showed up with a revised THEFT CHARGE ACKNOWLEDGEMENT OF RIGHTS for me to sign. I had already appeared at the arraignment for the theft charge over a month ago, but after Mr. Jent filed a MOTION TO DISMISS (see Document: 3237 @ www.ambrozuk.com), Ed Corrigan amended his original definition from March 26, 2007 (see Document: 3225 @ www.ambrozuk.com) and had re-filed it.

The two documents were practically identical, with only minor changes to the definition. Instead of stating that I had:

> . . . *purposely or knowingly, and with the purpose of depriving the owner of the property, exerted unauthorized control over the airplane belonging to Sol-Air Aviation . . .*

the amended theft charge now read:

> . . . *purposely or knowingly exerted unauthorized control over property of the owner, more specifically, a Cessna 150 airplane belonging to Sol-Air Aviation, and used, concealed, or abandoned that property knowing such use, concealment or abandonment will probably deprive the owner of that property . . .*

(see Document: 3248 @ www.ambrozuk.com).

Although technically the aircraft was rented—not stolen—from Sol-Air Aviation, more important was that Ed Corrigan found it necessary to re-file the court document (see Document: 3240 @ www.ambrozuk.com) after he had already refuted Mr. Jent's motion to dismiss the theft charge. In his court filing, my attorney argued that not only did the Canadian Crown Counsel not file any such charges, but that Ted Lympus, the Flathead County District Attorney in 1982, already had dismissed that same theft charge after it had been filed twenty-four years earlier (see Document: 3001 @ www.ambrozuk.com).

It was "déjà vu all over again" when I appeared in court on Tuesday with Mr. Sherlock at my side to plead *not guilty* to the same theft charge that I had already pleaded *not guilty* to a month earlier.

As before, Judge Stadler asked if I wanted to waive the reading of the acknowledgement of rights before accepting my plea.

But before he could adjourn the hearing, Corrigan stood up to explain some procedural changes to the case. There were three things on his list and without waiting for the judge to acknowledge began his rundown. First was the taped conversation between Tom and me from twenty-four years ago. He had found the original tape recording, but it would take time to get it prepared. "It's on one of those massive reels, and they're going to have to first find the equipment to play it on," he explained, showing the approximate size of the tape reels with his hands wide apart. He appeared almost giddy, gloating over his discovery with a smirk on his face.

His second item regarded my ground-school instructor whom he confirmed would not be attending the trial but would give a sworn deposition. The deposition was to take place during the upcoming week, and he wanted to notify the court so my attorneys could also make the necessary arrangements to be present.

His last item pertained to Greg Feith, Air Safety Investigator from Golden, Colorado, who created the National Transportation Safety Board (NTSB) accident report in 1982 (see Document: 3127 @ www.ambrozuk.com). The prosecutor had subpoenaed the NTSB investigator but wanted to clarify he would have to leave no later than 1:00 p.m. on Tuesday, and therefore asked Judge Stadler to change the trial start time from 9:00 a.m. to 8:30 a.m. so there would be enough time for him to testify and be cross-examined.

Throughout the prosecutor's announcements, Judge Stadler sat quietly and listened. But when Corrigan turned to him for a response, the reply was brisk. "The trial will proceed as scheduled!" The judge made it clear that this was his house and there would be no compromise—whether on the trial start time or the alternative option from the litigious prosecutor—to allow the NTSB investigator to come back and re-testify on Friday, the day after my four-day trial ended.

When the arraignment concluded, I fell in line with the other six detainees who had also finished their court appearances. We had begun our slow walk toward the exit door when something odd happened. Corrigan, sitting at his table with his head buried in paperwork, glanced up at me and for some reason decided to play the stare-down game. As I walked toward him, our eyes met, and what was to be a brief glance turned into a persistent ten second stare-off where neither of us was willing to concede the symbolic confrontation.

There were no words exchanged and both of our facial expressions remained neutral. But when I walked past the table and he slowly swiveled in his chair to maintain eye contact, the message was delivered.

For the last eight months I had been coerced and manipulated by both my attorney and him, but there was a limit to what I was willing to put up with when it came to games or his smug attitude of a few minutes before. I had put up with his courtroom theatrics long enough, and now that I had two new fresh-blood attorneys in my corner, we were going to war.

CHAPTER THIRTY-NINE

The Questionable NTSB Factual Report

May 11 – 16, 2007
Day 255 – 260

ON FRIDAY, I finally got the missing Flathead County Sheriff's Office Investigative Report— Follow-Up #6—that included the 1982 National Transportation Safety Board (NTSB) Factual Report (see Document: 3127 @ www.ambrozuk.com) created by Greg Feith. The 108-page report contained mostly instructions, much redundancy, and many inapplicable pages not used during the investigation. Its main purpose was to quantify and explain the events of the aircraft crash— specifically its attitude, aerial configuration, and the reasons behind the incident.

Unfortunately, what Mr. Feith produced using the cookie-cutter template, was a report full of holes and inaccurate critical assumptions, when compared to the stack of evidence that was gathering dust in my cell—and which he had had access to when creating his NTSB report.

For example, on page 7 of his report he wrote:

The pilot egressed from the plane, but the passenger was incapacitated after impact and drowned when the plane sank.

This was completely inaccurate based on my taped telephone conversation with Tom (see Document: 3111 @ www.ambrozuk.com) and Dianne's autopsy report (see Document: 3113 @ www.ambrozuk.

com). He assumed Dianne was incapacitated but didn't take into account her broken collarbone caused by the shoulder harness seatbelt on impact with the water. If she had been incapacitated, how had her shoulder harness become disconnected?

On page 11, he assumed the Kalispell authorities had begun their investigation on the same day Dianne and I attempted our landing on Little Bitterroot lake, stating:

> On August 22, 1982, the Flathead County Sheriff's office became involved in the search efforts . . .

which, again, was false. No one knew about the accident or the whereabouts of the aircraft until my first call to Tom on August 30, 1982, eight days later.

He also made several misleading statements on the same page that assumed the aircraft had landed right side up by reporting:

> The cameras showed the aircraft resting on the Lake bottom in a right wing low, nose low attitude.

In fact, the opposite was true. That may have been the aircraft's final attitude 240 feet below the surface, but that was not how it started out when the plane hit the water.

What he neglected to take into account was the recovery photographs that clearly showed the damage to the aircraft's tail fin (see Document: 7167 @ www.ambrozuk.com). If the aircraft had never flipped over, how exactly did the tail fin sustain damage?

But the biggest misstatement was his presumption about the seatbelts. On the same page, he stated:

> The investigation revealed that the passenger was restrained by a lap seatbelt. Shoulder harnesses were available to the pilot and passenger and used only by the pilot.

Again, that was inconsistent with the evidence. Why was the plastic front windshield completely broken outwards (see Document: 7156 @ www.ambrozuk.com) if Dianne and I were both strapped in with seatbelts? Why would she have a fractured clavicle (collarbone) if not wearing the shoulder harness?

These inaccurate interpretations—by the one man who was considered to be an expert NTSB air safety investigator—were responsible for misleading the Flathead County authorities, including Mr. Sherlock and Sheriff Dupont, into quoting false conclusions for the next twenty-four years.

Mr. Feith was no Sherlock Holmes, but it was his responsibility to correctly interpret the facts and evidence so that others could rely on his expertise. Three days before, Ed Corrigan seemed adamant about how important the NTSB investigator's testimony was. But from what I had read, his witness—along with the sketchy evidence report—would not be as solid as he believed in front of the jury.

Corrigan was clever, in a deceitful kind of way, but he was no dummy. He knew his chances at a trial were weak at best, so in a surprising twist after almost nine months, he reconsidered his position on the negligent homicide charge. After flying to Vancouver on Saturday to meet with Tom and the Babcock family, he conceded that the negligent homicide case was not as strong as he once believed. According to Mr. Watson, Tom spent four hours with the prosecutor, elaborating on my relationship with Dianne and what our lives were like in the early Eighties. That eventually opened the door for more negotiations. The prosecutor was not going to drop the charge entirely, but he was willing to replace it with another, considering the circumstances.

By the time I met with Mr. Jent on Tuesday, he had already researched and found an alternative to the negligent homicide felony: criminal endangerment. It was the first time I had met Mr. Jent face to face. Unlike Mr. Watson, he seemed less methodical and more driven by legal practicality when we discussed swapping the charges to satisfy the district attorney's crusade for a conviction. The catch was that in 1982 there was no criminal endangerment in the 1981 Montana Law books; therefore, it would take some court maneuvering to make the new charge work.

The understanding was that after they swapped the charges and dropped the weak theft felony, I would plead guilty to criminal endangerment and criminal mischief.

And that I could live with.

It was becoming clear that my new, expensive attorneys would not be successful in dismissing all the charges—barring a trial—and this was the best I could hope for. Looking at the definitions of negligent homicide and criminal endangerment seemed like splitting hairs, so my only requirement was that, despite being erroneous, there would be no negligent homicide attached to my name:

> **Negligent Homicide:** *a person commits the offense of negligent homicide if the person negligently causes the death of another human being.*

> **Criminal Endangerment:** *a person who knowingly engages in conduct that creates a substantial risk of death or serious injury to another commits the offense of criminal endangerment.*

The whole Flathead County court system seemed like a ridiculous circus, with Ed Corrigan trying desperately to pin something on me that would stick. He knew perfectly well that the nature of our elopement—and especially Dianne's voluntary participation—would not constitute negligent homicide, as Dianne's sister so boldly stated in her victim impact statement (see Document: 7073 @ www.ambrozuk.com).

But despite what was shaping up to be a disappointing ending to my state case, periodically there were times that put a smile on my face. One such moment happened on Wednesday when the private investigator mentioned Corrigan's intent to subpoena Genea as a possible witness for the trial (see Document: 3255 @ www.ambrozuk.com), as if to make me cringe at the possibility of her testimony. That was the prosecutor's idea of strengthening his case, hoping there was some dirt she would disclose about me during our past relationship. But to me this was karma, and he would be gravely disappointed.

Since my arrest, Genea had appeared anonymously on *America's Most Wanted*, where she unflatteringly tried to embellish our relationship and the reasons she eventually turned me into the authorities (see Document: 6802 @ www.ambrozuk.com). After spending thousands of dollars on her—including funding her all-expense paid vacation to Japan with me—I looked forward to hearing her version of our relationship under oath.

Genea was probably not the best choice of witnesses, but that was all the prosecutor had: an enraged Babcock family looking for retribution, an NTSB investigator with a report full of holes, and Genea, my ex-girlfriend who had nothing to do with the 1982 accident and could only strengthen my character and my case if we ever went to trial.

CHAPTER FORTY

The Second Change of Plea

May 17 – 20, 2007
Day 261 – 264

ON THURSDAY MORNING, two hours before my second change of plea court hearing, my attorneys showed up to go over, and for me to sign, the ACKNOWLEDGEMENT OF RIGHTS AND PRETRIAL AGREEMENT (See Document: 3265 @ www.ambrozuk.com). The document format was similar to that of my first sentencing, except for a few critical changes.

Paragraph 14 in the acknowledgement of rights contained a clause allowing me to withdraw my plea and go to trial if the judge rejected the agreement during sentencing. As that was exactly what happened the last time, I wasn't too confident these words meant anything in Flathead County, so I took its sincerity at face value—a definite maybe.

The pretrial agreement section contained clauses about agreeing to plead guilty to criminal endangerment—despite the statute not being enacted until 1987—along with criminal mischief, in exchange for the theft and negligent homicide charges being dropped. In both cases I would receive a ten-year suspended sentence that would run concurrently.

In the restitution section, the document stipulated I would not only be responsible for expenses incurred by Flathead County while pursuing my prosecution, and the Babcock family's burial costs, but also for the damage to the Cessna C150 aircraft. And that made no sense to me.

In 1982, that payment had been the responsibility of David Oliver's insurance company, which was no longer in business. Pointing this out to Mr. Watson, who had already discussed this with the prosecutor, he assured me the total restitution amount, including the aircraft repairs, would not exceed $15,000.

But the most interesting—and perhaps unprecedented—clause in the pretrial agreement was that I had to plead guilty to the passport charge in federal court. If I didn't, the Flathead County Attorney reserved the right to re-file my negligent homicide charge again.

Why would Ed Corrigan care what I did in federal court?

Mr. Watson explained that if I pleaded guilty, and had two state charges counted toward my federal criminal history points, I was sure to get penitentiary time rather than probation. Instead of going to trial and possibly losing the state case entirely, this was the prosecutor's way of passing that burden onto the federal judge he thought would do his bidding.

After the attorneys and I went through the entire document from cover to cover, I was disappointed with the final result but realistic enough to appreciate what prolonging the state case actually meant.

If I decided to fight and go to trial, could I beat all three charges and win? Perhaps. But that strategy would have been taxing on everyone, especially my family. As much as I wanted to challenge Ed Corrigan and prove him wrong, I was not willing to do it only as a matter of principle. Besides, given the unpredictability of people in a small town like Kalispell, where Sheriff Dupont and Ed Corrigan had been slowly brainwashing the media with their personal opinions rather than facts, it was anybody's guess how the jurors would react if we went to trial.

I was disappointed with my new high-profile attorneys because they were unable to dismiss all my charges as I was once led to believe, but my options were limited. Reluctantly, I signed the second plea agreement and appeared in court later that afternoon to make it official.

Unlike my first change of plea, this time the benches were practically empty when I walked into the courtroom, with only a few reporters and photographers sitting behind the prosecutor's table.

The hearing was administered by Judge Kitty Curtis, Judge Stadler's longtime girlfriend, who arrived shortly after I took my seat between my two attorneys.

Following a brief court introduction, I was motioned to the podium to go over the latest plea document line by line before pleading guilty to both counts of criminal endangerment and criminal mischief. During my meeting with the attorneys earlier, Mr. Watson handed me a handwritten statement (see Document: 3266 @ www.ambrozuk.com) that I was expected to read:

> *On August 22, 1982, I attempted to land an airplane on Little Bitterroot Lake, in Flathead County, Montana. My conduct created a substantial risk of serious bodily injury to another. I so acted with knowledge of that risk. I am guilty of criminal endangerment. I know that the airplane would be damaged or destroyed. I am guilty of criminal mischief. I waive any objection to jurisdictional issues. I acknowledge damage to the airplane in excess of $150.00.*

The words were few, but the paragraph covered everything the prosecutor wanted, including waiving any objections to jurisdictional issues related to the aircraft damage. Although that point seemed irrelevant then, it would play a significant role during the next few days.

When I finished, Judge Curtis turned to my attorneys to begin their staged questions about my relationship with Dianne, the reasons why we eloped, and a few details about the night of August 22, 1982. Its purpose was to disclose any relevant facts so that the prosecutor couldn't dissect or twist the case details out of context.

That theory sounded good on paper but in practice had never worked with Mr. Sherlock, and it would not work that day. Beginning his cross-examination, the prosecutor wasted no time jumping in with a slew of questions that demanded my input. Was Dianne aware of the elopement plan? Was it dark when we were attempting to land the aircraft on water? Did I turn off the beacon lights and the engine on our glide approach?

His questions came from all directions, and although I could answer most with a single word or sentence, there were a few that required a more detailed explanation. "It was like hitting a brick wall," I explained when asked what happened during our landing when the aircraft touched the water surface.

"We followed the outlined procedure from my ground-school instructor explicitly," I said, responding to the prosecutor's probe into the cause behind the aircraft flipping over.

It took me a while to figure out what Ed Corrigan was really after, but eventually it came out—it was about accepting responsibility. In Corrigan's eyes, if I just said it out loud in court, somehow the catastrophic accident would automatically be turned into a crime, and his conduct for the past nine months would be justified. Mr. Watson's objection to the question was overruled by Judge Curtis before the prosecutor reiterated the question.

No matter how I felt—or what I believed—this was neither the time nor the place to butt heads about responsibility, giving Corrigan an excuse to pull out of my plea agreement a second time. After a short pause to gather my thoughts, I simply said, "I loved Dianne very much and I feel responsible."

After nine long months of legal games, the Flathead County's self-proclaimed harbinger of justice could finally claim victory in front of the media. He appeared overjoyed, pausing for a moment as he relished his triumph before asking if I had any questions for him.

"No," I calmly replied.

"Are you sure?" he asked again, as if to bait me.

Did I have any questions for the egregious prosecutor who ignored the evidence showing Dianne as a voluntary participant in our elopement; a prosecutor who pulled out of our first plea agreement because I wouldn't take two years in prison; who currently was being investigated by the ACLU after being repeatedly reprimanded by the Montana

Supreme Court for similar unethical conduct; who added two more frivolous charges to my case just because he was on a self-righteous mission looking for scapegoat?

Sure I did.

But I wasn't about to give him an excuse to manipulate the case further. I politely, but sternly, confirmed "Absolutely!" and returned to my seat. Judge Curtis concluded the hearing by reminding everyone that Judge Stadler would be presiding over my sentencing that Monday.

Although the plea bargain negotiation, its signing, and the hearing all happened within hours after being prolonged for close to nine months, the courtroom drama was not over and would continue for the next several days.

It began with missing paperwork that Mr. Sherlock had dropped off on Friday. Among the stack of papers were several motions from Mr. Watson and Mr. Jent, including the DEFENDANT'S TRIAL BRIEF (see Document: 3244 @ www.ambrozuk.com) requiring that the state prove the accused conduct was the cause-in-fact of the victim's death. Another was the DEFENDANT'S NOTICE OF EXPERT WITNESS EXPANDED TESTIMONY (see Document: 3260 @ www.ambrozuk. com) that called for Dr. Stratford to testify as to the basic brain function of an eighteen-year-old, not only as a reference to responsibility, but also to explain how the short-term effects of trauma would impact the comments made to Tom Pawlowski shortly after the plane crash[ix].

But the most interesting was a copy of the Flathead County Sheriff's Office Investigative Report – Follow-Up #7. It contained a voluntary statement from David Oliver, the former owner of Sol-Air Aviation, and David Firth, my 1982 private pilot's license ground-school instructor (see Document: 3129 @ www.ambrozuk.com). The seventeen-page document included the aircraft's multiple change-of-ownership regis-

---

ix. If we went to trial, Dr. Stratford's testimony on the basic brain function of an eighteen-year-old would be based strictly on clinical data. He would attest to how a teenage brain worked, thereby allowing my attorneys to draw comparisons to what happened with me not only on the night of the accident, but in the weeks that followed during which I still appeared to be in shock.

tration certificates, and a ten-page, double-spaced voluntary statement from both men that was as colorful as it was long. It was designed not only to discredit me and my character, but also to reap potential financial gain they were seeking.

In its contents, David Firth implied I was responsible for ending the ground-school instructor's twenty-year career of *disseminating information to students.* David Oliver said that *the loss of the aircraft was the straw that broke the camel's back* and further blamed the unfavorable media publicity surrounding the aircraft's seatbelt equipment as the cause of his company's demise.

The entire document read like a big CYA (cover your ass) excuse, deflecting responsibility for their conduct, as they redirected away from the critical questions that still remained unanswered: Why did David Firth carelessly tell the class it would be safe to land a fixed-landing gear aircraft on water when even the flight-training manual stated otherwise (see Document: 1401 @ www.ambrozuk.com)? Why weren't lifejackets included as standard equipment on the aircraft? Why wasn't there a built-in transponder on board that could quickly pinpoint the aircraft's location in case of an accident? And why weren't the seatbelts upgraded to a single-release mechanism like most aircraft, thereby allowing a simultaneous quick release of both the shoulder harness and the waist seatbelt? That small equipment investment by David Oliver could have prevented Dianne's drowning, as she was not able to remove both of the restraining belts in time.

But it wasn't surprising that none of those answers were contained in their interpretation of facts and events from twenty-four years earlier. This was about building on what Ed Corrigan was executing, and the name of the game for the two opportunists was money.

Although the narrative from the Follow-Up #5 report summarized the aircraft repair costs and Blue Book value in 1982 at $7,614 USD and $8,500 USD, respectively (see Document: 3124 @ www.ambrozuk.com), David Oliver was looking for much more.

Financially the aircraft was a write-off if it was to be repaired by a commercial enterprise, however we thought through sweat equity and our industry contacts it was salvageable,

he wrote, explaining his inflated cost numbers.

So how much more was he looking for in order to cover his financial losses? According to his estimates found at the bottom of the voluntary statement:

Aircraft	20,000.00
Search	5,000.00
Rebuild	20,000.00
Loss of Revenue CG-ICK	50,000.00
Loss of Business General	50,000.00

The grand total was $145,000, although he explained it as *a conservative reality of the time without benefit of receipts*, and summed it up at $150,000.

In 1982, the aircraft repairs were estimated at $7,614 by Jim Keller, a certified aircraft mechanic, yet David Oliver decided to fix it himself through sweat equity at a cost of $20,000 and no receipts. What kind of a reputable business owner spends $20,000 to repair a used $8,500 aircraft?

It wasn't my place to speculate why his aircraft rental company ultimately went belly-up, but rather than unfavorable publicity, perhaps it was his business strategy, combined with his lack of algebra skills—as demonstrated in his voluntary statement arithmetic—that were fundamentally responsible for his company's failure.

What mattered, though, were not their undocumented estimates or their absurd reasoning, but rather what the court would ultimately decide during my second sentencing scheduled for Monday.

CHAPTER FORTY-ONE

I Is a College Student

1985 – 1994

A COUPLE OF years had passed since I arrived in Dallas, and I was finally beginning to turn things around. I was still fighting my inner demons, but after I made my money in construction and secured a college-appropriate job as a bartender, I was ready to try my luck at college.

Twenty minutes away from Lee's house, due east on Highway 30, was Eastfield College where I would spend the next two years taking prerequisite courses for my university degree. After consulting with one of the counselors, I was told that although all the courses would eventually transfer to University of Texas at Arlington (UTA), I would first need a high school diploma or a Certificate of High School Equivalency in order to enroll at Eastfield.

I already had graduated from high school back in Vancouver, B.C., and possessed many of the requirements necessary to pass the equivalency tests. My reading, writing, and comprehension were up to par, and although I excelled in math and science, I was lacking in American history. Taking home study material from the class covering history, I crammed for a week and got my Certificate of High School Equivalency on January 25, 1985.

Using the certificate, I walked into the Dean's office and signed up for a full load of generic spring semester classes, following several evaluation tests to determine my college English, mathematics, and science levels. Up to that point, I had no idea what I wanted to do or what degree I wanted to pursue, but I was sure it would be in the area of science.

I always was interested in mechanical devices, whether tinkering with and fixing appliances, taking apart and putting back together toys or, most recently, rebuilding car engines. Engineering blood seemed to run in my veins, and it was the most obvious choice based on my high school interests. After looking over the curriculum, including the differences between various engineering programs, I decided on Aerospace Engineering. It seemed like a prestigious job perfectly aligned with my past interests and my curiosity about the world.

With my slow return to a productive life, it also seemed logical for Lee and me to put on a family façade. It was a lot easier to explain to coworkers, fellow college students, and friends in general, that I was living with a family member rather than a stranger. And that is how Lee became known as my "Uncle Lee." By then we had a comfortable friendship that occasionally translated into lengthy political discussions over dinner. But over time, I would see him less frequently because of school, and my social life that was beginning to flourish.

Spending time at school during the day, and working at nights and on weekends as a bartender, left me with very little free time. Whatever spare time I did have, I split between my car projects and my social life—namely PJ.

Eastfield College was not only close to Lee's house, but the tuition and the books were half the cost of UTA. The trade-off was that when I finally got to university, all I had left were demanding engineering classes that required substantially more homework and lab work. While at Eastfield, I was told by one of the school counselors that after I had completed all seventy-four hours of transferable prerequisites to UTA, I would only need two additional classes to get an extra two-year Associate in Arts and Science degree from their college. Taking Physical Education class and an Appreciation of Art class for six weeks during the summer seemed like a small sacrifice for a second diploma, so that's what I did.

I received my Eastfield College degree in December of 1986, and continued to take prerequisites during the upcoming spring semester and the two summer sessions, before transferring all my course hours to UTA that fall to begin the final leg of my schooling. By then, I had parted ways with my bartending career and, in its place, secured part-time work at the Aerospace Research Center on the UTA campus, which would last almost the entire duration of my university attendance.

The paid co-op job was more of a place to do homework than any physical work, but it did have interesting perks. On occasion, I got to work with the graduate students performing experiments using on-site facility equipment, including subsonic, supersonic, and hypersonic wind tunnels. Having access to the research facility also allowed me to do an experiment in the hypersonic wind tunnel as my graduation project during my final semester. Taking advice from one of the engineering professors, I used the tunnel to determine airflow—more specifically turbulence produced over an airfoil—at speeds in excess of Mach 5. It was an interesting experiment, using oil droplets laced with red dye, to depict the patterns and vortices that simulated the turbulent airflow over aircraft wings while in hypersonic flight.

During my last semester at UTA, PJ and I parted ways, and that was also when reality about my career as an Aerospace Engineer began to set in. It was in the middle of the semester when one of the local aircraft company engineers came to speak to the graduating class about the industry we were about to enter and what to expect when we got in the job market. The guest speaker was very clear about the limited nationwide jobs that called for the design of the overall aircraft, saying that most engineers did a lot of grunt work designing small parts and calculating things like the aircraft's center of gravity, among other mundane tasks.

To add to the depressing outlook, after the end of the Cold War, the government steadily cut the defense budget, thereby awarding fewer contracts to aerospace companies, which, in turn, would need fewer engineers. That downsizing would eventually have a cascading effect, with General Dynamics laying-off close to 4,500 people in the Fort Worth plant and forcing our graduating class to compete for jobs against engineers who had years of industry experience.

Those were problems shared by everyone, but I personally had a bigger obstacle standing in my way: getting a security clearance. The aerospace industry revolved largely around federal government funding to build military aircraft, and that meant a detailed background check was mandatory. Getting a social security number and a driver's license seemed like child's play compared to what I would be facing. I had no illusion that my alias would be discovered if anyone started to dig deeper into Michael Smith's past.

Worried about remaining anonymous, I went through the motions with the rest of my classmates, pretending to be interested in finding a great engineering job. In reality, I knew that I had to find an alternative career. Fortunately, while in school, I got to use computers and FORTRAN 77, the preferred language of engineers at the time, which exposed me to programming and the possibilities of a new career path.

Graduating without an aerospace engineering job in sight, I turned my attention back to the business world. The previous summer, I had worked for GTE Directories Human Resources department through a temporary agency, and that opened the door to join their internal requisition department.

Hired as a full-time staff agency contractor, the job wasn't all that exciting, but working with six women in an office environment was educational in more ways than one. Sometimes it felt as if I was a rooster in a hen house, but the atmosphere was always fun and entertaining. I continued there until my contract ended in January of 1991.

Still trying to find my calling, I invested in an IBM 8088 PC and began taking evening classes at Eastfield College as I worked odd jobs through temp agencies, all the while continuing to apply for full-time positions at various computer-related companies. After several networking, PC repair, and programming classes, I found myself slowly drifting toward software development, when in the spring of 1992, I got hired as a tech support analyst at Software Spectrum, a software volume reseller to large corporations.

Fifteen customer services representatives, two supervisors, and one call-center manager were responsible for providing technical assistance to employees of companies that purchased their software. Stacked like books in a library, there were over 400 software titles at our disposal, and we were encouraged to install and try them all if it would help answer the customer's questions or solve their problems. To me, this was like being a kid in a candy store—every application you could buy retail was free for the taking. After several years of engineering problem solving, my mind was thirsty for more challenges, and this became the perfect outlet for me to thrive in.

Initially, my job was limited to providing spreadsheet support on applications like Lotus 1-2-3, Microsoft Excel, and Quattro Pro, but eventually I migrated to database support. Starting with flat-file databases, in time the company and our department expanded into the client-server and relational database area, making me the most qualified to take on that challenge.

Despite voluntarily taking Assembly, Basic, and C language programming classes on weekends at the community college, it seemed only natural to add training on products like client-server applications and SQL servers. I could then be of help to developers and database administrators calling in with questions and problems.

In time, I convinced my manager to send me to a Microsoft SQL Server Introduction and System Administration class in December of 1992, and then a PowerBuilder Workshop class at IBM in July of 1993. Those two training courses provided me with a springboard to transition from technical support into the client-server development arena. I continued with my technical support role while ramping up my software development skills on the side.

At the time, PowerBuilder, a client-server GUI tool comparable to Visual Basic, was the new kid on the block, and it became my focus.

Looking to hone my development skills, I voluntarily began developing a CD Select parsing application to help our tech support department be more efficient. CD Select was a database list of thousands of programs that analysts queried to find software matching specific search criteria from the customer.

Often staying up as late as 4:00 a.m., I spent three months creating the application I called MicParse. Its purpose was straightforward: after a search was executed in CD Select, the short list could be saved and imported into MicParse, allowing the analyst to further parse and compress the lengthy product descriptions. When done, the condensed version could be printed, faxed, or emailed right from their computer, thereby cutting down on extra work and saving time.

When it was unveiled, everyone in the department loved it—everyone, except for our manager. Although I created the entire application after hours and donated it to the department at no cost, he seemed perturbed and went out of his way to downplay my efforts. It seemed like a strange response to a tool that would ultimately improve everyone's productivity, but he refused to acknowledge the application even during our weekly staff meeting.

What he didn't know, but perhaps suspected, was that I was beginning to contact consulting companies in search of client-server development opportunities. Feeling comfortable enough with my new programming skills and the development environment in general, I rewrote my resume. When I faxed a copy to several firms in the Dallas Metroplex area, eleven called me back the next day. Everyone seemed impressed with my skills and was eager to discuss potential positions they were trying to fill.

After numerous telephone conversations with consulting companies to find the best fit, I decided to go with DCI—an agency staffing developers for a project Arthur Andersen & Company was building for one of their clients. It seemed like a convoluted employment structure, but that was when IT consulting and PowerBuilder development were at their prime, and everyone wanted to get a piece of the pie. The same day that I accepted the Senior PowerBuilder developer job offer, I gave my two-week notice resignation to my manager's dismay.

Spending the next couple of weeks under his watchful eye, I anxiously awaited the start of my new consulting job while continuing to provide support in the call center and fine-tuning my MicParse application. I had every intention of leaving my creation for the analysts to use when I left, but after repeated warnings from the manager about installing the upgrades during work hours, I felt my efforts were not appreciated, and that is when I had a change of heart.

With a minor modification, I released a final version of MicParse that contained a hidden Trojan. The software operated normally for the next couple of months until April Fool's Day. From that day onwards, a pop-up window would display a photo of the *Terminator* and the caption "YOU'VE BEEN TERMINATED," each time the analyst tried to print, fax, or email from within the application. Out of professional courtesy, I even included my contact information if they wanted to buy a corporate license to remove the lockout.

Needless to say, this did not go over well with the manager. According to several analysts, he spent the better part of the day trying to circumvent my lockout but eventually gave up and deleted the application from everyone's PC in frustration. Existential crisis it was not— with no harm done—but that shenanigan did earn me a standing ovation during our monthly ex-employee get-together at the end of the month.

Working at Software Spectrum was a great experience. I not only learned while being paid but met many talented and amicable employees during my two-year tenure. One of these exceptional individuals was Nancy—a call-center supervisor at the time—who not only became my close friend, but also a future business partner. Having similar interests and compatible personalities, we stayed friends for years as we eventually blended business with leisure while working on our startup: AJACOM.

CHAPTER FORTY-TWO

The Second State Sentencing

May 21, 2007
Day 265

MONDAY, THE DAY of my second state sentencing, turned out to be a strange one, and again, left me somewhat perplexed about the Flathead County justice system.

Preparing for my hearing in the afternoon, I met with my two attorneys to go over the court procedures and what to expect next with my federal passport case. Our discussion eventually got around to the congratulatory pat-on-the-back speeches expected in the courtroom after the plea bargain execution was complete. That was when Mr. Watson suggested I commend Ed Corrigan for finally coming around and honoring the plea agreement.

At first I thought he was joking. Then I realized he was dead serious about thanking the man who, for the past nine months, had plotted, schemed, and looked for ways to keep me detained for as long as possible if he was not able to secure my incarceration, whether in a Montana penitentiary, or a federal prison. Given all that, I had a difficult time mustering up any gratitude for such a man and his "justice."

Instead of debating the issue, I simply suggested Mr. Watson do the honors before we moved on to discuss my federal case.

According to Mr. Jent, when my state case was over, I would be picked up by federal agents. After being transported to one of their holding facilities for processing, I would be moved from one location to the next for several weeks before returning to Texas to deal with my federal passport charge. It seemed convoluted and unpredictable, but that was the way the federal government operated.

"But there are perks," Mr. Watson explained. "The federal facilities are more like a college campus compared to the city and state detention centers."

Mr. Jent had also spoken with the assistant U.S. federal attorney, Shamoil Shipchandler, assigned to my case. He was told Shipchandler intended to file a writ that week—an order issued by a court requiring that something be done or giving authority to do a specified act—that would start my "federal clock" accruing detention time. It was too early to speculate how my passport charge would play out, but the quicker I was on the federal radar, the better it would look to the judge during my sentencing if there was any hope for probation.

When we concluded our meeting, I changed into my civilian clothes and a few minutes later walked into the courtroom full of participants and spectators. My family was there, as were my three attorneys, several guards and court reporters, three prosecutors, Judge Stadler, a number of curious onlookers, and the media. Everyone was there waiting for the grand finale—everyone, except for the Babcock family.

As I sat down behind the defendant's table with the continuous clicking of the digital cameras, I noticed Mr. Jent engaged in a discussion with Ed Corrigan about the details of my restitution. From their expressions, it wasn't going well. In our meeting that morning, I was reassured by Mr. Watson, once again, it would not exceed $15,000, but as I watched my attorney butt heads with the cantankerous prosecutor, I could see that the negotiation was still not over.

It was exactly one o'clock in the afternoon when Judge Stadler hit his gavel on the wooden block to call for order and begin the hearing. Unlike my first sentencing three months before, this time everything seemed much more civilized, including the presiding judge who, after a brief introduction, asked my attorneys if there was anything I wanted to say. Whatever the Flathead County justice system was, first and foremost it was always about presentation and emotional apology in front of the media and the public. That was where my short, handwritten speech prepared earlier by Mr. Watson, and later edited by me prior to the hearing, came into play.

Your Honor,

I'd like to say that twenty-four years ago Dianne and I fell in love and eloped. I now know that it was a foolish and irresponsible thing to do. I have regretted that day ever since as I have paid for it dearly over the years.

I would also like to say again how truly sorry I am to the Babcock family for their loss of Dianne. I loved her very much and I hope that one day they too will find peace.

The room was silent when I finished, including Judge Stadler, who appeared satisfied with my atonement.

He then turned to Corrigan for his closing remarks. But the discontented prosecutor was not yet ready to capitulate. This was his last chance to confront me about the night of August 22, 1982 in front of the listening audience. Peppering me with numerous questions, he would occasionally interrupt to clarify. "So wait, when the press reports that you swam away and let her drown, that is not true?" referring to the aircraft prematurely sinking after filling with water (see Document: 6710 @ www.ambrozuk.com). He wanted no ambiguity about our landing, my conduct and, most importantly, my rescue attempt of Dianne if he was to do an about-face.

Well aware of the court of public opinion, and after nine months of pushing the case as far as he could take it, he finally conceded during his closing remarks and recommendation. Like a scene out of a scripted Hollywood movie, he stood up and began a methodical justification behind his plea agreement. Contrary to what the Babcock family believed, he was now convinced Dianne was a voluntary participant in our elopement, and that was why he agreed to two ten-year suspended sentences. In a sense, he did a 180 to what he had been preaching to the public for the past nine months.

But even during his triumphant victory, there was no reason why he still couldn't take a few cheap shots at me before moving on. With the authority of a clinical psychologist, he reassured the court he believed I was no longer a danger to society and had rehabilitated myself.

Rehabilitated myself? No longer a danger to society?

I wasn't aware I was ever a danger to society, but apparently to Corrigan, it was necessary to point that out to the listening audience.

And if that still wasn't enough, there was also the federal passport charge stipulation that was now part of the plea bargain agreement we had signed. Explaining its purpose, he expected me to plead guilty and get an additional two years in the federal penitentiary; otherwise, he had the option to re-file the state negligent homicide charge. It was a cleverly devious, well-orchestrated strategy by a prosecutor who now seemed satisfied with his accomplishment as he turned the floor over to my attorneys and their closing remarks.

Mr. Watson began with a five-minute speech that praised the prosecutor, heralding him as instrumental in working out the plea agreement, before transitioning into a recap of the night of the accident, and what my life must have been like after the loss of Dianne. Despite his sketchy recollection of my past, the accident, and the painful years that followed, I did appreciate his noble attempt at empathy, prior to turning over control to Mr. Jent for his closing summary.

Following suit, Mr. Jent began with his version of accolades for the prosecutor, before respectfully noting—in not-so-poetic words—that not unlike the Babcock family, I was also grief-stricken during the last twenty-four years. I had paid dearly for our mistake, the sympathetic attorney pointed out before bringing up the restitution dispute being debated with the prosecutor earlier. Although their initial verbal agreement was not to exceed $15,000, the district attorney was pushing for a valuation in excess of $43,000, based primarily on the unverifiable aircraft repair estimates provided by David Oliver in his voluntary statement.

The deliberation went back and forth for several minutes, before Judge Stadler stepped in and called for a restitution hearing on May 31, 2007 to resolve the dispute.

When my attorneys pointed out there was no reason for me to remain in Flathead County until then, Ed Corrigan once again disagreed. There was no specific reason he offered for my continued detention, but he was adamant I be present at the hearing in ten days.

My federal clock was already ticking, accruing my federal detention time, so I couldn't have cared less where I resided for the next ten days. But I was curious about how Corrigan and Judge Stadler would justify the $43,000 restitution the prosecutor was calling for.

With the hearing finally coming to an end, Judge Stadler turned to Mr. Sherlock and, out of respect, asked if he had anything else to add. But he seemed indifferent when he looked up at the judge and muttered, "I said it all in my brief at the last sentencing."

With everyone given the opportunity to say their piece, Judge Stadler began his own closing remarks that now seemed more complimentary than condescending. Twice during his short dialogue, he commented on how impressed he was that I was able to recover from the tragedy of losing Dianne, and how eventually I persevered, returned to school, and ultimately prospered. But after denying my preliminary hearing, siding with the prosecutor for the last nine months, and even taking Corrigan's lead to back out of our first plea agreement three months ago, his praise sounded hypocritical rather than sincere. Three months earlier, the probation conditions could not be enforced in Canada, but today that was all water under the bridge. Like the prosecutor, he had since changed his mind and decided Dianne was a willing participant in our elopement, and therefore he was now willing to go along with the proposed recommendations.

"My judgment is ten years committed to the Department of Corrections, suspended for both charges with time served," he proclaimed (see Document: 3269 @ www.ambrozuk.com).

It was a long nine months in the Flathead County Detention Center, and although I would be moving on to my federal case—to my family's delight—there was still the matter of the restitution hearing, including my daily fifty-dollar-per-diem and the court fine.

Being accommodating and liberal with my hard-earned money, Mr. Watson offered to leave that decision solely at the discretion of the court. Hearing my attorney out, Judge Stadler diplomatically confirmed that although I would receive the fifty-dollar-per-day credit, the net difference would be calculated based on the recommended $10,000 fine.

It was a walkabout way of stating that the casino never loses. No matter what the outcome of my upcoming restitution hearing, there was going to be a $10,000 fine on top of everything else.

After dealing with the Flathead authorities for the past nine months, I wasn't surprised by his comments and rationalization, but there was still ten days before the hearing, and plenty of time for my attorneys to come up with some solid arguments to defend against the prosecutor's ridiculous $43,000 restitution claim.

Other than restitution, the case was over, but not as far as Ed Corrigan was concerned based on his statements to the media. Prior to my sentencing, he had been telling local reporters for weeks about my no longer being a danger to society and rehabilitating myself (see Document: 2217 @ www.ambrozuk.com). But that night, after the hearing, when I watched the news and heard his follow-up comments to reporters, I was flabbergasted.

Their [the Babcock family] belief, if true, means that essentially she was kidnapped and murdered. And that is a terrible burden for a family to deal with over the loss of a child and if I was dealing with a prosecutor who felt otherwise, I wouldn't be happy with him either (see Document: 6711 @ www.ambrozuk.com).

Kidnapped and Murdered?

Really?

They were strong words from the lead district attorney of Flathead County, who instead of relenting, once again doubled down in front of reporters. Being the lead prosecutor allowed Corrigan much leeway;

still, it was disconcerting that he not only thought it appropriate to continue denigrating me in front of the media, but also saw no wrong in using the Babcock family's loss to justify himself in maintaining his delusion of morality on TV.

CHAPTER FORTY-THREE

The Curious Math of Flathead County

May 22 – 30, 2007
Day 266 – 274

IT FELT GOOD to finally have the state case behind me, but there was still the matter of restitution. Out of all the things I went through in Flathead County, this should have been a no-brainer, yet Ed Corrigan was determined to put his own spin even on that.

I had no doubt I was not the only one who had faced his wrath over the years—as his unethical conduct reprimands by the Montana Supreme Court and his ongoing ACLU investigations attested—but if anything, he was consistent and relentless.

Unfortunately for me, the law not only allowed him the liberty of ungoverned jurisdiction and ridiculous claims, but he also knew I had money. I seriously doubted there would have been a restitution hearing if I were homeless.

Nonetheless, we had to deal with his $43,000 demand. On Wednesday, Renata and I conferenced with Mr. Jent, who had since taken the lead on the upcoming restitution hearing because Mr. Watson left for his vacation to visit his son in Italy.

Referring back to the pre-sentence investigation report figures, we calculated the grand total for the restitution to be $13,840.25, based on the following reimbursement items:

- *Plane repair cost of $7,614.00*
- *Cost of extradition at $1,440.99*

- Dianne's burial costs at $4,285.26

- Plane rental for search and rescue efforts at $500.00

But, according to Mr. Jent, Corrigan had tacked on several other charges to that total. He was not only increasing the aircraft repair costs by another $20,000—based on David Oliver's voluntary statement estimates—but also wanted reimbursement for my first sentencing hearing in March, pretrial expenses, and trial date expenses totaling another $9,735.51.

The trial date expenses no longer seemed relevant as there was no trial because of our plea agreement. No airline tickets were required for the Babcock family, David Oliver, Tom Pawlowski, Lawrence Bodnar, and Greg Feith.

But most curious was the charge for Greg Feith, the 1982 NTSB Air Safety Investigator, now retired. The prosecutor not only intended to reimburse his flight but also pay him a consultation fee of $3,734.50 for his time, which was not legal. According to Mr. Watson, a witness could not be compensated for things like time, wages, or lost business.

When we ended the call, Mr. Jent assured us that he would take care of our concerns. But after a week of repeated calls to his office, only on Wednesday did Renata find out the discouraging news. Mr. Jent had increased the total restitution amount to $21,557.26, intending to file his MEMORANDUM REGARDING RESTITUTION the next day, in court (see Document: 3272 @ www.ambrozuk.com).

This was obviously well above the $15,000 maximum we were assured of on several occasions by Mr. Watson, but I was willing to look past the difference if it meant I would finally be done with Flathead County for good.

My state case may have been over, but there was still the matter of the probation conditions paperwork to review, initial, and sign. On Thursday, Keely Doss, Adult Probation and Parole Officer, showed up to go over the details. She was covering for Kyle Hinzman, who, after submitting his grossly distorted PSI report and testifying at my first sentencing had conveniently gone on vacation.

The two-page, twenty-two-item list (see Document: 3270 @ www. ambrozuk.com), in general mirrored the conditions recited by Judge Stadler at my sentencing. We reviewed, and I initialized, each item as instructed, but despite their intent, none would be enforceable in Canada—making this nothing more than an exercise in pointless diplomacy.

And just like every good old American establishment governed by the Second Amendment and the right to bear arms, Keely was also adamant I sign their FIREARMS REGULATIONS (see Document: 3271 @ www.ambrozuk.com). As I neither cared about nor ever owned a gun, this was strictly for their benefit, and I was more than happy to oblige.

The Civil War, American cowboys, the Wild West, and even hunting I could understand, but the modern American gun culture, recurrent school shootings, and their questionable obsession with guns I never did, and still don't get. Perhaps that's why I will always make a better Canadian than I ever did an American.

CHAPTER FORTY-FOUR

You Want $20,000 for a $7,000 Aircraft? I Can Help You with That!

May 31, 2007
Day 275

THURSDAY WAS MY restitution hearing, and things didn't go as well as I would have hoped, starting with my attorney, Mr. Jent. Renata did her best as a liaison, but we never got a chance to meet before the hearing to go over the obvious and relevant discrepancies between the evidence and what the district attorney was seeking. Forty-three thousand dollars was not a small chunk of change, and despite my repeated requests, I walked into the courtroom at two o'clock in the afternoon without a face-to-face meeting with the attorney solely responsible for defending me against the prosecutor's outrageous valuations.

Mr. Sherlock was already seated when I approached the defendant's table. He handed me several motions for my records that were filed by my attorneys and the prosecutor prior to the trial, with some dating as far back as May 3, 2007 (see List: 9000 @ www.ambrozuk.com).

Unlike my previous hearings, there were only a few onlookers in the audience when Judge Stadler called for order and began his customary introductory speech. Explaining the hearing's purpose, he turned to both parties and asked if they were ready to begin.

As if on cue, Ed Corrigan interjected and expressed his concern that my attorney didn't have a chance to talk to David Oliver, the 1982 co-owner of Sol-Air Aviation, about the repair costs. He was quick to suggest the hearing be postponed until further notice. Even at the eleventh hour he seemed determined to delay my departure from Flathead County. But by now everyone knew his game, including Mr. Jent, who simply addressed the court and said we were ready to proceed.

Forced to continue, the prosecutor began to list the restitution amounts individually along with his reasoning behind the proposed valuations. No one argued about the reimbursement for Dianne's burial costs, my extradition cost, the plane rental bill for search and rescue in 1982, Corrigan's pretrial expenditures, or even the Babcock family's questionable March sentencing hearing expenses. But when it came to the NTSB Air Safety Investigator's fees and David Oliver's absurd Cessna C150 repair costs, Mr. Jent finally objected.

Greg Feith's $3,734.50 reimbursement, the prosecutor explained, was largely based on the Air Safety Investigator's fee to generate a report in preparation for the trial. But there was no such report he could produce in court other than the NTSB Factual Report from 1982. When asked about any other receipts, including the questionable airline tickets, accommodations, and transportation for various individuals, Corrigan had none—not a single receipt or single shred of proof that anything was ever purchased. All we had was his word.

The more comical absurdity came when he tried to justify the $20,000 aircraft repairs from David Oliver. Already prepared, with a speaker phone that rested on Judge Stadler's bench, the prosecutor called the Sol-Air Aviation co-owner, who was sworn in and testified as if he were present in court. When nudged by Corrigan, the older-sounding man on the other end of the line explained that although the aircraft would have been considered a write-off by any reputable commercial enterprise, because he didn't carry any hull insurance, he decided it was salvageable through what he called sweat equity and his industry contacts.

Everyone listened patiently to his explanations about the expensive repair he undertook, but everything he said was old news—echoing his voluntary statement submitted to court a few weeks earlier (see Document: 3129 @ www.ambrozuk.com).

In 1982, Skip Faulkner, a mechanic from Red Eagle Aviation in Columbia Falls, Montana estimated the cost of the repairs to certify the aircraft as airworthy would be $7,614.00. Mike Strand, the owner of Strand Aviation, determined that in 1982 the aircraft Blue Book value was $8,500.00 (see Document: 3124 @ www.ambrozuk.com). But now those figures seemed irrelevant to both David Oliver and Ed Corrigan. The prosecutor seemed determined to make his witness's arguments stick by trying to misdirect the attention from the dubious $20,000, pointing out that Mr. Oliver was not asking for lost revenue but only the repair costs of the aircraft.

Even Judge Stadler was baffled by this logic. "Why would you spend $20,000 to fix a plane that was worth less than $7,000?" he asked, echoing the sentiments of everyone in the courtroom.

But there would be no plausible explanation given. Using a vague rebuttal, Mr. Oliver could only reiterate what he had stated before—that he didn't realize the cost until they got into the repairs.

No one questioned why he didn't have hull insurance, or whether the aircraft carried any insurance at all. Was there aircraft liability insurance? Or even passenger liability insurance against bodily injury/death? No one was curious if he or the Babcock family received any money from the insurance company. And no one seemed to care that the $20,000 Mr. Oliver allegedly spent on repairs was based on nothing more than his word—without a single receipt to prove that the out-of-business Sol-Air Aviation co-owner was actually telling the truth.

When you take your car to an automotive shop for repairs, you don't just take the mechanic's word for the completed work, and at the very least expect to see an invoice. Now imagine the cost of the repairs is three times the amount that the mechanic quoted you originally. Wouldn't you want to hear a valid explanation for his marked-up

278 • JAREK AMBROZUK

repairs and, more importantly, demand to see an itemized list of the parts and labor involved, before you would ever consider settling the bill? Even in Small Claims Court, the judge insists on proof of purchase receipts for products or services rendered. But apparently in Flathead County, Montana, that criteria is optional and only a gentleman's word on the telephone is required.

It was painful to watch my attorneys listen to these baseless arguments and not insist that Mr. Oliver provide at least some sort of proof to back up his word. Mr. Sherlock sat quietly next to me throughout the entire discussion, and like a "potted plant," as Mr. Watson once remarked, seemed indifferent to what the opportunistic ex-business owner and the prosecutor were trying to pull off.

Standing next to the judge's bench, Mr. Jent appeared ready to jump into action at any moment, but he too seemed disoriented when it came to questions for the witness who was spewing out his outrageous repair cost estimates.

With very little resistance from my attorneys, and giving everyone ample time for their cross-examination, Judge Stadler then concluded the question-and-answer period and asked both parties for their closing statements.

First up was Corrigan, who was ready to make his final plea on behalf of the Babcock family, David Oliver and, of course, the Flathead County justice. "Mr. Ambrozuk will not be punished if he doesn't pay for the damages to the airplane," the duplicitous prosecutor added at the end of his well-prepared speech.

Mr. Jent, on the other hand, was not as tactful and sounded unsure when it was his turn to address the court. He didn't have the polished presentation that Mr. Watson always strove for. His factual arguments fell short of convincing even me that the Flathead County prosecutor's case was designed to gouge me financially. His speech seemed choppy and disorganized, with his closing statement sounding more like a summary, rather than an argument with substance to impress the one man who would be responsible for the final decision.

Rarely interrupting during the hearing, it was now up to the District Judge to weigh in all the evidence heard and come back with a fair ruling for each of the items the prosecutor was seeking. But when Judge Stadler got through, there would be no compromise, and everything that Corrigan asked for, the judge granted, with the only concession being that half of the $20,000 Mr. Oliver was after would come from my $10,000 court fine. "Mr. Oliver could use the money more than the county," Judge Stadler declared. Perhaps this was his way to show his benign financial responsibility, but there was no mistaking it: this was money shuffling and, in the end, I would still be paying $20,000 for an aircraft that was worth one-third that amount.

The judgment read, "IT IS HEREBY THE ORDER OF THE COURT the defendant shall pay restitution in the amount of $19,500, the court shall suspend $9,000 from the fine, and the defendant shall pay all other agreed amounts." (see Document: 3273 @ www.ambrozuk.com). What the "all other agreed amounts" referred to were the fees, fines, and restitutions that would eventually be specified in the JUDGMENT AND SENTENCE document (see Document: 3274 @ www.ambrozuk.com), and would add up to *a grand total of no less than $41,577.08!*

Although done legally in the Flathead County courthouse, the whole charade felt more like extortion. Paying someone $20,000 for aircraft repairs that should not have exceeded its Blue Book value seemed not only preposterous to me but apparently also to Judge Stadler, who, at the end of his judgment, turned to Mr. Jent and asked for my consent. It was the most bizarre thing I had ever heard—a judge asking the defendant's attorney to see if his client was OK with the fines he just imposed. I didn't know if it was simply guilt, or if this was his way of buying my approval; in either case, his gesture seemed odd. Frankly, I had never heard of the defendant having a say in what the judge ruled.

What if I disagreed?

Would he change his mind and give David Oliver only the maximum Blue Book value? Or perhaps no money at all, because without receipts and no insurance records, there was the possibility he would be reimbursed twice.

Although they were thought-provoking questions, my attorneys—who had sat silent throughout the hearing—were now eager to help me with my decision. Leaning over and whispering in my ear, Mr. Sherlock urged me on, "Oh, that's a great deal Jerry . . . take it!" he repeated several times. Mr. Jent, on the other side of me, also spurred me on with the same sentiment. It felt like I was being tag-teamed by my own lawyers, who, instead of seeing the absurdity in all this, took the path of least resistance and joined the Motley Trio of Flathead County.

After spending an hour in the courtroom, watching my counsel unsuccessfully defend against the anecdotal—instead of verifiable—evidence, I was ready to stand up and fend for myself. Then I reconsidered. It was obvious that my questioning, reasoning, logic, and the need for documented proof would not only prove pointless but might also aggravate the judge. If Judge Stadler could give David Oliver $20,000 while he was in a *good mood*, imagine what he would do if I questioned his and the prosecutor's neatly-packaged, going-away present. They could jack it up to $50,000, $100,000, or perhaps even the $150,000 that Mr. Oliver alluded to in his voluntary statement for loss of business and revenue.

All of a sudden those figures didn't seem so farfetched.

It was during that moment I sadly realized my only recourse was to abdicate. As unfair as it seemed—and as much as I hated to be swindled by the Flathead County authorities—I had no choice but to agree to their extortion.

But now Ed Corrigan had a problem—collecting the money. Nine months ago, the prosecutor all but gloated when he announced during my bond hearing that Merrill Lynch had frozen my accounts. That misfortune had now come back to haunt him, because without access to my money, he could not collect the restitution.

While discussing my financial situation with Mr. Jent after the hearing, I noticed the prosecutor eavesdropping on our conversation. He was standing on the opposite side of the room and appeared fidgety in his silence, so I decided to appeal to his benevolence and see if he could help us both.

"Mr. Corrigan, you seem to have a lot of authority around here. Perhaps you can get Merrill Lynch to release my money?" I asked, without dwelling on the irony of his dilemma.

Everyone listening appeared to find that somewhat amusing except for the prosecutor, who now seemed speechless.

"Or perhaps I can work it off on a Texas chain gang at fifty dollars a day?" I jocularly suggested.

He didn't seem amused. Rather, he looked puzzled and after a brief pause, finally said, "I'm not going to let you leave the country until the restitution is paid!"

As much as he thought he was the king of the Flathead County castle, my attorneys, including Mr. Sherlock, all believed that once I was in the federal and immigration custodies, no one would care about Ed Corrigan or his petty demands.

And that is how my restitution hearing ended—with a grand total of $41,577.08, instead of the $15,000 that was verbally all but guaranteed by Mr. Watson, the man who was absent while I was ruthlessly pillaged by the Kalispell authorities.

But be that as it may, I was finally done with my state case and would soon be leaving the clutches of Flathead County.

Although the road ahead was still unclear, my family and I were very much excited about the future ahead. In the last nine months, we had endured and persevered many a game from Ed Corrigan and Judge Stadler—all in the name of justice. Now all that was behind us, and it was time to move on to the next stop—the federal court and my passport charge.

CHAPTER FORTY-FIVE

AJACOM: The Middleman Alternative

1994 – 2006

MORE THAN TWELVE years had passed since the accident. Every time I closed my eyes, I could still clearly see the night that changed my life forever. But over time, my rage—along with my rebellious anti-authoritarian persona—had mutated into a more productive lifestyle. With help from my close friends like Nancy, and Dave, whom I met playing racquetball at a local gym, my social life slowly improved and it was once again becoming enjoyable.

My relationship with PJ ended just before graduating from UTA, and since then most of my leisure time was devoted to friends and working out. During evenings, I lifted weights three times a week and on other days alternated by playing racquetball with Dave. But during work days it was all about business. The Dallas hub, surrounded by adjoining suburbs, had plenty to offer in terms of corporate businesses where talented consultants could practically write their own paycheck as they moved from one project to another.

The client-server industry was hot, and good developers were hard to come by, so finding work as soon as the last project ended was never an issue. Along with experience came the rewards, and I found myself repeatedly increasing my hourly rate by five to ten dollars an hour each time I started a new project.

Although I saw Lee less frequently because of work and my social life, on occasion we would grab a bite and talk about the latest news on TV, or what had recently changed in our personal life. He was always understanding, generous, and a good friend, so it was hard to see him go when he got cancer and passed away within months. Never asking for anything and always there to lend a hand with an open heart, I can honestly say I considered him a true friend and was deeply saddened to see him go so quickly.

After his funeral, I stayed in his house for another half year before moving out when his sister made the decision to sell the property. I had very few possessions, and other than my school books I kept for sentimental reasons, the outdated Software Spectrum software hidden under my bed, a few garage tools, my Corvette, and my immobile, never-ending MGB project car, there was very little else to my name, making it convenient to relocate from one place to another. I moved several times in the next few years, cohabitating with various roommates, but my main focus was always on work.

By 1995, I had worked on IT projects in the Dallas area for many well-known companies: Arthur Andersen, Kaiser Permanente, Fujitsu, GET Directories, IBM, The Associates, and Deloitte & Touche, to name a few. With each project my development skills built on themselves, and it wasn't long before I started to see an opportunity to create a product that was superior to what other companies were using. The tool was called PowerArchitect, and it marked the beginning of AJACOM—our new company that would not only develop, sell, and provide training to developers who purchased our software, but would also act as an IT staffing/consulting agency.

Our product was an application architecture, or a class-library, providing a foundation and a set of pre-built tools that a project team could use to save months of initial development work. But the PowerBuilder market, especially the class-library arena, was fierce. Everyone wanted to get in on the action, not only selling their product and training services, but also assisting clients with staffing the project using their own developers, technical leads, and managers.

It was a great model structure, and after discussing the possibilities with Nancy, we decided to jump in headfirst with our better mousetrap. After years of IT consulting, it was time to reap the middleman benefits for ourselves. On July 21, 1995, we incorporated, and while Nancy took on the challenge of sales, I continued to consult through AJACOM to bring in spending capital, as we worked long hours to complete our flagship product.

Our architecture could run circles around the competition, but as typical start-up companies go, with minimal employees and no financial backing, the road was tough. Nancy did her best at networking and finding new clients with projects to staff, but in a male-dominated IT industry, that was easier said than done.

I, on the other hand, worked on getting PowerArchitect to a stage where it could be boxed and sold, but being a perfectionist, there were always things to tidy up and document. During the week, I spent fifty to sixty hours on projects at client sites, leaving only evenings and weekends for Nancy and me to devote to finishing our masterpiece.

Toggling between two jobs meant a lot of work and long hours, but I still made time for a social life. Whether it was a few beers at a pub, or a Halloween costume party dressed up as "Hans and Franz" or "Marvin the Martian" (see Document: 1418 @ www.ambrozuk.com), Nancy, Dave, and I would always take time to blow off steam. There were weekend camping trips with a church group, visits to Florida to spend time with my friends, vacations in Bahamas and the Walt Disney World Resort, and of course, Mardi Gras, one of my most memorable trips. On the spur of the moment, Dave and I hopped into his gold Lincoln Continental with "The Lincoln Hotel" painted in white shoe polish on the back window. We spent the entire week partying, catching a few winks in his car each night because there were no vacant hotel rooms left in New Orleans.

But in between the diversions, there was always work. Being a seasoned PowerBuilder consultant allowed me to pick and choose projects I wanted to be involved with. On occasion, I would be asked to step in and help on existing programs that needed enhancements or bugs fixed, but I always preferred new development where coding was done from the ground up. From a custom application at Kaiser Permanente for a radiology department that needed a new patient X-ray tracking system, to a Fujitsu factory program that used hand-held barcode scanners to track circuit boards on an assembly line in real time, it was always exciting to meet new clients, learn about their industry, and develop a solution to improve their productivity.

The most notable and rewarding projects, though, were ones where AJACOM had complete autonomy. In the late 1990s, we sold PowerArchitect across the world to countries like France, Australia, China, Canada and, of course, the United States, but we were never directly involved with the tool's development cycle—not until we landed a large-scale project at a private-equity fund firm in downtown Dallas. There, our architecture's potential would be fully realized. The enterprise-level application we redeveloped managed a $4.5 billion fund portfolio, and over a period of three years we not only replaced the front-end GUI interface but also the back-end database infrastructure, while continuously synchronizing the data between the two databases with stored procedures and triggers during the ongoing live transition.

Although that large-scale project would finally put us on the map, it came at a price. Overseeing and managing the development of various application modules—with multiple developers and database administrators (DBA's)—was exhausting, as I was forced to divide my time between the full-time project downtown and running AJACOM. With our credit cards maxed out and unable to cover our salaries and all the overhead, Nancy left AJACOM, leaving me to run the company by myself just as the downtown project was beginning to evolve.

Starting conservatively with one day per week, the project eventually scaled to a full-time gig over months. Requiring additional developers and DBAs to join the team, it subsequently provided AJACOM with the necessary capital to hire a new salesperson to continue growing the company. And that was when, purely by accident, I ran across Kim, a head-hunter at the time, who joined AJACOM as a self-motivated go-getter to head up sales. With a recruiting background, Kim seemed perfect to staff and market AJACOM as a project management company. Unfortunately, by then the economy had taken a turn for the worse in 2000, and the dot-com bubble burst along with opportunities for new IT projects.

Watching the IT staffing and consulting momentum fizzle out—along with our downtown client of three years that had replaced our entire project team with permanent employees to save money—our focus quickly turned to the medical industry and healthcare staffing.

Although profit margins in healthcare staffing were negligible compared to that of the lucrative IT sector, the name of the game was efficiency, persistency, and volume. With a well-funded corporate bank account to float paychecks of medical candidates for months, Kim and I opened our healthcare staffing division.

Returning full-time to our corporate office in Richardson, Texas, I took on the task of overseeing the entire operation. In addition to working with Kim to hire medical recruiters and grow AJACOM, I started developing our internal application, iStaff, to help manage not only candidates, but also clients and their job orders. Using bits and pieces of code from previous projects, I quickly pieced together an application that would help with the daily tasks of recruiting—complete with digital resumes for candidates and tracking conversations between clients. Eventually the goal was to create an all-in-one system, where the candidate skills could be automatically matched with the client requirements.

But my vision would never be fully realized, because after a couple of years of hard work and barely breaking even, my focus and expectations changed. By then, Kim had moved on to head up an orthopedic surgeon's office as office manager. After hiring her replacement to lead our staffing division, it became too exhausting to continue motivating the young recruiters so that we could maintain the 1,300 billing-hour minimum needed to cover our $32,000 monthly overhead. Despite the $1,300 bonus for each employee every month if they maintained the billing hours, no one seemed motivated enough to work more than forty hours per week.

In time, I ran out of patience and made the executive decision to shut down healthcare staffing and concentrate on the new IT project for Honda Racing.

Finding us on the Internet, a Honda representative from California contacted our company about taking over the development of their existing logistics applications. Looking to replace the IT consultants who were currently developing and maintaining their internal IRL/CART software, AJACOM won the bid and began redevelopment of the system that Honda despised after having spent $900,000 and six years on it.

Redesigning the workflow, replacing the database, and upgrading the GUI interface with a more intuitive and user-friendly one, iRace became a hit. After extensive testing for a year, including keystroke tests to show how much more efficient it was compared to its predecessor, they put us in contact with Honda Formula One to redesign their logistic applications that were much more complex, largely due to the shared data between offices in England and Japan.

Our first Formula One meeting was at the Texas Motor Speedway in Fort Worth, Texas (see Document: 1413 @ www.ambrozuk.com). Eventually I would have to go to England and Japan several times, not only to meet and conduct JAD (Joint Application Development) sessions to iron out the application features and functionality, but also to install and test the software after development.

Until then, I had travelled only within North America using my driver's license, but if I wanted to fly internationally, I had to apply for a passport. Less than three years after 9/11, and with the federal authorities still on high alert, I was hesitant about filling out the passport application, even though I had lived as Michael Smith for the last twenty-two years without incident. Worried, but determined to continue with the project, I walked into the local post office on May 24, 2004 with my identification and filled out the application. A couple of weeks later, I received the passport in the mail, no questions asked.

In between gathering requirements, my trips to England and Japan, and the application development for Honda, Kim and I also slowly began to rebuild our friendship. We had parted ways for personal and professional reasons but eventually reconciled to begin a new venture in the medical industry. Working as a manager in an orthopedic surgeon's office, Kim recognized the need for better software to manage everything from patient check-in to HIPAA compliant billing and insurance collections. Her foresight would lead to the development of MedCube—our all-in-one application designed to target healthcare facilities with multiple offices, not only across the Dallas/Fort Worth area, but eventually across the country.

But after maintaining a grueling twelve-hour-a-day work schedule for years, I was exhausted, and it was time to throttle down. Initially an escape from grieving over Dianne, the long work hours eventually began to take a toll.

By then, I had managed to pay off the mortgage on my two lakefront properties, pay off my 1996 Firebird Formula, purchase and pay off my house in Plano, Texas in order to save a preposterous amount in interest, and got my ultimate boy-toy: a red 2003 Dodge Viper I bought on eBay from a Las Vegas seller (see Document: 1410 @ www.ambrozuk.com). After so many years of reflection, sorrow, and pain, I was finally done running and no longer needed to prove myself. I was comfortably set, and the only thing missing was someone to share it all with. I had friends and acquaintances I played racquetball with during the week, played Halo on Friday nights, and went out with to pubs on the weekends. But what I was missing was that significant other to spend time with.

Up to that point, all my relationships always revolved around work. Reluctant at first, I was determined to change my habits and try online dating. Many of my friends had found success on the Internet, so I followed suit and signed up on several dating sites to try my luck. Dating for months and spending an absurd amount of money on dinners with women I would never see again, eventually I met Carolyn in January of 2004. She was young, fun, bubbly, single, and had no kids. She was also the first serious long-term relationship I would have since Dianne where I made a conscious decision to get involved. During the next three years, we spent a lot of time together, whether with her close-knit family, going to clubs, or just relaxing at the house. But in the end, we did have our differences, and a few months before my last trip to Japan, we broke up.

Still undeterred from finding that perfect companion, I rejoined the now dreaded online dating world, and that was when I ran across Genea, the girl responsible for my second "life reboot" and ultimately my return to Canada and my family after twenty-four years.

Act II: Federal Case

CHAPTER FORTY-SIX

"Club Fed," Here I Come!

June 1 – 20, 2007
Day 276 – 295

AFTER NINE MONTHS of dealing with Ed Corrigan and the Flathead County, I was finally moving on to my federal passport case. Friday morning at 6:30, a guard told me to roll up because the U.S. Marshals made good on their Federal Detainer (see Document: 3705 @ www.ambrozuk.com) and were ready to pick me up.

Anxious to leave, I changed into the civilian clothes I wore at my last sentencing and packed the evidence papers and personal letters into a grocery paper sack to take to my next destination. Whatever wouldn't fit, I signed off to Mr. Sherlock, who would forward the items to my sister in Canada.

Since my arrival in Kalispell, I had built a rapport with many of the guards at the detention center—chatting with them, finding out intimate details about Flathead County and its dirty politics and, of course, being frisked by many for contraband after every court appearance and attorney visit—so I appreciated their subtle, yet sympathetic words of farewell. No one shared the sentiments of the outspoken Sheriff Dupont and his lies about my conduct at the FCDC—including when he went on record and falsely stated I had refused to talk to him and only complained about my cell conditions (see Document: 2230 @ www.ambrozuk.com). They genuinely wished me luck when I left Kalispell under the guard of two immigration officers, once again in full restraints.

After a two-hour ride south through the countryside, we arrived at the Missoula County Detention Facility (see List: 9160 @ www.ambro-zuk.com) for my initial appearance in front of a judge for identification. Accompanied by Jessica L. Weltman, a court appointed attorney, the judge asked if I wanted an identity hearing. Having lived as Michael Smith for the past twenty-four years, the first order of business was to establish my true identity. But since I saw no reason to delay the process by forcing the government to prove who I really was, I waived the option. The judge placed me in the custody of U.S. Marshals before noting my final destination—the Eastern District of Texas to eventually face my passport charge.

Until then, I would begin my unpredictable journey through the federal court system, starting with the Missoula County Detention Facility, where I was booked and outfitted with "indigent" essentials—blanket, mattress sheet, comb, toothbrush, and a second pair of socks and underwear—to confirm it was not a one-night sleepover.

My new temporary home was Pod 2A, a general population designated area with eight cells—four on each floor and two beds in each. It was much larger than Flathead County but also much quieter, with very little echo emanating from the 35-inch TV suspended in the middle of the pod, or the social conversations that filled the room during the day. Located not far from the border, the pod also contained several Canadians waiting for their turn in court, with one in particular who also had Mr. Watson and Mr. Jent as his attorneys.

I was housed in what they called the "Celebrity Pod." Practically everyone there had been on local or national television whether for drugs, homicide, or for burning down half of Montana's forests. Because of the publicity, over time everyone got assigned a nickname appropriate for his case. The Montana firebug was known as *Pyro*, and after several days of bonding, I became *The Pilot*.

Talking with some of the more seasoned occupants, I was told that my route to Texas would most likely first include relocation to Great Falls, Montana, before the federal aircraft, Con-Air, would transport me to the Federal Distribution Center in Oklahoma City, Oklahoma. Depending on who you talked to, I would then spend anywhere from one to three weeks being processed at the distribution center before being moved to the federal facilities in Texas. Nothing was certain with the federal government—except that unpredictability was by design—and I would have to remain patient with the U.S. Marshals and their shell game.

Fortunately, I didn't have to wait long. On Tuesday afternoon, I was transferred to the Crossroads Correction Center (CCC) in Shelby, Montana, a 660-inmate private state prison facility that was owned and operated by a third-party company called Corrections Corporation of America.

Processed out and back in my civilian clothes, the guards handcuffed the four of us using the traditional leg and belt irons, before loading everyone into the transport vehicle. The extended van had three rows of bench seats inside, steel mesh on all windows, and a mesh fence partitioning the back of the van from the driver and the passenger seats that the guards occupied. Buckled down with seatbelts, we were given a brown-bag, paper-sack lunch for our long journey to the CCC facility. Although very much appreciated, there was a catch—we had to make and eat the sandwich while fully restrained.

The first challenge was making the sandwich itself.

The bread, cotto salami, and cheese were all individually wrapped and required some creativity for assembly. Normally that task would be trivial, but when your handcuffs are attached to a chain belt around your waist and another around your ankles, your maneuverability is drastically reduced. Now imagine that in addition to all this linkage restricting your movement, there is also a rigid black box covering your handcuffs to not only provide additional security, but inadvertently immobilize your hands further.

Using great care and control, I managed to unwrap both the meat and cheese slices out of their plastic covers and stack them on top of

296 • JAREK AMBROZUK

the two bread pieces now lying on my knees. That was only half the battle—eating the sandwich proved even more difficult.

Although I could lean forward, my back would not arch enough for my mouth to reach the sandwich I extended toward my face using my fingertips. It took several tries and adjustments to take a single bite, but eventually, like a drinking-bird toy that bobs ever so closer to the water, I managed to eat the last well-earned bite to everyone's amusement.

Despite all of us being in the same boat that day and taking turns at the sandwich eating challenge, only a few were brave enough to also attempt drinking the quarter-pint of milk. Opening the paper carton didn't seem that difficult, but drinking it was another matter. How do you raise the milk container above your mouth to take a drink if your hands are tied to your waist? With ingenuity and great flexibility it *is* possible since several of the guys managed to do just that during our bumpy ride. Unfortunately, for their full bladders, there would be no bathroom break during our three-and-a-half-hour journey, and that would prove more than a challenge when it came to their bodily fluid control. Toward the end, many were pleading with the guards to stop on the side of the road, as they crossed their legs in pain, but there would be no pit stop until we reached the detention facility in Shelby.

Booked in, photographed, and fingerprinted, I was given a picture ID with an agency and commissary number for making phone calls and ordering items from the commissary. I also filled out a form so all my paperwork would be mailed to Canada the day I was transported by Con-Air; other than glasses and medicine, nothing else was allowed on the aircraft.

Processed and waiting to be housed, we were served dinner in the temporary cell. But unlike the city and state detention centers, this was more than just a meal—this was gourmet food. We got home-made meatloaf, real mashed potatoes and gravy with potato skins clearly visible in the mix, an assortment of vegetables, some fruit and, of course, real apple pie for dessert.

Showered and dressed in new yellow attire, I was given a large, white plastic storage box with indigent-inmate supplies before being moved to Pod-H, Cell #117. Unlike the small pod in Missoula, this one contained forty-eight detainees—twelve individual cells on either side of the pod—with two bunk beds in each cell. There were two TVs mounted overhead, and several amenities, including two telephones, a microwave, and two large shower areas that could be used during designated times throughout the day.

Mr. Watson was right—this was like a college campus.

On alternating days, we had the option to either go outside and roam for an hour over a large, fenced-in field partially covered with gravel and patches of grass, or use the gym facilities. There was a Universal weights machine available to work out with, a designated area to play a game of round-robin hand-ball, a full-size basketball court with spectator benches, and an adjacent room full of games—Ping-Pong and air-hockey tables, and seven PlayStation 2 machines where video gaming skills could be honed.

Even the commissary was beyond what I expected. In addition to the standard food and candy supplements, there were also playing cards, an AM/FM radio, and Squirt (a refreshing citrus pop) on the menu to purchase (see Document: 4203 @ www.ambrozuk.com).

But just when things were finally looking up, everything ended abruptly.

During my first full day at the CCC facility, a stabbing during dinner occurred between Native and African Americans. It was the result of a dispute between the racially divided six-on-six basketball game players over some chocolate bars, but it was enough to place the entire pod on full lockdown with restrictions for thirty days (see Document: 4204 @ www.ambrozuk.com). Full lockdown meant we were confined to our cells twenty-four hours a day, with "Johnnie[x]" paper-sack breakfast,

---

x. A "Johnnie" paper-sack lunch consisted of a single slice of bologna and cheese, sandwiched between two slices of white bread. Depending on the facility, an apple or an orange may also have been included in the bag.

lunch, and dinner for the first ten days, no recreation or commissary for fourteen days, only three showers per week under supervision, and no communication with my attorneys or my family.

It wasn't easy spending twenty-four hours a day in a small cell with nothing to do. But within a week they began to loosen their reins and let us out for two hours—half a pod at a time—so we could take a shower and use the telephone. It was great talking to my family again, but the curse of Flathead County lingered on even after my departure. Speaking briefly to Renata, I was told there were still issues with not only the state case, but also the jury consultant.

According to Mr. Sherlock, Flathead County miscalculated my credit for time served. Since the fines and restitution amounts were already set at my final sentencing, Ed Corrigan and Judge Stadler were in the process of nullifying the $4,000 three-month credit I had accrued between my first and second sentencing by simply raising my fine to make the numbers match. In other words, the house never loses, especially in Flathead County.

After finding out that Mr. Sherlock took it upon himself to resolve this, and was still billing us accordingly, Renata asked him to stop immediately. There was no need to pay him extra for something that Mr. Watson was perfectly capable of handling directly with the prosecutor via an email or a phone call.

But the most disturbing news was regarding our jury consultant who was keeping the bulk of our pre-payment because of a technicality. On recommendation from Mr. Watson, she was hired for her expertise on jury selection, but since the trial never occurred, we expected most of the money back. Instead, she refunded only $8,470, out of $26,300, and kept the rest as payment for her services and so-called cancellation fees. My sister was outraged when she read the invoice stating the reason for not refunding the rest of the money: we failed to notify her on time about reaching a plea bargain agreement—literally missing her twenty-four hour cancellation deadline by minutes. She was in direct contact with Mr. Watson throughout the plea bargain negotiations and knew the status better than anyone. Because Renata didn't contact her in time, she billed us double the amount, including several frivolous charges for airline tickets and accommodations in Kalispell that my sister took the time to verify.

Dealing with Merrill Lynch about my frozen accounts, and even John Bodnar about the release of my Corvette, I could almost understand. But not this! Not Mr. Sherlock billing us extra for something he knew Mr. Watson could do for free; and not the jury consultant for using a technicality to keep the bulk of our initial payment.

It was tough to swallow all the gauging by people we had hired, all of whom seemed sincere and honest before we signed their contracts and paid them money.

CHAPTER FORTY-SEVEN

Con-Air—The Federal Airline of Choice

June 21 – July 2, 2007
Day 296 – 307

JUST WHEN THINGS were about to return to normal after the full lockdown at the CCC facility, I was once again uprooted. On Thursday, an hour after breakfast, two guards came to my cell to verify my ID, told me to roll up, and escorted me out into the booking area for processing. No one would disclose where I was going, but in all likelihood it was my turn to *catch the chains* on the infamous "Con-Air." Unable to take any personal items, including legal paperwork, I quickly stuffed all my possessions into a large FedEx box for shipping to my sister in Canada.

I was given a quick physical inspection to make sure there were no hidden weapons on my body. Stripped naked, the officer said "open your mouth, lift your nut sack, bend over, spread your butt cheeks, and cough." I never had an opportunity to point my naked arse at an officer before, but I was more than happy to oblige if it meant a farewell to the Crossroads Correctional Center, and the lockdown.

Dressed in the freshly-washed civilian clothes I came in with, I joined seventeen others in two transport vans that took us to the airfield at Great Falls, Montana—a stop along the way for the Con-Air aircraft making its way around the country. While the one-hour morning ride to the airport was pleasantly cool, the three-hour wait on the tarmac in the hot, ventless vehicle was brutal.

When the plane arrived, detainees and prisoners from their respective buses were marshaled out and separated into small groups of parallel lines for sorting. Armed guards patrolled the outskirts of the fields for any possible escape attempts. It was like the old Wild West with lawmen and their loaded shotguns at their side, guarding the stagecoach, ready to defend against a possible robbery attempt.

Standing in front of the large Boeing 737, several U.S. Marshals kept order, calling out names and swapping bodies from one line to another. Some boarded the aircraft while others disembarked and would be transported to either a local federal penitentiary, or a detention center, by bus. When the reshuffling was complete and verified twice over, my group was motioned to board the aircraft in a single file, slowly walking up the stairs with chains around our ankles, before taking seats, starting at the back of the aircraft. The front seats were reserved for females, with two empty rows separating the genders to keep the interaction and sexual taunts to a minimum. Ten U.S. Marshals were spaced strategically throughout the plane to keep order.

The Boeing aircraft had a capacity of 150 seats and for the most part looked like a typical passenger aircraft. Resembling nothing of what the movie "Con-Air" portrayed, the non-reclining seats were more or less cushiony. But there were a few minor modifications: the tray from the back of each seat was removed and any loose flaps, like ashtray lids, were glued shut.

My ultimate destination was the Federal Distribution Center in Oklahoma City, but the plane was scheduled to make several stops along the way to drop off and pick up detainees and prisoners. Heading in a counterclockwise direction, our first stopover was SEATAC in Seattle, Washington, before turning south for San Bernardino, California.

For security reasons Con-Air didn't fly at night, so after three hours, we landed at the Victorville, California airport. We were unloaded, placed in several uncomfortable Greyhound-type buses, and taken to the San Bernardino Detention Facility.

Sitting in a crowded holding tank for hours with no food, it was close to seven o'clock in the evening when the guards finally came by to give us their "welcome" speech. Unlike Shelby—where many of the guards appeared to have spawned from the same recessive gene pool—these were the complete opposite, with pompous attitudes and a body-building, muscle- beach mentality. Every guard who walked by looked as if he came straight from a Mr. Universe contest, complete with a bulging chest, arms and legs that barely fit into his two-sizes-too-small uniform. It was difficult not to smirk at the eccentricity, but despite the occasional heckle from the restless crowd, the guards tried their hardest to maintain order. We were all exhausted and hungry, and by then no one cared about their disciplinary rules and procedures. What we really needed was food, a few personal hygiene items, and blankets to lie down on and get some rest.

It would be another hour before we were given a paper-sack dinner, met with the nurse to answer the same suicide questions every detention facility asked, and moved into cells to begin our processing. We were sorted by whether we would return to Con-Air the next day or be transported to a local facility by bus.

But in between the discomforts, there were also comedy relief moments from the local county patriots being booked in. A short, stocky fellow, who appeared to be high as a kite, with sweat pouring down his face and blotches of perspiration seeping through his shirt, managed to singlehandedly entertain the entire gloomy crowd. Arrested after allegedly throwing a stone at a passing vehicle—a felony in his county—he described every hilarious detail of his saga while the entire cell roared with laughter. His neighbor had peeled his truck tires on the gravel road in front of his house—no less than three times! This, of course, had created an ongoing feud between him and the neighbor in the past few days.

304 · JAREK AMBROZUK

A fifty-ish black man, sitting quietly in the back of the cell listening, jumped in and asked with a chuckle, "Did they find the rock?"

"I never threw no rock!"

But when the accused confessed that he had only shot a *paperclip* at the neighbor's truck from his front porch using a rubber band, the black man, with most of his front teeth missing, enunciated in a voice echoing O.J. Simpson's attorney, Johnny Cochran, "If the rock is not legit, they must acquit!" It was all about the delivery, and between the two, half of us had tears in our eyes, listening to each up the other's ante. Their Abbott and Costello routine was much appreciated after the exhausting day everyone had endured.

Tired and hungry, it wasn't until 1:00 a.m. when the guards finally handed out the bedding for the night. With only two blankets each— one used as padding on the cement floor and the other rolled up into a pillow—I found an empty space on the floor, made my bed, and turned in for the night. But the rest was short-lived because three hours later we were awakened for breakfast.

Lined up in single file, we silently headed for the cafeteria, passing through a metal detector at the door before entering the large hall-like room with dozens of long metal tables and seat benches.

The place was dead silent, with only the shuffling of feet and the knocking of sporks against the metal trays resonating between the echoing white-walls. Not unlike the modern version of the movie *Cool Hand Luke*, the guards maintained order through silence, and the only dialogue allowed was during the replacement of dirty cups or utensils.

"Cup!" a random detainee would call out, raising it in the air.

"Cup here!" the guard repeated, pointing in his direction with a baton. One of the six inmate workers standing at the kitchen line sprinted to exchange the cups before quickly returning to wait for his next task. It was an eerie scene. Fortunately, I was a quick eater and managed to scarf down most of the food before the guards ordered everyone to stop, drop off their tray at the kitchen counter, and return to their cells in the same orderly fashion as when arriving.

Preparing for our departure, we were given new photo IDs as identification for the U.S. Marshals. Processed and checked-out within an hour, we were shackled and returned to the airport to continue our journey to the next destination of Atwater, California—a military base that housed hundreds of large gray cargo aircraft. Our final leg took us to the Federal Distribution Center in Oklahoma, where every federal detainee and prisoner was cycled through before being moved to his permanent location.

Landing at approximately six o'clock, we waited for almost an hour as they unloaded another Con-Air aircraft that covered the eastern part of the U.S. It had managed to beat us by ten minutes.

Unshackled and moved into a temporary holding tank, everyone received another inquisitive federal "special" inspection before being booked-in, photographed, and dressed in the standard detention facility attire. The clothes we wore we could either donate or mail to our families. During the visit to the nurse's office to review the medical papers we had filled out earlier, the few of us who were still newbies were assigned a classification—a security level based on charges, criminal history, and previous behavior in other prisons or detention centers—that would determine our housing and privileges during our stay.

After a brief glance at the monitor by the guard in charge, I was given the designation of "Medium," and taken to Pod 5E on the fifth floor via a large, industrial-type elevator, where I was assigned Cell 628L for the duration of my stay.

The pod typically housed up to 108 people, with the entire facility cycling through somewhere close to 1,800 detainees or inmates at any given time. There were four TV rooms, the largest one comparable to a basketball court-size area that was open to fresh air at the top of either end. There were four phones available for use throughout the day, a commercial-size ice machine, and even a microwave that remained a mystery as there was no commissary to order food from. Everyone was there temporarily, except for the few permanent inmates who resided on the floor above and were responsible for the facility maintenance and regular cleaning.

My new cellie was a scrawny, nerdy man who seemed to have a chip on his shoulder. Instead, I spent most of the day with Terry, a more social fellow I met on Con-Air. To pass time, we walked on the upper deck—back and forth for hours—getting exercise while discussing everything from our cases to what the federal prisons were like in general. Terry was about to be released, but after five years of incarceration in the federal prison system, he had learned and seen things that I continued to find fascinating.

Of particular interest was a story by Barbara Walters. Several years back, she had done a documentary special on federal penitentiaries, and that was when the term "Club-Fed" was coined. In her report, one of the California prisons was highlighted, noting how the inmates had access to a full-size Olympic swimming pool. The abandoned military base was eventually converted into a prison years later—along with all the military perks still intact—but after her report aired on TV, the pool was filled with sand a few weeks later, never to be used again.

From low-level security inmate golf course access in California and New York, to medium-security prisoners in Florida who watched movies in a stadium-seating theater complete with drinks and popcorn, to the "super-max" federal prison wing in Colorado where the government kept their worst criminals in a fifteen-by-twenty-foot Plexiglas cell for life, Terry's stories were eye-opening.

But my fascination with the federal prison system would be cut short; after six days in the Oklahoma Federal Distribution Center, I was moved to Texas. Thursday morning at 2:30 a.m., I was told to roll up, and along with a few others, placed on a refitted Greyhound bus that dropped each of us off at various detention facilities across the state. Heading southeast, our first stop was Texarkana to swap out nine inmates before turning west and ending up at the Seagoville Federal Correctional Institute (see List: 9190 @ www.ambrozuk.com). It was already afternoon when we arrived, got unloaded, processed, and dressed in the orange, one-piece jumper suit before waiting another three hours to be moved into general population.

Pod H2, Cell 229, was my new home, and I took the top bunk, sharing accommodation with a somewhat unhappy South-African man, who immediately protested to the Corrections Officer in charge that he wasn't supposed to bunk with others because of his medical condition.

The place was definitely a downgrade from where I came from—disorganized about even the smallest tasks like finding an empty bed or a mattress to sleep on. Because I didn't have a PAC# that each inmate was assigned after being sentenced, I couldn't make calls to Carolyn or my family. And even after filling out a telephone-number request sheet, I was told by the C.O. that no one would be added to my approved caller list until their background checks were verified, which could take several days.

Luckily, that problem was alleviated a day later when I was once again told to gather my belongings because I was moving on. After a quick checkout and another cavity search of the most intimate cracks, I was instructed to put on a dark blue jumper suit made entirely of paper for the trip. This time I was transported in the back of a squad car with an African-American man who had been on the bus that brought us to Seagoville.

We arrived at the Hunt County Detention Center in Greenville shortly after, which turned out to be the undisputed crowning shithole of Texas (see List: 9200 @ www.ambrozuk.com). I was housed in the northwest wing of the 300-inmate facility, Cell 353, along with four other men. With four double-stacked bunk beds, I took the first available top bed. The cell was small, dirty, and unsanitary—with a shower area that had black mildew covering the bottom of the walls.

As luck would have it, on Saturday an inmate worker, along with a supervising guard, came into the pod and painted over the black mildew. Nothing was cleaned before they slapped on a fresh coat of paint to cover the black spots in preparation for an inspection by the detention facility chief. The paint was still drying, with the fumes saturating the musky air, when he showed up unannounced a few hours later and did his five-minute walkthrough.

He checked a few bunks and talked to a couple of guys, but little did he know that three of them were making hooch. To make alcohol, all you needed was bread, sugar, and some citrus, like oranges, which they gave us regularly. Mix it all together, let it sit for a week, and presto—the beginning of happy hour. Of course, the drawback was that during the fermentation process, the pressure built up inside the plastic cups used for mixing the pruno (prison wine), and periodically the top popped off with a loud bang. Although humorous throughout the day, it would not be as entertaining during an inspection. But the chief left without incident, and the three men averted fifteen to thirty days in the hole with loss of privileges, if caught.

Despite the poor living conditions, there was a positive side to the Hunt County Detention Center—it was the closest I'd been to Dallas in almost a year. On Sunday, Carolyn showed up for an unexpected visit—she, as always, with her glowing, tanned face and a cheerful smile, and me, for some unexplainable reason, in full restraints. The visitor booth was completely enclosed in Plexiglas with a telephone for communication, so the handcuffs and chains around my ankles seemed ridiculous. From what I could tell, conjugal visits were definitely out of the question, and all we could do was laugh about their policies during the twenty minutes we got to spend face to face.

Talking on the phone to Carolyn and my family on a daily basis had kept me in good spirits since all this began, but there was no substitute for seeing a friendly face, if only for a few minutes at a time.

And that sentiment would continue for months to come because on Monday, three days after my arrival in Hunt County, I was transported to Grayson County Jail in Sherman, Texas (see List: 9210 @ www. ambrozuk.com), bringing me that much closer to my final federal destination in Denton. Showered with a lice-cleansing fluid and dressed in a new orange jumper suit, I was housed in Pod 2B at eight o'clock that evening. Although the twenty-four bunk bed pod was an upgrade—

with three toilets, two showers, and much more privacy—it was also loud with the sound bouncing off the concrete walls as if we were in a congested subway station.

The strangest thing during my travels from one detention center to another was the tuberculosis test the facilities insisted on upon arrival. The first one I had received ten months before in McKinney, Texas, after my arrest. The second one was in Shelby, Montana, and the third one here in Grayson County Jail.

A few months before, the news had reported that the U.S. Government quarantined an attorney because he tested positive after returning from Europe with his fiancé. Ever since then, everyone seemed to be on high alert. Although I could appreciate one TB test, repeating it several times over the course of months could only compound my chances of actually contracting the infectious disease because of the multiple TB antigens they kept injecting under my skin to see the reaction. It would have been prudent to simply call the last place I was detained and ask for the results.

But try explaining that to the nurse insistent on administering it again!

CHAPTER FORTY-EIGHT

The Federal Passport Arraignment

July 3 – 8, 2007
Day 308 – 313

AFTER SEVERAL WEEKS of shuttling between federal detention facilities, July found me in the Eastern District of Texas in my
first federal court appearance: the arraignment.

On Tuesday morning, July 3 at ten o'clock, I met with Camille
Knight, a local Texas lawyer hired by Mr. Watson, to go over the upcoming hearing in the afternoon. A younger attorney with a laid-back
and pleasant personality, she seemed well informed about how the federal process worked and what to expect.

For those still keeping score, we're up to eight attorneys: Clancy
(dismissed), Davis (Texas), Sherlock (Montana), Palmer (Cor-
vette release), Cohen (Merrill Lynch), Watson and Jent (Montana
State and Texas Federal cases), and now Ms. Knight.

She brought with her a couple of power of attorney documents to
sign for my car title transfers—the four previous ones I had signed
in Flathead County obviously meant nothing —before we went over
the revised plea agreement she received from my Montana lawyers.
We were still in the middle of our conversation when a guard showed
up with restraints and escorted me to a van with two female detainees also scheduled to make their court appearance. The courthouse was
only two minutes away, but the arraignment was not what I expected.

Instead of the traditional courtroom, the federal government had gone "virtual," and we found ourselves sitting in a small room in front of two TV screens.

Ms. Knight and I sat at a table on the right. Shamoil Shipchandler, the federal assistant prosecutor, was on our left. It was the first time I had seen Mr. Shipchandler, who looked older than what Mr. Sherlock described. He seemed laid back as he sat quietly, waiting for the hearing to begin.

Within minutes, Judge Caroline M. Craven, the magistrate from Texarkana, popped up on one of the television screens to begin the arraignment. Video screens displayed both parties, with the hearing being recorded to serve as court evidence (see Document: 3712 @ www.ambrozuk.com). To expedite the process, we waived the reading of the indictment (see Document: 3701 @ www.ambrozuk.com) and went straight to pleading *not guilty* to my one and only federal charge, *Violation 18 U.S.C. 1542, False Statement in Application and Use of Passport.*

Toward the end of the arraignment, when Judge Craven was about to set my detention hearing date for August 17, Ms. Knight interrupted and explained that my pending immigration detainer would prevent me from being eligible to bond out. Acknowledging the complication, the magistrate muttered a few words to the court clerk before smacking her gavel on her desk to the words "Court adjourned!" thus ending the first step in resolving my federal charge.

Returning to Grayson County Jail, I met again with Ms. Knight to finish our detailed first draft walkthrough of the plea bargain agreement. As we sifted through the legal document, we both agreed she would contact Mr. Shipchandler regarding the included FACTUAL STATEMENT, specifically to remove paragraphs 4, 5, and 6 that were irrelevant to my federal case (see Document: 3718 @ www.ambrozuk. com).

But the most valuable piece of advice Ms. Knight gave me that day was to read the book, *Busted by the Feds*, by Larry Fassler. It was considered somewhat of a federal-procedures bible not only by detainees, but also by many attorneys (see Document: 3755 @ www.ambrozuk. com). A comprehensive summary of how the federal system works, it served as a great reference into its intricate and sometimes confusing laws, regulations, and procedures.

How hard was it to get access to such a book while I was in Grayson County Jail? As it turned out, not that difficult! After returning to the pod and making a few inquiries, I got my hands on it a couple of days later, courtesy of a few resourceful individuals generous enough to get it moved from another pod.

Thumbing through the pages, the book was a great source of information that explained the federal court process from beginning to end—from the first day you were arrested all the way through to your sentencing and appeals.

First published in 1992 as a four-page handout, I had the 7th Edition 2007[xi], with the latest federal sentencing guidelines I was very much interested in reviewing. Written in laymen's terms, I found it refreshing that the author warned the reader to be skeptical not only of the federal prosecutor, but also the defendant's own attorneys, who often manipulated the facts and the law alike to get the desired results, which were not always in your best interest.

As I dove deeper into the book, I found it very helpful to understand what I was actually facing with regard to my charge. One of the first things the book recommended was to calculate my sentence guidelines using my offense level and criminal history category. Using these two values, it was then possible to cross-reference the federal sentencing table and fairly accurately predict the probation/months of imprisonment.

---

xi. *Busted by the Feds* – the book used during my detention, was the 7th Edition 2007, containing the latest federal information at the time. To keep up with federal law changes, the book is republished each year with an updated version. It contains not only the latest guidelines, but also current developments in the law, along with appropriate advice for the defendant. See www. bustedbythefeds.com for more information about the latest edition.

Part L – Offenses Involving Immigration, Naturalization and Passport, stated that:

2L2.2. Fraudulently Acquiring Documents Relating to Naturalization, Citizenship, or Legal Resident Status for Own Use; False Personation or Fraudulent Marriage by Alien to evade Immigration Law; Fraudulently Acquiring or improperly Using a United States Passport

the Base Offense Level is 8.

Furthermore:

If the defendant fraudulently obtained or used a United States passport, increase by: 4.

This brought my offense level total to 12. By taking responsibility for my actions and pleading guilty to my passport charge, I was entitled to a reduction of two levels, thereby reducing my offense level to 10.

So far so good. But the criminal history points, based on the criminal history category, were not as simple to interpret because they were based on my prior criminal convictions and sentences.

To compute the points you had to:

(a) Add 3 points for each prior sentence of imprisonment exceeding one year and one month

(b) Add 2 points for each prior sentence of imprisonment of at least sixty days not counted in (a)

(c) Add 1 point for each prior sentence not counted in (a) or (b) above, up to a total of 4 points for this item.

Underneath each item, there were also "Important Notes" that further clarified where my prior sentences should fall, and/or if they should even be counted in my computations. One of the notes stated:

A sentence imposed more than ten years prior to the defendant's commencement of the instant offense is not counted.

If I was reading it right, my probation of twenty-two years ago, having come up after my arrest and extradition to Kalispell, would not be counted because it occurred more than ten years before.

So the only accountable charges were the recent criminal endangerment and criminal mischief felonies in Montana, for which I received two ten-year suspended sentences. Although I had spent nine months in a detention center in Kalispell, officially I had received no imprisonment for either charges, and therefore I would add one point for each prior sentence as specified in (c) above.

To compound the complication, a second note under (c) also stated that judgments levied in cases related to the original finding were treated the same as the original court decisions:

Prior sentences imposed in related cases are to be treated as one sentence.

I understood this to mean that since my criminal endangerment and criminal mischief charges were a result of a single incident—and furthermore were imposed during one sentencing—they combined for a single criminal history point.

And therein lay the ambiguity.

According to Mr. Watson, Mr. Jent, and Ms. Knight, I fell somewhere either in Category II (2 or 3 points) or Category III (4, 5, 6 points). But the way I had computed the points using the book, I was in Category I (0 or 1 point) (see Document: 3751 @ www.ambrozuk.com).

So the $64,000 question was: Who was right?

Could the attorneys be mistaken about interpreting the sentencing guidelines as the book had suggested?

I wanted to believe the three of them, backed by years of experience, knew what they were talking about, but I also had to trust my logic and what I was reading. I was still in the middle of understanding how the system worked, but I believed that the name of the game was to assist the judge—in any way possible—by giving him every excuse for probation rather than incarceration.

Judges have some wiggle room with the sentencing guidelines, as *Busted by the Feds* pointed out, so if we could give him enough excuses, he might play along.

According to Ms. Knight, Judge Bush, my sentencing judge, was one of the more reasonable and fair magistrates, but he would have to justify why he was deviating from the sentencing guidelines if he decided on a downward departure in my particular case.

Based on discussions with my attorneys, and what I verified through the book, the whole sentencing process worked something like this:

The judge had to select a sentence that not only fell between the statutory sentence range (0 to 10 years) for my charge, but was also within the sentencing guidelines. The problem was that, even at Offense Level 10 for Category I, the sentence prison range was six to twelve months. This meant that if he went by the book—and had no valid reason to do otherwise—he would have to give me six months minimum. For Category II, the range increased to eight to fourteen months, and for Category III it was ten to sixteen months. It was, therefore, in my best interest to convince my attorneys, the probation officer, and ultimately the judge, that Category I was where I needed to be.

Fortunately, because of some precedent-setting cases, that was also where the judge could exercise his discretion. After the *United States v. Booker* and *United States v Fanfan,* effectively spelling the end of the federal guidelines as being constitutional in June of 2004, the strict guidelines were no longer mandatory and essentially became advisory only. This gave judges the flexibility for upward and downward departures during sentencing based on several factors, including but not limited to the sentencing guidelines, which could carry a different, and more significantly, lesser weight.

That significant change in the law allowed the judge to look at other defendant characteristics such as job history, family ties, etc., and not just the defendant's criminal history to decide on the appropriate sentence. His decision had to be warranted and justified but he could, in my case for example, decide to decrease my minimum sentence from six-plus months to time served and release me to immigration, thereby applying a downward departure.

Busted by the Feds mentioned that very few defendants got lucky enough to receive a downward departure—and if they did, it was because of some other unusual circumstances that were rare and not taken into account in the formulation of the guidelines.

Fair enough. So how about this for being unusual and rare:

First, my criminal record had been unblemished for the past twenty-plus years and the two state felonies, although considered recent convictions, happened twenty-four years ago. That, in itself, enforced my positive past over the last quarter of a century.

I had obtained an aerospace engineering degree, and through my IT and healthcare staffing company had provided jobs for over 230 people in the last seventeen years. I had personally, and through my company, paid a substantial amount of money in taxes to the federal government over the last quarter century. Over the same time period, I had also managed my personal and business affairs like an exemplary citizen of the United States.

Secondly, the only reason I obtained the passport was to work on international IT projects. I did not get the passport for pleasure purposes or for illegal activities; it was strictly to secure work. Although it was ironic that the federal government—the same government I paid taxes to because of the money I made in England and Japan—was now charging me for obtaining the passport from them in the first place. Without a passport, there would have been no projects that brought revenue back into the United States.

And finally, there was the matter of economics and my Canadian citizenship. By the time we went to sentencing, I would have spent nine months in state detention centers and approximately four months in federal detention centers, patiently awaiting due process. With my track record, and given that I would inevitably be deported to Canada, why would the judge waste taxpayer money to incarcerate me further?

The Federal prosecutor agreed to recommend the minimum sentence, and it would now be up to my attorneys to convince the probation officer—the underwriter of the PSI report—and eventually the judge, to consider downward departure because of my unusual circumstances.

But if all those points still were not enough of an incentive for the judge, there was also the early-disposition option to consider. According to *Busted by the Feds*, early disposition allowed the judge to give the defendant sentencing concessions in exchange for a prompt guilty plea and a waiver of procedural rights, such as the right to appeal. This fast-track program, if applied to aliens, required immediate deportation, which I would inevitably face anyway when I got to immigration.

This was not rocket science. After reading all the compelling arguments in *Busted by the Feds* book, I was feeling much more confident about my odds in front of the federal judge. The only thing left was to convince my attorneys to see my optimistic rationale through their own eyes. With any luck, everything would fall into place, and hopefully the prosecutor, the probation officer, and most importantly, the sentencing judge, would side with probation when the time came.

CHAPTER FORTY-NINE

The Black Widow Cometh

March 2006

HER FULL NAME was Genealen Marss Johnson and I met her on an online dating website. Her first name was a concatenation of her mother's and father's names, but she went by her nickname Genea (pronounced Gina).

Genea contacted me via email on Wednesday, March 1, 2006. Like me, she had a profile on Yahoo Personals. But unlike mine, it was hidden so no one could find it using search criteria. I was up late the night when I got her first email. A night owl in general, on Monday and Wednesday nights I was usually up well past midnight because of racquetball. The time stamp on her email envelope read 11:02 p.m. when I checked the laptop sitting on my living room coffee table. Included in the email was a profile URL that linked back to her private Yahoo Personals webpage containing her personal details, a three paragraph write-up, and a couple of photos (see Document: 7200 @ www.ambro-zuk.com).

When I first glanced at her profile, I must say I was impressed. She had much of the criteria I was looking for—5'7", thirty-three years old, no kids but wanted some, athletic and toned, drank socially, and didn't smoke. The only thing that stood out was her divorce. Although I was always looking for a Catholic, unmarried woman, over the years I had learned to compromise, so neither of the two seemed like a deal-break-er. Being no spring chicken myself, I'd also had a reality check and decided I would be perfectly happy with someone who at least met some of my criteria, including someone who not only wanted, but still could have kids (see Document: 3115 @ www.ambrozuk.com).

After looking over Genea's profile and reading her comments, I wrote her back that same night. I assumed I would not hear from her until next day but had a reply an hour later. The email not only explained why she was writing so late, but also included a phone number to call after 11:00 a.m. the next morning, because she usually slept until then.

After months of online dating, that was the first time a girl skipped the formalities and gave me her telephone number the same day we made contact. I was a bit surprised at her forwardness, considering her profile was hidden from the public. But I was not complaining. I was more than happy to bypass emailing for two weeks before she was comfortable enough for us to talk on the phone.

As instructed, I called her the next day around 1:00 p.m., and our initial chat went well. There were no dead spots I sometimes experienced with other women where I tried to come up with the next topic to avoid that awkward, uncomfortable silence.

She said she worked at a chip manufacturing plant in Dallas and was a Fabrication Lab Technician, maintaining the wafer production. After graduating from a two-year technical school program, she had taken the job and worked there for the past ten years. She switched to the graveyard shift years ago to accommodate her ex-boyfriend, Hoyt, and decided to continue that schedule because of the higher pay.

During our first conversation, it was mostly Genea who did the talking. She went on about her life story, her likes and dislikes, and pet peeves. I listened for nearly two hours, trying to live up to my Yahoo profile headline that read, "I have this uncanny ability to listen and pay attention to the conversation at hand." I had read so many profiles from women looking for guys who could listen and engage in intelligent dialogue and thought my blurb was straight to the point. The more Genea and I talked, the more I found her fascinating. She was raised in Longview, Texas by her mother and grandmother. Her biological father was basically a bum, she said, who was currently living off of, and shacking up with, another woman.

She went on about her mother and how she always had been there for her—not only educating her to be independent, but passing on some of her domestic skills. From an early age, she was taught how to use a hammer and fix things around the house, which, in general, would have been considered man's work. She talked about her passions, including cooking, gardening, and the Honda crotch-rocket bike she got because of Hoyt and periodically rode for fun.

Genea and I spent the rest of the week continuing our daily phone calls for hours at a time. The daytime and nighttime talks went so well we decided to meet face to face that Saturday night at 7:00 p.m. at a local Hibachi restaurant in Plano, Texas. She loved sushi, but since I was not as fond, I thought that would be a good compromise.

Despite our extensive phone calls and pictures on her profile, I was still nervous about meeting. I had gone out on first dates that initially sounded great, but when we finally met, the women either didn't look like their photos or there wasn't that click between us. I was hoping for the best but prepared for the worst.

Trying to sync our arrival time, we were still on our cell phones when she pulled into the parking lot of the shopping center and parked her car a few spaces away from mine. At that moment, my jaw almost dropped. She was driving the same car that Carolyn had: a dark blue 2000 Volkswagen with black bottom accents. The only difference was that Carolyn's car was a Passat, an upgrade from what Genea drove.

Stepping out of the vehicle under the glare of the parking lot lights, she was dressed in casual jeans and a light shirt with long sleeves that complimented her figure. She had long, straight blonde hair almost down to her thighs and looked just like the pictures in her profile.

Approaching each other, I greeted her with a simple, "Hello," and gave her a friendly hug, gently pressing against her body. To break the ice, I playfully asked, "Are you disappointed?"

Without hesitation she said, "No," and asked me the same.

322 • JAREK AMBROZUK

In jest, I stepped back, scanned her from top to bottom, and enthusiastically replied, "No, definitely not!"

We both smiled in relief and went into the restaurant. After a twenty minute wait, we were finally seated in the Hibachi grill area along with six others, including a young couple across from us who also appeared to be on their first date. But unlike us, from the looks of things, their night was not going as well.

Normally, I don't have a problem with public display of affection, but for some reason Genea came out of the gate running. Throughout the evening, she would fling her long hair from side to side, wiggle in her seat to get closer, touch my hand or arm each time she made an interesting comment, and literally move her face inches from mine every time she spoke.

Oblivious to everyone sitting around our Hibachi table, we must have looked like two sixteen-year-olds in heat who couldn't keep their hands off each other. At first, all her sexual innuendos made me somewhat uncomfortable, but eventually I decided that if she didn't mind, neither did I.

Other than Genea's forwardness, our first date went great, and it was largely due to our conversation. Transitioning from one discussion to another, we covered the gamut of topics, with most ending in a smile or a giggle to punctuate our mutual agreement. Everything seemed great until the subject of school came up.

Grabbing my hand to examine the university graduation ring I wore, she rotated my hand to get a better look from every angle. She was surprised I got my BSAE degree the same year she had graduated from high school, even though we were only one year apart in age according to my Yahoo profile. Impressed by my early academic accomplishments, she said nothing else, so I simply smiled and changed the subject.

Throughout dinner, our conversation flowed so well we literally lost track of time. A waitress eventually came by and asked us to leave because they were waiting to seat another party. I quickly paid the bill and we walked out of the restaurant, still chatting away but now holding hands.

During the week, Genea and I had discussed an exit strategy if for some reason things didn't work out between us on our first date. The plan was to end it without any hard feelings if either of us felt uncomfortable. If everything was going smoothly, though, the alternative was to drive to my house to watch movies and relax.

Now standing in the parking lot, holding hands, it seemed as if we both knew where this was heading. Being a gentleman, I still asked her for a confirmation. She agreed without hesitation and followed me to my house less than fifteen minutes away.

Once there, I gave her a tour of my bachelor pad. We started off with an introduction to my blue-fronted Amazon parrot, Cal. He was not the friendliest bird to strangers, but Genea nonetheless thought he was adorable.

After a quick peek outside at the pool and the hot-tub, we made our way upstairs to my game room where a dart board was mounted next to the bookshelf with all my aerospace engineering books from college (see Document: 7512 @ www.ambrozuk.com). Since I now worked in the IT industry, they were there collecting dust simply for sentimental reasons, but to Genea, they meant much more. She looked at the thick books all nicely arranged on the shelves, pulled out a couple to thumb through the pages, and made a strange remark: "They are real!"

During our week of conversations, she had shared many details about her previous online dating experiences, and one thing that came up repeatedly was *trust*. She had plenty of stories to tell, and every one of them had something to do with a guy who was dishonest about his previous relationships, his marital status, how much he earned, or what he did for a living. She eventually confessed this repetitive behavior was so prevalent in her life that even her coworkers encouraged her to verify everything I said.

Genea had two favorite quotes she lived by: "three strikes and you're out," and "I give guys just enough rope to hang themselves." She explained all her previous relationships had failed because, eventually, every guy would fulfill her expectations.

Listening to her that night, I could not help but wonder if she was determined to catch every guy in a lie or if those were words of caution. Since it was our first date, I put aside my doubts about the girl who came across as happy-go-lucky on the phone and tried to look for a brighter side in our future.

Making our way back downstairs to the living room, I was ready to show off my greatest boy-toy of all time—the THX 7.1 Dolby Digital Surround Sound theater system I had put together over the years. Girls had their hair salons, massages, shoes, and shopping, but for guys like me, there were toys for big boys. At the top of that list were my two Texas-sized 73-inch TVs, each accompanied by their corresponding surround sound systems. Although the house was not designed with a state-of-the-art media room in mind, watching movies in my living room was comparable to a night out at a theater. All my friends and ex-girlfriends were always impressed by the setup, so I was very excited to show Genea one of my greatest possessions.

Queuing up a DVD with the intro THX logo, I cranked up the volume on the receiver to amplify its crystal-clear sound and waited for Genea's reaction. Most people were awed by the full and thundering resonance that encompassed the room, making my black leather sofa shake.

But not Genea.

As the THX sound filled the room, she put both of her index fingers in her ears and started yelling, "Too loud! Too loud!" With her face scrunched up, she bent over and hopped from one foot to the other like a five-year-old in pain.

I immediately turned down the volume but was surprised at her unusual reaction to something that most people regularly experienced at the movies without causing a scene. Trying to diffuse the situation, I suggested we get comfortable on the sofa while I picked out a DVD that she had not seen before. Pausing frequently for comments and side stories along the way, we eventually got through the movie and decided to adjourn to the bedroom for Round Two. Her unconventional work schedule meant she was still wide awake, and we agreed to get more comfortable on my bed if we were to watch another film on my other big-screen TV.

After changing into a pair of shorts and a T-shirt I loaned her, we reclined on the bed. I queued up the next DVD that would last until 4:00 a.m., while she snuggled up with her head on my chest.

When the movie ended, I offered her the option to stay the night either in the spare bedroom upstairs or in the bed we were already in. There was plenty of room on my California King bed, so she opted to crash next to me as we both turned in for the night.

I had a hard time falling asleep that night. Everything was going great, and the sheer adrenaline of finally finding someone who shared many of my interests made it difficult to wind down. I tossed and turned for a while, but eventually I too fell asleep and didn't wake up until half past nine that morning.

Since it was Sunday and neither of us had any plans for the day, we decided to continue our date by watching another movie. I loaned her a brand-new toothbrush, we both quickly freshened up, and within minutes were back in bed cuddling, ready for another round of chitchat between the DVD pauses.

After the movie and a quick lunch, I suggested we get out of the house and take a ride in my Viper. It was early afternoon when we finally got into my Firebird and left for Kim and Ken's house less than fifteen minutes away. After a brief introduction and a few minutes of small talk, I pulled my Viper out of Kim's garage and put the convertible top down.

Although it was March and reasonably cool, there wasn't a cloud in the sky. With the car heater fully cranked, it was a pleasant drive to my land on Lake Ray Hubbard where I eventually planned to build my home. Making our way through thick shrubs and grass to the bottom of the properties that terminated at the shoreline, our visit was brief. But it was enough for her to confirm that my plans and my two lakefront lots we had talked about previously were real.

When we returned to Kim's house to swap cars again, Kim and Ken had already started the party and were waiting for us with drinks in hand. They insisted we share a toast before we left, and Genea and I reluctantly agreed. Everyone seemed to be getting along great as the magic of alcohol kicked in, and we began dancing in the living room. From our clubbing days, I knew Kim had moves, but that night Genea stole the show. After years of going to clubs by herself because her ex-husband refused to participate, her dance moves now rivaled the best of the exotic dancers. Dancing with Kim and Carolyn was always fun, but for some reason, with Genea it felt distant and awkward right down to my lap dance at the very end. I appreciated the lap dance—what guy wouldn't?—but it felt more staged and artificial than genuinely passionate.

When we eventually settled down for another round of drinks and more conversation, that's when the subject of my work and upcoming trip to Japan came up. I was working on a project for Honda Formula One and would be heading back to Asia the next month for a week of business meetings to finalize some of the logistic application features we were developing.

"Are you going to take Genea?" Kim asked, out of the blue.

Everyone looked at me, waiting for an answer.

I was caught off guard and wasn't sure how to respond. I had known Genea for just over a week and had only met her in person the day before. Now I felt pressured to commit to a weeklong vacation. On one hand, it seemed like things were moving a little too fast, but on the other, I felt like everything was going great between us so far. Without much deliberation, I replied, "Sure I will!"

As soon as I had said it, I realized how absurd the idea was. I pledged to take Genea, a woman I had just met, on an all-expenses-paid trip to Japan!

But she seemed excited about the holiday. She even told us that it always had been her grandmother's dream to visit Japan.

It was no doubt a hasty decision on my part, but it had its benefits: travelling together would inevitably show if we were actually compatible.

After an exhausting evening of dancing and surprising conversations, we said our goodbyes and left for my house. That night, Genea stayed at my place again. We watched more DVDs in my bedroom, making it the longest first date ever.

The next day, she invited me to her house in McKinney to see her home and meet her three cats. It was a quaint little bachelorette pad that wasn't extraordinary . . . with one exception: when we walked into her bedroom, a loaded two-barrel shotgun rested against the nightstand next to her queen-size bed. She explained the gun was for her protection, despite the house already being armed with an alarm system. Sure, this was Texas, and she did live alone, but a shotgun was the last thing I expected to see.

In the short few weeks I was with Genea, with the exception of venturing only once to a local bar for half an hour, watching DVDs and talking was all we did, whether at my house or at her place while she did her StairMaster exercises before heading to work. We found out a lot about each other—from things we enjoyed to things we still wanted to do to things we could now do together. Our conversations always flowed, and the more I learned about Genea, the more I thought she was my twin.

We both liked science-fiction movies, the same type of music, and working on projects around the house, to name a few. At times, it seemed like whatever one of us said, the other felt the same way. With an endless supply of topics to discuss and agree on, we slowly became the couple who would finish each other's sentences.

On the surface, things were progressing splendidly between us. But there was still my curiosity about the loaded shotgun in her bedroom, and it wouldn't be long before I found out the reasons behind Genea's trepidation.

CHAPTER FIFTY

Champagne Wishes, Caviar Dreams...
and Wall-to-Wall Carpeting?

July 9 – 16, 2007
Day 314 – 321

IT WAS JUST after lunch when they "pulled chain," and I was transferred from Grayson County to Denton County Correctional Facility (see List: 9220 @ www.ambrozuk.com), my home for the next several months where I would get to live it up in luxury as I waited for my federal case to resolve. Other than my legal papers and the bare minimum clothes on my back—a pair of socks, a T-Shirt, and boxer shorts—I had to leave everything else behind, including thirty dollars' worth of commissary food and hygiene products I had just received. After distributing the items among the guys who had helped me get the ever so valuable *Busted by the Feds* book, I was checked out and transported by van to the new facility along with five other detainees.

Waiting eighteen hours in a temporary cell to be processed and housed, we were first disinfected one at a time. Standing naked in the shower area with arms in the air, head bowed and eyes closed, a guard misted de-licing fluid all over our bodies like an exterminator fumigating for cockroaches, using what looked like a professional-grade bug sprayer with a long nozzle attached to a propane tank. Sanitized, sterilized, and decontaminated, only then were we allowed to take a shower and assigned new clothes—orange two-piece uniforms for state detainees, dark blue for federal, and the classic prison chain-gang, black-and-white stripes for inmate workers—before being moved to Pod P-16 at six o'clock the next morning.

The newly built unit held forty-eight intermingled state and federal detainees, and was, hands down, one of the cleanest and nicest facilities I'd had the pleasure of visiting so far. The L-shaped pod had twelve bunk beds fanning out from the center in each direction, three telephones, a small PlayStation 2 gaming console room, and a larger area on the right used during visitation. Just beyond the guard desk, ahead of the main floor area, there was a forty-by-forty-foot outdoor REC yard, enclosed by cement walls with the ceiling exposed to the open sky. There were also two bathroom areas with several sinks, toilets, and stalls on either side of the pod, and three showers on the left side that could be used throughout the day.

But the main area in the center was the most impressive. It contained not only two TVs, mobile chairs, and square tables each with a built-in checkers game board, but also *berber carpeting* that covered the entire floor. It was just like the guys in Sherman had described.

The entire place was run like a military camp, neat and tidy, right down to folding and placing your blanket at the foot of the bed when leaving your personal area. Other than the questionable food, when hot meals were served with a soybean-like meat extract having no flavor, I very much appreciated the upgrade in accommodations—everything except for the fourth TB skin test. My last test spot from Grayson County was still visible when the nurse injected more of the tuberculosis protein under my skin, uninterested in the explanation of my test history.

But despite the nonexistent medical tracking between the federal detention centers, everything else seemed to be as good as one could expect from a federal facility. In fact, things got even better on Thursday, when I was moved to Pod 4 in the old wing, with more seasoned detainees and a much calmer and quieter atmosphere. There the ratio of federal to state detainees was reversed—with federal dark blue colors outnumbering the handful of orange coats—and other than the REC courtyard walls painted tan instead of white, the two pods were practically identical.

Discipline was strictly enforced, requiring permission for the simplest of tasks like using the phone or changing the TV channel. Out of respect, even the TV volume levels were kept at a minimum, with complete silence required several times a day during rack down for a headcount after every meal, and during pod cleaning.

When I finally settled down, got a PIN number, and called Renata, there was good news and bad news. The good news was that my change of plea court appearance was scheduled for Tuesday, July 17, 2007, thereby expediting the court process and ultimately my sentencing. The bad news was about more pillaging of my finances. Not only was the jury consultant still making excuses about refunding the bulk of our pre-payment, but now there were more questionable charges from my Montana attorneys.

The latest was an itemized invoice from Mr. Jent calling for an additional $4,720.00 for legal research fees (see Document: 5260 @ www. ambrozuk.com), which in his email, Mr. Watson referred to as consulting fees. But was that really what they were? First, according to our contract, any expenditure over $1,000 needed to be approved by me in writing. But the real question was whether that legal research was the attorney's responsibility instead of being farmed out and billed to the client as an extra expense. Exactly what did the $150,000 retainer we had already paid Mr. Watson and Mr. Jent cover?

As vexing as their audacious looting seemed, more amusing was the lengthy article my sister found on the web from Paul Peters, a reporter from the *Missoula Independent* newspaper, who attempted to summarize my state case. "A Fugitive Truth" (see Document: 2230 @ www. ambrozuk.com) was the reporter's version of events pieced together from available information and various newspaper articles, with a few

332 · JAREK AMBROZUK

interesting highlights conveniently supplied by none other than my
nemesis, Sheriff Jim Dupont.

Now retired, the Sheriff found himself in the spotlight once more,
as he indiscreetly voiced his opinions about the twenty-four year old
accident. In 2005, he called me "an S.O.B." in a *Daily Inter Lake* article (see Document: 2201 @ www.ambrozuk.com), but since then I
had escalated to the status of a sociopath. Based on his interpretation
of the evidence, his judgment was that I didn't save Dianne and should
have. He was as loud as he was opinionated, with an excuse and finger-
pointing at everyone except his own incompetent actions. When asked
why he never went to Texas to track me down, he told the reporter that
the County didn't have enough money back then to pay for his airplane
ticket and hotel. Dupont was known by many for his arrogance and colorful exaggerations over the years—including his fellow deputies—as I
eventually learned during my stay in Flathead County. What he lacked
in deductive reasoning, he more than made up with lies, false accusations, unprofessional conduct, and pure flamboyance.

Take, for example, the three phone calls I made to Tom between
September and November of 1982. The calls were made from two different telephone booths within blocks of each other. They were all well
documented in the evidence (see Document: 7500 @ www.ambrozuk.
com). All he had to do was look at the available evidence and call the
Dallas Police Department to pick me up, and yet this pride and joy of
Flathead County couldn't even do that correctly. I don't know how that
man ever got to the rank of sheriff.

Renata and I had a good laugh about the article, but a putz like
Sheriff Dupont was not worth getting perturbed over. Instead, I focused
on much more important and pressing issues: taking my turn at cleaning the toilets and sinks, sweeping and mopping the floors, vacuuming
the carpet, wiping off tables and counters, and cleaning the windows. I
wasn't going to learn a trade in the federal detention centers, but when I
eventually returned to Canada, there was no doubt I would make some
lucky lady very happy with all my newly acquired domestic skills.

As much as I enjoyed wallowing in betterment, there was still a case pending. Monday evening, Ms. Knight showed up to go over the ambiguous sentencing guidelines. She also gave me the PSI report questionnaire to fill out before my meeting with the federal probation officer after the change of plea hearing. As before, we didn't make much progress with the sentencing guidelines, but I hoped that at least some of my deductive reasoning had sunk in. After all, it was Ms. Knight who recommended *Busted by the Feds*, the main reason why I was now questioning my attorneys' computations.

CHAPTER FIFTY-ONE

The Federal Change of Plea and the P.O. Interview

July 17 – 27, 2007
Day 322 – 332

I ARRIVED AT the courthouse during the late morning hours on Tuesday for my scheduled change of plea hearing in Sherman, Texas. Before the hearing, I met with all three attorneys in a small Plexiglas-divided room, next to the courtroom entry doors, to go over several outstanding issues.

The first priority was obtaining a notarized legal court document to prove my true identity. Renata had taken on the task of changing all my property titles into my proper name, but without a certified document that identified "Michael Lee Smith" and "Jaroslaw Ambrozuk" as one and the same person, she was running into complications.

This was not your typical everyday problem, but a court document like my INDICTMENT (see Document: 3701 @ www.ambrozuk.com) or ORDER FOR WRIT (see Document: 3706 @ www.ambrozuk.com), that already contained both names—JAROSLAW AMBROZUK a/k/a MICHAEL LEE SMITH—should have worked fine. Yet after a month of repeated attorney requests, none seemed willing to get it notarized through the court system. They also felt that asking the judge for such a document during my change of plea hearing would be inappropriate, but eventually Mr. Watson agreed to get it notarized in the next few days.

In preparation for my court appearance, we went over the entire contents of the plea agreement, with Mr. Jent taking the lead, before moving on to the more important computation of my criminal history points. Everyone was in agreement about my Offense Level 10 in the sentencing guidelines—+8 for the passport charge, +4 for using the passport in the U.S., and –2 for taking responsibility—but my criminal history points were still in question.

Being the authority on federal law among the three, Mr. Jent agreed that because my criminal endangerment and criminal mischief state charges resulted from the same incident, they should be counted as a single felony. Where we differed was with the number of points that it carried. With a stack of photocopied legal papers he had brought to support his argument, he insisted I would receive two points rather than one for the state charge, based on the fact I had spent more than one month in jail. But his reasoning seemed in direct contradiction to what *Busted by the Feds* stated. I did not spend any time in jail. I had spent nine months in a *detention center*, waiting for my sentencing and/or to go to trial, and that was not the same thing.

What would happen, for argument's sake, if I had bonded out the first day I arrived in Flathead County? Since there would have been no jail time, would my criminal history category then also be zero? That made no sense; my jail time should not be an arbitrary number based on whether or not I could bond out. It should be based on the judge's ruling at my sentencing—in my case, ten years suspended with no prison time. Jail, detention center, and incarceration might be synonymous to most people, but to Mr. Jent, whom Mr. Watson referred to as a "federal expert," there should have been a distinct difference, especially if his interpretation could be the difference between my probation and incarceration.

Unfortunately, the resolution to that dilemma would have to wait for another time. It was getting close to my hearing and I wanted to throw out a couple more options for the attorneys to think about that I had recently come across during my reading—specifically, Downward Departure and Early Disposition.

Early Disposition[xii] was not available in all districts. They would have to do some digging to verify if that proceeding even existed in the Eastern District of Texas, but I was determined to give the judge every excuse to send me home to Canada during my sentencing.

None of the attorneys offered any comments about my newest findings, but eventually Mr. Watson ended their silence by bringing up two other possibilities: 5K1.1 Letters[xiii] and the Safety Valve[xiv]. Although I had read about them both and knew I was not eligible for either, I did appreciate his attempt to at least look outside the box.

When our time was done, I was briskly escorted by the U.S. Marshals into the courtroom to begin my hearing. A large, round, bronze crest with the words "Eastern District of Texas" was proudly mounted on the wall behind the judge's seat. I sat down on the side bench and noticed my three attorneys engaged in conversations with the prosecutors. In addition to the court stenographers, there were also a couple of lawyers representing two other detainees there for arraignment. Within minutes of my arrival, the judge walked in and began the hearing.

---

xii. Early Disposition, available only in certain districts, allows the judge to give the defendants sentencing concessions in exchange for a prompt guilty plea and a waiver of procedural rights such as the right to appeal. This fast-track program, if applied to aliens, requires immediate deportation due to state and/or federal felonies.

xiii. 5K1.1 Letters allows non-mandatory minimum offenders to remain eligible and receive a departure from the applicable guideline range by providing substantial assistance to the government. For example, when a defendant cooperates with the prosecutor and helps the government investigate or prosecute someone else, the sentencing court may "depart downward" and recommend a shorter range of sentences.

xiv. Safety Valve is a provision in the Sentencing Reform Act and the United States Federal Sentencing Guidelines, authorizing a sentence below the statutory minimum for certain nonviolent, non-managerial drug offenders with little or no criminal history.

U.S. Magistrate Don D. Bush presided over my change of plea on behalf of the sentencing judge—Richard A. Schell—and immediately got down to business. Taking my place next to Mr. Jent in front of a podium, the judge warned me against making any false statements on record as they could result in additional charges. He then went over the entire plea agreement one paragraph at a time. Pausing periodically only for my acknowledgement, he accepted my change of plea to guilty at the end of his reading, wished me good luck, and I was motioned by one of the U.S. Marshals to head for the exit door.

It was quick and painless, and with my attorneys in tow, we all returned to our original small visitor room, where a federal probation officer was now also waiting behind the Plexiglas.

Lori A. Carlson was a middle-aged woman who seemed pleasant, yet reserved, as she introduced herself and commenced with the PSI report questionnaire I had filled out the day before. Page by page, she reviewed the document, asking non-confrontational questions until we got to my state charges. She seemed curious not only about the case, but also why I didn't return home after the accident. As my federal charges had nothing to do with my state case, her line of questioning seemed irrelevant, but I answered her all the same, with sincerity and without a second thought.

In general, our conversation flowed without incident or uncomfortable pauses to warrant skepticism. But before our meeting ended, she asked a couple of questions that Mr. Watson and I found curious—specifically, where I would be moving to after my federal case was over, and if I intended to sell my house in Texas. Asking once was understandable, but when she asked again at the end of our interview, her persistence seemed suspicious. Was her heightened curiosity a foreshadowing? Perhaps she was privy to some federal insider information that no one else was yet aware of. But at that point my attorneys and I could only speculate. We ended the interview on a positive and seemingly sympathetic note.

My sentencing was tentatively scheduled two months from the date of our interview in order to allow time for the PSI report revisions. According to Ms. Knight, the probation officer would have up to thirty days to come up with her recommendations in the PSI report before we could review it and correct any mistakes through motions in the ten days that followed. Until then it was simply a waiting game.

And what better way to spend time than with my inspiring family close by. On Thursday, Renata and her kids flew into DFW Airport, intending to party it up at my house by the pool for the next three weeks. Because they were out-of-towners, they would get to visit me three times a week—Tuesdays, Thursdays, and Saturdays—with their time extended to forty minutes instead of the usual twenty minutes given to locals. Between my sister and her family, Carolyn, and a few visits from my weekly Friday night Halo gaming tournament friends, it wasn't difficult to maintain a positive outlook, despite what seemed like a never ending list of unresolved issues: my Corvette release, the jury consultant refund, my loan repayment, and even Merrill Lynch added more stipulations before they would release my frozen accounts.

According to Mr. Cohen, Merrill Lynch was willing to free my assets only under the condition that I sign an agreement preventing me from suing for punitive damages—including, but not limited to—depreciation of stock values, maintenance fees, and attorney expenses. If I decided to fight, I would have to pay another $5,000 upfront for an independent arbitrator at NYSE Inc., and $12,000 for my attorney to fly to New York to argue the case, which, at best, according to Mr. Cohen and the account agreement I originally signed with Merrill Lynch, would only get my attorney fees back.

How was that for Merrill Lynch treating their clients with fairness and professionalism while looking after their best interests? I may not have been an attorney, but I could tell the difference between right and wrong—and this was, without a doubt, wrong.

But given all the drawbacks, at least things in Denton County were getting better over time. With the warm Texas sun shining brightly overhead, it was sometimes hard not to feel as if I never left home. Tanning and playing handball to get some exercise during the day, and watching TV in the evening for entertainment, it seemed only natural there would also be a solution to supplement the mediocre food being served daily at the facility. Everyone called it "cooking," and it included the participation of practically the entire pod.

Close to nine each night, we would split into small groups of four or five men before beginning the daily ritual. Everyone in the group would contribute their commissary items—ramen soup, jalapeño peppers, cheese, refried beans, and sausage, among other food items—to make a concoction of sorts that would eventually be rolled into a burrito. The ingredients were first mixed in a sealed plastic bag, before the pouch was placed in the sink full of hot water to "cook" for several minutes. Using a separate plastic bag, the flour tortillas were also warmed in hot water before being rolled into burritos that were as tasty as the ones from your favorite local Mexican restaurant.

What was astonishing was the generosity most detainees demonstrated, beginning with Phillip and V—two guys I met the first day I arrived. It was not often that complete strangers were kind enough to feed someone for a week, using their own commissary items until I could contribute to the meals myself.

I don't know if I would go as far as to call the federal detention facility experience "Club Fed," but it came pretty close.

CHAPTER FIFTY-TWO

Keep Calm and Carry On

July 28 – August 20, 2007
Day 333 – 356

"HURRY UP AND WAIT" seemed to be the norm as I awaited the probation officer's PSI report. Fortunately, there was always something fascinating going on in Denton County to keep me amused. From making full-size soap bars using shampoo, lotion, and the small, brittle bars that were readily available, to making tattoos using a sharpened staple and black ash from burnt plastic, there was never a dull moment thanks to the many creative detainees who often appeared antsy. But in between their entertainment and the occasional humor from my friends and family to keep me grounded, my focus remained steady on the passport charge. I continued the quiet battle with my attorneys regarding the criminal history points.

I was disappointed, and quite frankly dumbfounded, that it was I who had to convince *my own attorneys* about their incorrect computations. I could read just as well as they could, and by then I was sure they were wrong. Perhaps none of their clients challenged their legal expertise, but I was not about to pass up an opportunity to make them see things from my perspective.

To that end, on Sunday morning and Monday night I went to the detention center legal library to get information and do more research about my charge. Unlike Kalispell, where the library consisted of twenty law books, Denton had a small room filled with all kinds of digests

342 • JAREK AMBROZUK

and legal material. Most of the books were specific to state cases, but I did find several federal ones that pertained to my passport charge, specifically the 2006 edition of the Federal Sentencing Guidelines Manual—the source material for everything *Busted by the Feds* talked about.

The key to the ambiguity between how Mr. Jent and I computed my criminal history points was based on our interpretation of the definitions of "prior sentence" and "sentence of imprisonment."

USSG 4A1.2 (a) (2) confirmed that my two prior state sentences were to be treated as one because they were related and happened at the same time.

But more importantly, USSG 4A1.2 (b) (2) stated that the portion of the sentence not suspended was to be used in computing my criminal history points.

In my case, I received two ten-year suspended sentences—meaning I did not get any prison time and therefore should fall into Category I with only one point.

I understood that eventually my sentencing would come down to what the judge decided, but his ruling would also take into account the recommendations from the prosecutor and the probation officer. If I could convince my three stubborn attorneys, then perhaps they, in turn, could convince Ms. Carson and Mr. Shipchandler to correctly compute my criminal history points. Sitting helpless in a detention center, it seemed like a long shot. But I had plenty of time and patience, and perhaps with a bit of luck my persistence would eventually pay off.

On August 9, my parents arrived at my house in Plano, Texas. Instead of flying from Vancouver to Dallas, they drove down in their 1987 Toyota Landcruiser (SUV), traversing over 3,900 kilometers (2,400+ miles) in three days. They undertook the exhausting road trip because my dad planned on towing my Firebird back to Vancouver after my sentencing. But until my hearing, they could relax by the pool for the next two months and enjoy the sunny Texas weather as they took over house chores and repairs from my sister. Dad was never one to sit still, and I could tell he was aching to put his maintenance skills to work so we could eventually put the house on the market.

Knowing I was about to get regular visits from my parents, on Thursday I decided to get a haircut and look more presentable. My last one had been over two months before in Kalispell, and it was time to get my personal grooming in check. My two choices: let one of the detainees in our pod cut my hair using a contraband razor blade wedged in between a comb's teeth, or get my haircut from a worker trustee who had access to an actual electric hair clipper.

Looking at it from a scientific perspective, I went with the latter and learned the lesson of dire consequences. The former automotive-mechanic-turned-barber butchered my hair—cutting holes in my head while leaving clumps of long strands hanging down the sides. Rushed by the officer, he tried his best after deviating from his standard crew-cut special. But in the end, it would be the entire pod that got the last laugh.

When I returned to our bathroom and glanced in a mirror, I looked like a child hair-styling project gone wrong. It was so bad even my little niece pointed at me during our visit and said "*Włosy* funny" (*Włosy* means hair in Polish). You know there's something majorly wrong with your haircut when a three-year-old makes fun of it. But the good news was that it would eventually all grow back.

After Renata and her kids left for Canada on Sunday, it wasn't long before I began to miss our face-to-face visits. My parents were great, but it was just not the same as with my sibling when laughter filled our every conversation. It was tough to return to the once-a-day phone calls, but I did my best by compensating with sun tanning and trying my luck at handball.

Equipped with a new pair of sneakers from the commissary, I joined the boys in the fast-paced game that was played throughout day. With my court shoes, I could now move about the concrete floor without slipping, but my hands were another matter.

Because of no manual labor for the past year, it was quite painful when forcefully striking the ball with my bare palm. The first few games were tolerable, but eventually the pain set in as the blood vessels popped, turning my fingers purple. It wasn't long before the guys began calling me "royalty." But that quickly subsided after my ingenious idea: the "Denton County Special" prototype gloves.

Instead of sulking on the sidelines until my hands toughened up, I put my engineering skills to good use. Using a pair of socks, I cut holes for my fingers in the toe area and inserted a piece of thick notepad cardboard backing in between my palm and the sock to act as padding. The gloves were crude, but worked brilliantly. I could play all day, and to everyone's surprise, it wasn't long before I started winning games.

It was inevitable that my ingenuity would be deemed contraband by some guard, but until that day, "Look out, Texas!" because I was on my way to becoming the Denton County Detention Center Hall of Fame Handball Champion!

CHAPTER FIFTY-THREE

Sex Yes, But the Kissing Sucks

March 2006

EXCEPT FOR HER work hours, Genea and I never left each other's side for the next four weeks. Things were going so well in the beginning that within days we exchanged house keys to better accommodate our schedules. On her days off she came to my place, and during the week I drove to her house before 4:00 a.m. to greet her when she got home from work. Spending so much time together at the beginning of a relationship suggests smothering, but with Genea it didn't feel excessive.

Comfortable with each other, it wasn't long before she opened up about her dark past. During one of our nightly movie marathons—she kneeling on my bed, and I reclining with the TV playing in the background—Genea began a systematic rundown of her past relationships along with the pain that she endured over the years.

One of her first traumatizing experiences, at the age of five, revolved around a break-in and her mother, who also had a double-barrel, loaded shotgun next to her bed for protection that she showed off when we visited her a couple weeks later in Longview, Texas.

Not very popular with other girls, Genea was a shy tomboy as a child and spent much of her time with boys riding bikes and skateboards. It wasn't until her late teens when she finally started dating and had a steady boyfriend. He was controlling and possessive and she referred to him only as "Asshole!" They broke up after a year and a half; he not only cheated on her but slept with her afterwards without telling her about his indiscretion. That was unforgivable to Genea—the gravest sin of all.

Mike, her next boyfriend, was very supportive about her modeling career, and they remained friends after their relationship ended. Because of his encouragement, the next few years following high school, she went on to model part time and compete in local and state swimsuit competitions. Occasionally, she won second or third place but eventually threw in the towel and concentrated on her two-year program at a vocational school to become a lab technician.

Lending her my sympathetic ear, I listened and slowly began to see a different side of Genea. Opening up about her other painful experiences from her past, I could only sympathize as she explicitly acted out the vivid details. Kneeling on the bed next to me, she leaned over and grasped my forearm firmly with both hands, "I grabbed him just like that, looked him in the eyes and said, 'Please don't try anything tonight while we're in the hotel room. No sex of any kind, OK?'"

It was heartbreaking to watch her emotions pour out. I wanted to reach over and give her a comforting hug, but I was unsure how she would react. Instead, all I could say was, "I'm sorry, I'm so sorry!" over and over.

It was obvious that Genea was not the bubbly, friendly, and carefree girl she presented herself as during our telephone conversations and on our first date. There were many painful memories she still harbored after so many years.

But among all her adverse relationships, there was one guy who stood out above the rest. His name was Hoyt, and to Genea, he was what Dianne was to me. Like me, he was the only other guy her mother approved of if only during the first time they dated. But, unlike my relationship with Dianne, their love seemed conflicted. Pressured by his friends during their second time around, Hoyt took her on a cruise-ship vacation and got down on his knee to utter the phrase she so desperately wanted to hear. But what his proposal lacked were the words, "I love you." Disappointed but patient, she waited for the rest of the night and eventually confronted him about it the next day. When he still couldn't bring himself to say it, she gave him back the ring and called off the marriage.

They remained friends after the breakup, and although he moved on to another relationship, it often seemed Genea still hoped for his return.

Lying on the bed listening, I wondered what our future would hold. Could we overcome her long dark history and cheaters? Could we get past Hoyt? Those were tough questions that could be answered only over time.

No doubt I appreciated her openness about her turbulent past, but instead of reciprocating in kind with my own history secrets that night, I decided to wait at least until after we became intimate.

Since we first met, Genea and I held hands and snuggled in bed watching movies, but after a week, we still hadn't kissed or made love. Her cardinal rule was no sex for the first two to three weeks or until she felt she was ready, and I had no problem conforming.

On Monday evening, we finally ventured out to a pub for a change of scenery. My friends and I usually went out to bars and dancing on Friday and Saturday nights, but because of her unconventional work schedule, that seemed as good an evening as any.

She took forever to get ready, but when she finally emerged from the bathroom, it had been worth the wait. With her hair straightened, she looked ten years younger, and with a little make-up and flashy clothes, she turned a few heads when we walked into a local pub in Plano. They had a good selection of beer, great food, and, of course, fabulous salsa—the main reason why my friends and I occasionally visited that particular establishment for a pint or two before heading out on the town.

I was looking forward to spending time and having fun with Genea outside our homes, but things didn't work out as expected. As soon as we walked in, the mood between us became awkward. She insisted on sitting at the bar rather than a booth, and with her acting prim and proper, we struggled for words. It felt like I was on a first date with a girl who was there for show rather than to have a good time.

I had a couple of beers and she a glass of wine before I paid the bill and we left for the next pub, hoping to improve the atmosphere. The Irish bar had darts, live entertainment, and an incredible selection of 120 beers on tap, but it was closed on Mondays. Disappointed but undeterred, we decided to head back to my place to continue the evening on a more casual note.

Looking forward to something other than watching DVDs, I turned on some music as we quickly changed into more comfortable clothes. Intending to play Cricket darts, I was still setting up the scoreboard when Genea finally came upstairs wearing one of my T-shirts and her Victoria's Secret undies.

We were not even at first base and here she was half naked with her derriere exposed. But who was I to complain? I complimented her on the choice of clothes with a witty remark, and we transitioned into our first game of darts. Not even halfway through the first round, Genea suggested we start doing beer shots each time someone scored. And that was fine by me. After a week of listening to depressingly sad life stories, I was ready to add some excitement to our somber evening.

The darts kept flying and the shots kept flowing for almost an hour before both of us called a truce. Looking for a change of scenery, we relocated downstairs for another round of DVD watching in the bedroom. But unlike our previous nights, things were about to get more intimate.

Genea made herself comfortable on the bed, lying on her stomach with her butt cheeks flashing out of her tight undies. Although I wasn't blind to her sexual come-ons, after hearing about her past I was not about to take the initiative without her approval. I waited patiently for her to make the first move, and it didn't take long. She jumped to her knees, lunged over in my direction, and planted a long kiss on my lips.

It wasn't the worst kiss I ever had, but it wasn't something I would remember for the rest of my life. Like our trip to the pub, it was awkward, and for some reason it felt choreographed and unnatural. But neither of us said anything other than her making a comment about satisfying her curiosity.

Kissing may have been awkward, but sadly our intimacy turned out to be even worse. Rather than feeling natural, we seemed to struggle, and the more I concentrated, the more my mood shifted from excited and anxious to optimistically cautious. I made an effort to be as gentle and considerate as possible, but the more I focused, the more I could not get past her icy stare.

From Dianne to Carolyn, lovemaking was always pleasurable, and I went out of my way to make sure it was mutual. Occasionally, there were initial jitters, but I never had to deal with such extremes. All the things I once thought were remarkable about Genea now took a backseat to our intimacy issues. In time, this would become our undoing, just like her relationship with Hoyt that was also plagued by similar frustrations.

In the days that followed, we continued to talk on the phone when she was at work, and spent the weekends at my house and work days at hers, spooning in bed as we fell asleep. Sometimes, we even had sex with relative success, but the passion and the excitement I had experienced before was never there. Instead of affection, our relationship mutated into more of a tolerable acceptance infused with an underlying fabric of hostility.

A case in point was our shopping experience for a digital video camcorder I intended to buy for our trip to Japan. Browsing the aisles of an electronics superstore, we came across various keyboard instruments, including a thin piano keyboard made of cloth that could simply be unrolled, turned on, and played. Genea hadn't touched a piano for over eight years, but she played it like a pro.

Recalling the years of my accordion lesson disappointments, I was genuinely impressed and made an innocent comment about her skill after so many years. Rather than appreciation, she responded with irritation because I was complimenting her too much. I should have done it in a different way, she said, and not put her on a pedestal.

After almost three weeks together, things were not getting any better. But like a hopeless romantic, I was still determined to salvage our slowly deteriorating relationship by trying a new approach—appealing to her need for honesty.

There would never be a perfect time to tell her about my past, the accident, or age, but if I was going to do it, it had to be before we left for Japan. I had already bought her plane tickets, and despite my initial thought of saving the big news for when we were relaxing in a hot tub in Kyoto, I felt convinced this could not wait. She seemed to have so much animosity built up inside about honesty, and after seeing her outburst in the electronics store, I was not about to take a chance 4,500 miles away to see what her reaction might be.

It was a typical sunny Texas day when we decided to get lunch in her part of town. Genea often visited the cafeteria attached to a large chain grocery store located in a McKinney shopping center. We ordered our food and found a table upstairs surrounded by a few patrons sitting on the outskirts of the small dining area. As always, there was trivial conversation between us before we got to the subject of education and college. And that was when I told her my real age.

Looking at her expression and trying to gauge her reaction, I could see she was not taking the news well. Clenching her mouth, she hit the table with the side of her closed fist, and with a vexed voice blurted out, "I knew it! "

Our age difference seemed so negligible compared to all the problems we were experiencing with our relationship and intimacy. Personality, physical attraction, and how they inspired and made you feel, were so much more important than the number of years in between. If actor Catherine Zeta-Jones could fall in love, marry, and have children with Michael Douglas—a man twenty-five years her elder—then perhaps so could Genea, given a chance and the right circumstances. If there had been no connection when we met, at worst she got a free dinner with no strings attached. But it seemed silly to pass up an opportunity for a meaningful, long-lasting, and loving relationship because of something as trivial as age prejudice.

Hearing me out, she seemed understanding but questioned why I didn't tell her earlier—specifically several nights before while going over her twenty-item, "how to find the perfect man," criteria. Yes, she actually had a checklist based on her friends' successes, which included the declaration, "He will not be more than ten years older than me." When I confessed it hadn't felt right before now—and pointed out that our age difference was still within her range—she seemed empathetic, albeit somewhat more reserved.

Given our latest discord, I wondered about our vacation plans and bluntly asked if she still intended to go to Japan. She briefly thought it through and, to my surprise, confirmed that she was still in. I had expected a much bigger reaction, but since everything appeared to be back on track, we finished our lunch and left the cafeteria shortly after still holding hands.

Back at her house, before heading off to work, she changed into her workout clothes and got on the stepper machine, while I turned on the TV and sat down on the couch with her cats. In between the movie scenes and our usual commentary, I debated whether this was also the right time to tell her about my past.

My alias was a secret that only Kim, Ken, and Carolyn knew, but if I was to build a stronger bond with Genea and earn her trust, I needed to come clean about that too. By doing so, I might not only help bring us closer but possibly solve our intimacy problems in a single swoop. Until then, she knew only as much as everyone else did about Dianne: she had been my high school sweetheart and had died tragically in a plane accident. I never went into much detail about how she died or what my mental state was like afterwards. Most people, including Genea, were content not to dig deeper.

There was no easy way to interweave into a conversation what I was about to divulge. I opted to use the movie we were watching to find what seemed like an appropriate moment to disclose that Dianne

352 • JAREK AMBROZUK

did not die in just any plane accident. I explained how we were in love, how we came up with the crazy plan to elope, and how, in the blink of an eye, my life changed forever.

Without a big reaction to the startling news, she listened curiously while continuing to bop up and down on her exercise machine. Every now and then, she asked a question, but in general, the details of our elopement didn't faze her enough to pause her exercise routine.

But the light bulb went off when I got to the part about coming to Texas and getting a new ID. It finally dawned on her that Michael Smith was not my real name, and neither was my birth date. I explained how I had obtained my new identification, but she was more interested in my real birth date. It seemed unusual to focus more on that than the details of the accident, but I would later find out the reason behind it—Genea was a firm believer in astrology and horoscopes.

While at work, she would read me our daily horoscopes, elaborate on their significance, and explain how we were compatible based on our astrological signs and how the suns, moons, and stars aligned. Coming from a science and technology background, I could never understand how someone's birth month had any bearing on their disposition. If I was born six months earlier, would I now have a different personality and be more compatible in a relationship?

But this wasn't random to Genea—this was religion. It was all about the cusps, and how we were compatible in some things and clashed with others. Now that she had learned my real birth date, all her prognostications would have to be reevaluated because I was suddenly a Cancer, not an Aries.

Moving past the name and birth date dilemma, I went on to explain the details of the accident, including the sinking of the plane with Dianne still inside, and that was when I got teary-eyed.

Genea was still on the stepper machine, but when she saw my emotions pour out, she finally paused and came over to give me a gentle hug of sympathy. Unlike the age disclosure earlier, she seemed much more understanding about the accident and my new identity.

That night at her work, while we were still on the phone, she googled my last name and found the only article referencing my case. It was a piece from *The Daily Interlake* that Chery Sabol, a reporter in Kalispell, Montana, had written in February 2005 (see Document: 2201 @ www. ambrozuk.com). The article corroborated my story, but we were both in disbelief over the negligent homicide charge attached to my name.

The article stated I was featured twice on *America's Most Wanted* program, but when she searched their website, there was nothing. Discussing the article in detail, she didn't appear bothered by the charge and was surprised that the Flathead County authorities were treating this like a crime of passion.

When we hung up the phone that night, Genea seemed fine with the new developments, including the details of the accident. I waited patiently through several days for her to truly appreciate the gravity of my past before I again asked if she was still on board with our vacation. She may have been confused about some things—perhaps a bit standoffish at times—but she never wavered about the trip.

And so our plans for our first excursion began.

CHAPTER FIFTY-FOUR

The Federal Pre-Sentence Investigation Report

August 21 – 29, 2007
Day 357 – 365

THE FIRST DRAFT of my probation officer's PRE-SENTENCE INVESTIGATION REPORT arrived on Tuesday (see Document: 3724 @ www.ambrozuk.com), and although not as controversial as my state case, it had its share of questionable facts and details.

Created on August 16, 2007, the eleven-page report included a cover letter stating that my attorneys had fourteen working days to file objections with the U.S. District Clerk regarding any outstanding issues that could not be resolved by telephone with the probation officer.

Compiled by Ms. Carlson using various sources—details from our interview, the Equifax Credit Report I had signed off on, and documents she resourcefully had obtained from various city, state, and federal governments—the majority of my demographic information appeared correct. All except for my release status date that read July 3, 2007, rather than May 21, 2007, the day of my state sentencing and officially becoming the property of the U.S. federal government. Adding another month and a half to my federal detention time would be significant when the judge looked at how long I had waited for my sentencing. Fortunately, that was easily correctable by my attorneys.

What was not simple to fix was Part B of the Defendant's Criminal History, where Ms. Carlson computed my criminal history category as II. Based on my two state felonies, she defined it as "10 years' probation, 270 days jail." Like Mr. Jent, she assumed the time I had spent in the detention center was considered jail time, thus counting it as if I had been incarcerated.

More surprising was the Other Criminal Conduct section, where for the first time a complaint for forfeiture in rem appeared on any federal government document against me. Filed by the United States District Court for the Eastern District of Texas, Sherman Division, the complaint alleged that "the defendant stole the identity of Michael Lee Smith from a deceased child and used it to commit the following offences:

False Statements in violation of 18 U.S.C.§ 1001,
Loan and Credit application Fraud in violation of 18 U.S.C.§ 1014,
Identity Theft in violation of 18 U.S.C.§ 1028,
Mail Fraud in violation of 18 U.S.C.§ 1341,
Wire Fraud in violation of 18 U.S.C.§ 1343, and
Bank Fraud in violation of 18 U.S.C.§ 1344."

Because I had used my assumed identity on various loan and title documents to purchase my two cars, my house, and my land, the federal government was now in the process of repossessing my legally bought property.

As absurd as these allegations were, I was more angered than surprised because of what I was told by my lawyers. Since the day of my arrest, I repeatedly asked every attorney if the government could take any of my property. Every single one of them, including Mr. Watson and Mr. Jent, had reassured me that because everything was purchased legally—with no stolen funds or drug money—I had nothing to worry about. But despite their confidence, every one of them turned out to be *wrong*. They may have all talked the talk, but apparently they knew diddly about federal civil law, and now I faced the possibility of losing everything.

I recalled the interview with Ms. Carlson at my change of plea hearing and her repeated inquiries into whether or not I was planning to sell the house. Now her questions made a lot more sense. The civil lawsuit by the federal government had obviously been in the works for some time, but somehow they managed to keep it off the radar from even my attorneys.

Those may have been serious allegations, but there were also a few humorous paragraphs in the report that reminded me of Flathead County. They read as if all the probation officers graduated from the same school of pessimism. Unable to find any unfavorable references to my model conduct over the past twenty years, Ms. Carlson wrote:

An Internet search for assets was conducted, but due to the fact that the defendant has been using a false name, a very common one at that, and a false Social Security Number, the reliability of the report was suspect.

False name and false social security number? Suspect? I think not! My IDs and social security number had been issued by the U.S. government, making them as legitimate as they could possibly be. In fact, they were the reason why she was able to run my Equifax credit report, look up my criminal history, verify my employment, and find all records pertaining to my assets, including my cars and my properties.

Putting aside her attempt at embellishment, what really mattered was Part D—the sentencing options at the end of the PSI report. Going by the book, she noted that statutory provisions carried a maximum term of imprisonment of ten years. Furthermore, the guidance provisions—based on my offense level of 10 and criminal history category of II—put me in a range of eight to fourteen months of imprisonment, as defined in Zone C of the SENTENCING TABLE (see Document: 3751 @ www.ambrozuk.com).

My proposed fine was also computed using both statutory and guidance provisions, with $250,000 maximum and $2,000–$20,000, respectively.

That brought us to the last page of the report—sentencing recommendation. There, the probation officer split the middle of the guideline provisions and recommended I get eleven months in custody and pay a fine of $10,000.

A recommendation of eleven months in the penitentiary would not help me with the judge at my sentencing if I was hoping for probation. After a quick call to Renata, we conferenced with both my Montana attorneys that same afternoon to get their feedback. In his typical manner, Mr. Watson downplayed the severity of the report and tried to reassure us everything was going according to plan.

I didn't know which plan he kept referring to, but it was definitely not mine, considering very few things had turned out as expected, at least from where I sat.

Instead of the Montana negligent homicide being dismissed, I ended up with two charges after his negotiations with the prosecutor. My state restitution, which he all but guaranteed would not exceed $15,000, turned out to be in excess of $41,000 because he was on vacation in Italy and left Mr. Jent in charge. And after reassuring me that my property was not in peril because everything had been bought legally, the federal government had just slapped on a complaint for forfeiture in rem lawsuit, where I could potentially lose all my assets on a technicality.

So exactly how was all this going according to plan?

But the worst of it was that it was the third time I had to ask Mr. Jent—the federal law expert and the man responsible for the court filings—to again look into the sentencing guidelines definitions we disagreed on. After paying them a ridiculous amount of money, at minimum I expected a relentless pursuit from both attorneys to reduce my eleven month recommended jail time—preferably down to probation.

It was not my responsibility to find ways to minimize my sentencing; that was their obligation—without my having to nudge them repeatedly along the way. What I expected was for them to do their job.

CHAPTER FIFTY-FIVE

One Year and Counting

August 30 – September 18, 2007
Day 366 – 385

AUGUST 30, 2007: It was official—I'd been in detention centers for over a year. Surprisingly, after all that had transpired and all I had endured mentally, physically, and emotionally, I still felt pretty damn good.

I had my family back in my life and talked to them and Carolyn daily, and that largely contributed to my positive outlook. Even though I was still in the middle of the federal passport case, with immigration pending, it felt like the end was within reach.

On Thursday I received news from Mr. Jent regarding my complaint for forfeiture case. After some research, he believed it to be a case of double jeopardy[xv], because the federal government agreed not to prosecute me for any other non-tax related charges in our plea agreement.

Surprised at the forfeiture, even the federal prosecutor was going to call the district attorney handling the civil case to see why they were pursuing the lawsuit. But at the end of the day, the responsibility laid squarely on the shoulders of my two Montana attorneys.

---

xv. The double-jeopardy clause—based on the Fifth Amendment to the U.S. Constitution that states, "No person shall … be subject for the same offence to be twice put in jeopardy of life or limb"—prohibits state and federal governments from prosecuting individuals for the same crime on more than one occasion, or from imposing more than one punishment for a single offense.

During our conference call Friday, Mr. Watson explained that from the way paragraph #8 was written in the PLEA AGREEMENT (see Document: 3719 @ www.ambrozuk.com), I should have been protected against the government filing any other federal or civil non-tax related charges. Obviously that was not the case. Because of their oversight, Mr. Jent then drafted a letter to Mr. Shipchandler, hoping, in turn, that he would convince the civil case prosecutor to dismiss the lawsuit given his ample rationale.

But despite all the promises and back-pedaling, their efforts seemed futile. If they couldn't produce an iron-clad plea agreement to prevent the forfeiture from being filed in the first place, what were the chances a letter or a phone call to the civil prosecutor would have a different result? With no bargaining chips and no incentive for the district attorney to dismiss the forfeiture case, their after-the-fact efforts seemed like nothing more than pointless busywork.

Luckily, for every disappointment I faced, there always seemed to be an equal and opposite force to balance out the unfavorable. This time, that miracle came on Thursday in the form of capitulation from both Mr. Jent and Ms. Knight. After weeks of persistent nagging and frustration, they finally agreed that my criminal history points should be counted as Category I rather than II. If they could likewise convince the prosecutor and the probation officer, that would reduce my federal sentencing guidelines incarceration range down to six to twelve months. Perhaps a negligible difference by itself, but by the time my sentencing hearing arrived, I would have spent over four months in the federal detention center. That might be just enough to convince the federal judge to give me probation—and let me move on to immigration.

With my passport case somewhat stagnant until my sentencing, fortunately there was always something tumultuous happening in the pod to break up the monotony. Early Sunday afternoon, a corporal came into our pod with an aerosol can to set off the smoke detectors and force a rack down.

As the alarm echoed between the pod walls, six guards showed up and began moving everyone into the REC yard, systematically checking every locker and mattress. Looking under the bunks with a mirror and a light to make sure nothing was hidden underneath, they overturned even the dayroom tables before returning to the courtyard to administer a somewhat personal if unorthodox inspection.

Cracking down on the few brave souls engaged in tattooing, the purpose of the inspection was twofold: find the homemade needles and ink and identify the culprits.

Following a five-minute warning speech about the severity and consequences for those involved, the corporal instructed everyone to spread out against the four walls and begin removing one article of clothing at a time, shaking it in front to make sure nothing was hidden inside. The disrobing went on for several minutes before we all stood in the courtyard naked as jaybirds, our hands cupped over our crotches, wondering what to expect next.

Inspecting each of us from head to toe, looking for fresh ink markings or tattoo swellings on the body, the guards eventually located the guilty parties before allowing us to dress.

Like tattoos, gambling and Fantasy Football were also against the rules in Denton County. Before leaving, the corporal in charge made sure everyone understood the repercussions. "If you don't stop, you will be racked down for an entire week with no REC and no privileges."

Limiting what forty-eight ornery men could do in a confined space for twenty-four hours a day was not easy. But after my personal experience with the rack down in Shelby, I was hoping that the agitators would mellow out—at least until after my sentencing.

On Tuesday, a half-inch thick package arrived from Renata, who had been busy digging up information about my latest civil case with the federal government. After some Internet research, she came across PACER—a government website that contained a list of documents pertaining to my complaint for forfeiture in rem case (see List: 9050 @ www.ambrozuk.com).

362 • JAREK AMBROZUK

At the forefront of the list was the affidavit from Alejandro L. Johnson, Federal Special Agent, who had spent close to a year researching me, my background, and my assets (see Document: 3802 @ www. ambrozuk.com).

On the surface, the civil case appeared justified, but aside from legality, it didn't make sense from a moral perspective. If I had used stolen or used drug money to buy any of the properties in question—or if I had taken over an identity and then defrauded the individual—I could see how they would have a valid argument. But that was not the case. I took over a deceased child's identity and never harmed anyone in the process; there was no stolen property to recover, and there were no victims of identity theft. But after wasting so much time trying to prove me a criminal, this was about finishing what the government agents started whether justified or not.

It was several days later when I finally received a copy of Mr. Jent's letter to Mr. Shipchandler, stating his reasons why the forfeiture case should be dismissed (see Document: 3726 @ www.ambrozuk.com). Although his arguments in the three-page letter were compelling, the litmus test would obviously be the reply from the federal prosecutor, who held my fate in his hands—not only in my passport case, but now also in the forfeiture lawsuit.

CHAPTER FIFTY-SIX

The "Complaint for Forfeiture In Rem" Summons

September 19 – October 10, 2007
Day 386 – 407

EVER SINCE MY PSI report, I was aware of the pending COMPLAINT FOR FORFEITURE IN REM civil case, but it would be Wednesday morning when the federal government made it official. At 9:00 a.m., a U.S. Marshal showed up in the detention center and presented me with the SUMMONS papers (see Document: 3806 @ www.ambrozuk.com).

At the same time, they went to my home in Plano, Texas and—to my parent's dismay—seized my house and my cars. Until it was official, Renata and I kept the forfeiture under wraps so as not to worry our family. Imagine my parent's surprise when U.S. Marshals knocked on the front door and told them they were confiscating all my property. With my Viper already on its way to Canada, they towed my 1996 Firebird Formula—which my father planned to haul back north—and placed a seizure note on the front door of the house. When my parents asked for an explanation, they were told it was due to my involvement with *drugs*.

Obviously, that was pure nonsense—perhaps nothing more than a jerk reaction from the U.S. Marshals who automatically assumed the worst scenario. But until everything got straightened out, we had no choice but to take the house off the market.

Selling my property after my arrest would have been the smartest course of action. But since every one of my attorneys—beginning with Leigh Davis from Texas to Chuck Watson and Larry Jent from Montana—were convinced I had nothing to worry about because I had purchased my properties and cars with legitimate non-drug money, I now had another federal government case to deal with, forcing Renata to return to Texas earlier than necessary.

While my sister and I searched for federal civil attorneys, on Monday I received a copy of the letter from Mr. Shipchandler refuting Mr. Jent's plea to dismiss my civil forfeiture case (see Document: 3727 @ www.ambrozuk.com). Naively hoping the assistant U.S. district attorney would also look at this from a moral perspective, my optimism was quickly crushed after reading his three-page retort.

Using historical case references to counter my attorney's arguments, the prosecutor pointed out that my civil case was not in breach of contract with respect to my plea bargain, because it was not filed against *me* but rather *my property*. He quoted the case of "United States vs. URSERY," 518 U.S.267 (1996):

> *a forfeiture proceeding in rem means that '[i]t is the property which is proceeded against, and, by resort to legal fiction, held guilty and condemned as though it were conscious instead of inanimate and insentient' Id at 275.*

". . . property . . . held guilty and condemned as though it were conscious?"

What the hell was that all about? A *resort to fiction*, indeed!

Could you not make a similar—equally absurd—argument about your cell phone being conscious and sentient because the personal assistant talks to you when it answers your questions and gives you driving directions?

It was hard to believe the law allowed attorneys to make up such piffle and get away with it as legitimate arguments in court. That was the federal government's best argument despite no one else claiming rights to my property and everything already converted to my proper name with help from Mr. Cohen over the past several months.

The most damning part of the prosecutor's letter, though, was a footnote he included as a warning. If my attorneys decided to pursue this further, possibly bringing it up at my sentencing hearing, Mr. Shipchandler cautioned their intentions might be construed as not taking responsibility for my criminal actions. This "may be viewed in a less favorable light at sentencing," he admonished. Meaning that if my two points for taking responsibility were taken away, my sentence would put me in a range of ten to sixteen months rather than six to twelve months, and perhaps make it less appealing to the judge who would ultimately decide between probation and custody time.

I still had a difficult time comprehending how everything I had bought throughout twenty-four years could be treated independently, as if there were no rightful owner. At the same time, I could not ignore the possible consequences at my sentencing. I had not heard anything from my attorneys regarding the rebuttal letter, but I was sure they were well aware of the risks and realized how they had grossly underestimated the United States government.

On a lighter note, I became acutely aware of how small our world really is—even within the confines of my current habitat. What were the odds that in 1982, a teen in Alaska who had heard about our elopement, would now be sitting next to me, asking about the case details? He recalled many debates between his parents and their friends as they sifted through the facts reported by the media on TV and in the newspapers. Listening to my side of the story and the reasons behind the elopement, the man—now in his late thirties—could only shake his head in disbelief.

Like so many others, he had heard all the hype and speculation behind a possible sinister plot that may have been involved. With people like Sheriff Jim "Hollywood" Dupont and Sheriff Al Rierson—a gung-ho, wannabe writer of our elopement story in 1982 (see Document:

3129 @ www.ambrozuk.com)—it was no wonder their embellishments over the years had painted a dismal picture of what actually happened. Their public opinions on what they thought happened, why they thought it happened, and how they would have done things differently, may have been the Flathead County standard of professionalism, but by the time our conversation was over, at least one misinformed detainee had discovered the truth.

On Thursday—while playing handball outside with the boys—I was called out by the guard on duty to meet with a potential civil federal attorney, Mr. Mickelsen, to go over my forfeiture case in person. Unshaven and covered in sweat, I walked into the visitor booth to meet with the clean-cut, middle-aged man there for a job interview.

For those still keeping score, we're up to nine attorneys: Clancy (dismissed), Davis (Texas State), Sherlock (Montana State), Palmer (Corvette release), Cohen (Merrill Lynch), Watson and Jent (Montana State, and Texas Federal cases), Knight (Texas Federal), and now Mr. Mickelsen.

During the last few days, Renata and I had spoken to several civil federal attorneys about taking on my forfeiture case. Out of all of them, he sounded the most optimistic and promising.

Two days before, we had conferenced with a more seasoned lawyer, who cautioned we should be prepared not to get back 100 percent of my seized property. My circumstances were unique and non-drug related, but throughout his career he saw many cases where the client got back anywhere from 90 to 10 percent of their assets once the dust settled. Despite his experience, and being the most qualified to predict the final outcome, I wasn't ready to concede to the U.S. government with a defeatist attitude just yet; hence our opting for Mr. Mickelsen.

In his nineteen years of experience, he also said he'd never seen a circumstance where the defendant recovered 100 percent of their property. Optimistically, he speculated that my case had the potential. He went as far as to suggest that because of my situation—specifically no guns or drugs involved—the case could set precedence for governing regulations, including how the government seized personal property in the future.

As with every previous attorney, he sounded sincere and made a lot of compelling arguments, all but suggesting a favorable ruling in the end. It was the typical sales job from an attorney who was there to solicit business, but I felt comfortable enough with his presentation to possibly accomplish what my two Montana attorneys were not capable of doing—dismissing the civil case altogether.

Along with a claim to sign that he intended to file in court by Friday, identifying me as the rightful owner of my seized property (see Document: 3809 @ www.ambrozuk.com), he brought a couple of contracts for review. One was for a straight $300 per hour rate with a $60,000 cap, and another for a $20,000 non-refundable retainer with an additional $20,000 if we pursued a jury trial (see Document: 5450 @ www.ambrozuk.com). As that was a substantial money commitment that—until my Merrill Lynch money was released—would have to be funded by my parents, I had to discuss it with my family before any decision could be made. And that was how we parted ways.

With my federal sentencing date set for October 11, it was Monday when Renata and I contacted my attorneys, who had been keeping a low profile after receiving the reply from the prosecutor thwarting their efforts to dismiss my civil case. There were courtroom protocols to discuss and what to expect when I appeared in front of the federal judge.

But that was not what my attorney wanted to talk about once we got on the phone. What Mr. Watson was more interested in was *Vanity Fair*. This was the fourth time he brought it up in as many months, and it was becoming irritating. My state case hadn't turned out well—a hefty restitution and two felonies rather than the negligent homicide charge being dismissed—and the federal case was not looking that promising either. Yet publicity from a *Vanity Fair* article by one of his acquaintances, an author who had previously written several New York best-seller books, now seemed to be his priority.

When I denied his request for a phone interview and expressed my disappointment with the forfeiture case, he mitigated the extent of his liability by casually pointing out my civil lawsuit was not accounted for in our contract. To that extent, he was correct, but neither was publicity at my expense. I asked that he drop any further discussions with reporters until both of my federal and immigration cases were over.

Following our conference call, I returned to my daily routine for the next ten days, until I "caught the chain" the day before my hearing. Generally, detainees wouldn't be moved to another detention center if they were expected to get prison time, so things were finally looking up on Wednesday when I was told to roll up because I was going ROA, or "Release to Other Agency."

Starting at 9:45 a.m., the transfer to Grayson County Jail took the entire day. They shuffled me from one temporary cell to another, re-booking me as if it were my first time, before I dressed and was moved into a pod at close to 4:00 A.M that morning. I had spent six days there three months previously and was quite familiar with the routine, including another attempt at a TB test by the nurse on duty. Eventually, I got settled in and managed to get a couple of hours' sleep before they woke me to get ready for the big day in court.

CHAPTER FIFTY-SEVEN

What? A Free Vacation? Sure, I'm in!

March – April 2006

THE CLOSER IT got to the day I was supposed to leave for Japan, the more hesitant I was about my vacation with Genea. I had committed to the trip the second day I met her, and ever since then our relationship had gotten worse. It was perplexing to think I had been paying for everything—buying her groceries, six bottles of wine she never drank, and now I was about to drop thousands of dollars in Japan—all while we were still drifting further apart. But being a man of my word, and considering she had already reserved her vacation days at work, I decided to make the best of our trip.

The plan was for me to leave in the beginning of April, and when my business meetings were over with Honda, I would rendezvous with her a week later at the Narita International Airport in Tokyo. The timing seemed perfect, because that was the start of cherry-blossom season. The two-week event was well known on the island, and the ultimate place to experience it was in Kyoto. I had hoped the spectacular, blossoming trees (see Document: 7222 @ www.ambrozuk.com) would also set the mood for us to rekindle our romance.

But Genea seemed lackadaisical about our trip and uninterested in making any plans, including booking our accommodations for the ten-day stay. I didn't mind being spontaneous, but going to a foreign country where you didn't speak the language was no time to wing it. The annual phenomenon was incredibly popular with tourists, making it next to impossible to get a hotel in Kyoto at such short notice. Instead, based on my Honda meeting schedule, weather patterns, and meteorological predictions of the event, I let the Honda Logistics department I was working with book our lodging.

While I was away, Genea offered to look after my house, my pool, and my parrot. When it was her turn to fly out, Kim would take over and not only watch my house but also feed Genea's three cats.

After my week of productive meetings with Honda, it was time for Genea to join me in Japan to kick off our vacation. But during her drive to the airport with Kim, she burst into tears and had an emotional meltdown. I didn't find this out until after we returned from Japan; according to Kim, Genea confessed she didn't know if she could fall in love again, that she probably wouldn't have agreed to go on the trip except that I had already purchased her ticket by the time I told her my age, and a slew of other confusing mental hang-ups. Kim said she was quite a mess and almost missed her flight because she couldn't pull herself together and wouldn't get out of the car. Eventually, she did stop sobbing and boarded the plane along with my new video camcorder I ordered at the last minute and had shipped to her house.

She arrived at Narita Airport in Japan on Saturday, and as soon as she walked through the arrival gates, I could tell from her body language that this vacation was not going to be what I hoped. Walking towards me, she seemed unenthusiastic, and the sparkle in her eyes that one would expect when beginning a romantic holiday was nowhere to be found. We greeted with a gentle hug and a cordial kiss before grabbing our suitcases and heading for the train that would take us to Tokyo.

There, I purchased a pair of round-trip tickets on the Nozomi Shinkansen—the fastest of the three bullet trains—and we left for Kyoto. Holding hands, kissing, and intertwining our legs, we spent the next three hours on the train discussing my Honda meetings and our upcoming sightseeing tours we were about to undertake. But her confusing romantic signals were unmistakable. She seemed receptive to being intimate, yet I could still feel a cold distance between us.

When we disembarked in Kyoto, we found ourselves in an underground subway station trying to find the right street exit to the surface. There were hundreds of people hurrying past us as we tried to orient ourselves using a station map to figure out which of the four exits would put us on the right path to our ryokan. Although the map accommodated four different languages, including English, the exits on the map didn't seem to match the signs in the subway terminal. We must have looked at the map for over two minutes before I finally walked up to one of the uniformed subway conductors to get some assistance. When I returned to the spot where Genea was still standing with the map in her hand, she looked furious. In a harsh tone and with an indignant look on her face, she said she was just about to figure it out and couldn't believe I asked for help.

To that I had no rebuttal. I stood there dumbfounded about her outburst regarding such a trivial matter. We were disoriented, in the middle of a busy subway station in a foreign country, and I just got reamed out for asking about directions. In that moment, I realized the tone for the rest of the trip was set.

Genea would eventually attribute this outburst to her PMS at the time (see Document: 7240 @ www.ambrozuk.com), but there was more to her temper than she was willing to admit.

We spent that night in the Takaragaike Prince Hotel outside of town, returning the next day to Kyoto for sightseeing and accommodations at our first traditional ryokan later that evening.

Pulling a few strings, the Honda Logistics team managed to book us in Hiiragiya Ryokan—a Japanese inn dating back to the Edo period. Conveniently located in the center of town, it was just what we needed after an exhausting day of touring and aching feet. Hidden among the city buildings, the ryokan from the outside appeared unspectacular, but inside it captured the traditional authenticity of old Japan and its culture. From the water-covered rock entryway, to the century-old sculptures and artwork in our room, the mood was set for a relaxing evening. The accommodations consisted of a single room where one ate and slept, with the staff simply swapping the two-foot high table and chairs for a futon bed at night. The floors were covered with tatami mats on which we walked barefoot while wearing the traditional *yukata* robes that were also included (see Document: 7223 @ www.ambrozuk.com).

With hours to spare before dinner at eight—and the weather forecast calling for possible rain the next day—I was ready to venture out to the nearby parks and see the picturesque cherry-blossom scenery I had heard so much about. But Genea was not interested. She appeared apathetic and said she was tired and wanted to stay in. There were a thousand places to go, and a million things to explore in this new world of unknowns, but we ended up spending the next four hours in our room taking photos with my camera and testing my new digital camcorder.

Our traditional Japanese cuisine dinner consisted of a number of small, varied, seasonal and regional specialty dishes known as *kaiseki*. (see Document: 7225 @ www.ambrozuk.com). The host, dressed in a kimono, a maiko wig, and white facial make-up with contrasting red lipstick to complement the cultural authenticity, brought out a few delicacies at a time—every ten minutes for an hour and a half—before we were both full.

When booking the room through Honda, I also requested access to a private bath. It was Japanese custom to take a "soaker bath" after dinner in a large, cedar-type spa. Although everything was extra, I spared no expense because this was meant to be the experience of a lifetime. Typically referred to as a public bath, that night it would only be us during the allotted time slot. The room was enclosed in cedar paneling, with the fresh scent permeating the steam-saturated air. To set the mood, a small nature scene was visible from behind the glass window, but even that was not enough to spark romance between us. In the end, we settled for a few kisses and more mundane conversation.

During the next couple of days we continued to explore Kyoto, alternating between paid tours with English speaking guides and our own excursions. Using the local trains and buses, we visited the city's major popular attractions, including the Kyoto Emperor Palace and Park (see Document: 7221 @ www.ambrozuk.com).

The sightseeing may have been spectacular, but Genea's behavior was confusing. She kept her distance for the most part, but would occasionally surprise me by laying her head on my shoulder during train and bus rides, holding hands, or insisting we browse the Kyoto jewelry stores for engagement rings to compare our styles and taste.

Perplexed by her polarizing behavior, I could have spent the next ten days figuring it out but instead decided to cut to the chase. Choosing my timing carefully during one of our complimentary breakfast buffets, I brought up the subject of us. When I confessed I didn't know why we were having intimacy problems because this had never been an issue, Genea flipped out. She took my comments personally, thinking I was blaming her. I repeatedly tried to explain that was not what I meant, but by then she was furious and wouldn't listen to any reasoning.

That was our first major argument, and for the first time I became genuinely uncomfortable around her. She appeared hostile and bitter by the time our breakfast was over, and we returned to our hotel room to finish packing before heading to our next ryokan. Confused but considerate, I bluntly asked if she wanted to cancel the rest of the trip, reschedule our flight tickets, and head back home to Texas.

But Genea wasn't about to end the trip of her lifetime that easily. Realizing what was at stake, she quickly changed her tone and opted against the cancellation.

The next three days we spent touring Todaiji Temple, Nara Park, and Kasuga Shrine, before returning each night to the more modern Shoenso Ryokan. Although the hotel was also equipped with our own private soaker bath on the balcony that overlooked a wooded area, the romantic setting made little difference to our now subdued evenings of tolerance.

After an exhausting week in Kyoto, we boarded the Shinkansen and headed back to the more modern city of Tokyo and its wonders. Checking into our hotel, we continued our self-guided tour of attractions for the next several days. Having visited the city on two separate occasions, I offered to take Genea to some of the more interesting places I had previously explored. We went to the Tokyo Imperial Palace, in the heart of the city, with its surrounding gardens, sculptures, and scenery, the orange Eiffel-like Tokyo Tower with its spectacular skyline during the evening—where we opted for a cheeseburger at McDonald's after many days of nothing but traditional Japanese meals—and Akihabara, the Electric Town as it was known.

While shopping in Kyoto's small, local shops, I bought Genea and her mom a couple of expensive kimonos and a bunch of souvenirs for her friends and co-workers. But during our excursions, we never found the perfume and men's cologne she was looking for. In Tokyo, surrounded by hundreds of department stores in the middle of Electric Town, that was no longer a problem. Still being optimistic and believing we could reconcile, I once again splurged and bought her a large bottle of perfume, expensive lipstick, and a make-up kit that I thought would at least buy me some brownie points. Although I was now starting to feel like a sugar daddy, it seemed a small price to pay if it improved her mood and possibly our disintegrating relationship.

During our wanderings through shops along the subway route, we came across a small boutique that reminded me of a Halloween costume store. There were lots of fairly inexpensive casual clothes for men and women—including shirts, pants, and dresses—but there were also a few garments that seemed a bit more risqué and right up Genea's alley. One such item was a black dress that had a large, wavy gap running the length of the front. The dress was held together by three strategically placed clasps in front, but because of its design, no undergarments could be worn without being seen. The knee-length dress seemed more appropriate for a lingerie show than a night out on the town, but since it was under $50 and we both liked it, I bought her that too.

Exhausted from sightseeing and shopping, I looked forward to going to Roppongi Hills—a nightlife area of Tokyo where lots of tourists and locals came to party on Friday and Saturday nights. But when we returned to our hotel, Genea had other plans. She immediately went into the bathroom and after what seemed like half an hour, she came out with her hair in a bun, wearing the black dress. Slowly walking toward me, she looked nice, but looking good in a dress was not her problem—being sexy was. Her movements seemed awkward when she began her lap dance, and her attempt at seduction seemed artificial. Although we eventually got through our klutzy game of foreplay and sex, I don't think neither of us found it enjoyable before we turned in for the night. Spooning on the small bed pushed against the wall, watching some meaningless Japanese program on TV, I tried to figure out why we seemed to have everything going for us yet couldn't get over this hurdle.

On our final full day in Japan, we spent the better part of the afternoon at the Tokyo-Edo Museum. It was a large building with many exhibits ranging from ancient Japan to World War II. Our mood was dismal, and Genea now appeared to go out of her way to keep her distance. Understandably, we were both frustrated and fed up with each other, but she took it a step further. Throughout the day, she made subtle comments and hints about how we should split up for a while and remain friends. We had touched on this once before during our walk to the Tokyo Tower, but it was now undeniable that she just wanted out.

While I still had hope things would eventually work out, in reality I was also ready to end the pointless struggle and simply move on.

We tolerated each other throughout the day at the museum, but when we finally returned to the hotel later that evening, that's when the "shit hit the fan." Relaxing in our room watching TV, we eventually got to the subject of relationships, Carolyn, and, of course, Hoyt. Genea went on about how once, in a record store, he nonchalantly mentioned her moving in, and how great those words made her feel. That was at the beginning of their relationship, but even now it seemed he was still very much on her mind.

When Genea and I first met, and I heard about her traumatizing history, I told her I had no problem waiting until she was ready. But

I didn't think that meant getting over a guy she had broken up with years before (and dated many others since). If you've tried twice with a guy you loved, but since then he's moved on to someone else, take the hint and get on with your life. It's good to talk about your past, but unhealthy to still live in it. Normally, I am very understanding about people's emotional baggage, but even I have a breaking point.

We sat on opposite beds in our tiny hotel room as Genea rambled on about Hoyt, how great he was, and what a wonderful relationship they had. For the last month and a half, I had showered her with gifts and paid for everything—including her trip to Japan. But now instead of a thank-you, all I heard was how Hoyt was this and that.

I had reached my limit, and out of frustration finally said, "So, I guess you just weren't good enough for Hoyt!"

I had spent weeks trying to cater to her physically and emotionally, hoping until the very end we could still get past our romantic problems. But all Genea could do was to give me the cold shoulder as she walked around moping about Hoyt. I felt used, unappreciated, and didn't know how else to make her snap out of her delusional fantasy I had no place in.

In retrospect, that probably wasn't the nicest thing to say to someone who was still hung up on a guy from years ago, but to Genea, my comment was the straw that broke the camel's back.

She looked furious as she got up from the bed and stormed into the bathroom. She emerged a minute later and said that was the first time in twelve years that anyone had made her so angry. You could see the blood rushing through her veins on her face as rage boiled inside her. I never found out what had happened to her twelve years earlier that made her as livid, but I suspected it was in reference to her husband.

Furious and perturbed, she disappeared into the bathroom for the next twenty minutes as I sat on the bed wondering what the hell just happened. Hearing the water running, I went in to make sure she was all right. Sitting naked in the bathtub—her hands wrapped underneath her bent legs, and her head resting between her knees—she stared aimlessly into the water pouring out of the spout. I asked if she was OK, but all I got back was, "Leave me alone!"

I tried asking again, but she raised her voice once more and told me to leave her alone. Confused about why she seemed so violated by my comment, I wasn't sure if I should continue to console her out of fear for her safety, or just let her be so she could calm down. But by then, I had exhausted my patience with her attitude and said, "I'll leave you alone soon enough," and walked out of the bathroom.

It took another ten minutes before she came out with a towel wrapped around her body and started explaining how this was the worst thing I could have possibly said or done. I still had no idea why she took such offense to my trivial comment as her voice rose and her tone became contemptuous.

"Genea, please don't yell at me."

"I'm not yelling at you!"

"Then please don't raise your voice at me," I calmly reiterated.

The more time I spent with Genea, the more frustrating our relationship became, and the more I felt like she was here only because of a free trip to Japan. I felt taken advantage of.

When I brought it up, she quickly denied it, "I didn't use you!"-

"I didn't say you used me. I said it feels like you used me."

She was taken aback by my observation and realized that our trip, along with her intentions, were not as noble as she wanted to believe. She took a long pause and, perhaps out of guilt, offered to pay for her half of the vacation. I didn't care that several days before, she had broken my $700 digital camera when she tripped in the Tokyo Imperial Palace and it smashed on the concrete sidewalk, so I wasn't expecting her to pay this back either. Knowing she was on a strict month-to-month budget, I sympathetically said, "Don't worry about it. Just look at it as a gift," and left it at that.

Without so much as a thank-you, we turned in for the night.

The next morning, after I got out of the shower, I felt bad about what had happened the night before. I asked Genea as she sat on the bed ready to go, "Can I talk to you about something?"

All I wanted was to apologize again and clear the air, but she still seemed on the defensive. "Oh God, what did I do now?"

Appearing much more in control, I ignored her lingering irate attitude, said my piece, and asked for a friendly hug to reconcile. We must have stood there for over two minutes in silence, holding each other motionless with our arms wrapped around our bodies. This wasn't some cheap pat-on-the-back hug a girl gives a guy knowing she'll never see him again after a bad date. It was a full embrace hug that seemed sincere yet confusing.

I didn't know what to make of it, but I was done analyzing. Our trip was almost over and at least we cordially tolerated each other until the very end.

Our flight out of Narita Airport was not until early afternoon, giving us a few hours before departure. We checked out of our room, stowed our bags with the hotel concierge, and decided to find a café within walking distance to get brunch.

Being mid-April, the Tokyo weather was still a bit chilly. I was bundled up in a long- sleeve shirt and my long, black wool business coat. Genea, on the other hand, decided to make a statement with her wardrobe. She wore her thin black, shiny, loose-fitting, polyester pants and a negligee-like sleeveless top. Her braless slipover top was silk, with two thin straps holding it up, and her always-erect nipples clearly protruded through the thin material in the brisk, windy day.

As we walked past all the conservative Japanese business locals in their black suits, it was hard to miss their eyes glance first at her, then at me, and then back at her chest. At first, I ignored the stares, but when I finally pointed it out, she seemed surprised. I didn't know if her flamboyance was a way to get back at me, or to make her feel like she was in control, but I smiled and let her be as we walked side by side to the nearest café, oddly still holding hands. She would continue in her skimpy top not only for the rest of the day in Japan but also on our flight back home. Walking through the airport toward our departure gates, I could only smile politely at the oncoming pedestrians glancing in our direction.

We hadn't arrived in Japan together, but when I bought our airline tickets, I made sure we would return home on the same flight—direct to Dallas and lasting approximately thirteen hours. My round-trip business class tickets cost over $8,500 and came with all the amenities, whereas Genea's tickets were substantially less expensive because they were economy class. Despite all that we went through, I harbored no hard feelings and, as my parting gesture of goodwill, offered her one last act of kindness. Realizing that she would probably never fly in business class again, I asked one of the flight attendants if we could swap seats. We traded places, but Genea remained cold to the very end—no acknowledgment of our seat exchange, and once again, not even a thank-you!

CHAPTER FIFTY-EIGHT

The Day of My Federal Sentencing

October 11, 2007
Day 408

UP AT THE CRACK of dawn and excited about the upcoming sentencing later in the afternoon, I started the day by first meeting with my family.

Shaven, showered, and in freshly washed clothes the trustees brought in that morning, I was called out for a surprise visit with only my parents. I had expected to have a visit from Renata as well, but my sister had broken the cardinal rule of visitation—her pants were four inches too short. Women were allowed to wear long pants and skirts, but not if the ankles were exposed in her stylish crop pants. It was a strange rule that we could only snicker at. Our visit was brief, but Mom and Dad were both delighted my federal case would soon be over and I was that much closer to coming home.

After my return to the pod, I expected to head to the courthouse next, but instead, they called me out again at 12:30 in the afternoon for another visit; this time with my sister and my little niece. Laughing almost the entire time, I could not believe my ears when Renata told me she was wearing my dad's long pants to get around the silly wardrobe restrictions. I could only admire her tenacity as I pictured my father sitting in the back of their vehicle in his tighty-whities.

Our visit lasted but ten minutes before I was escorted by two guards to the federal courthouse two blocks away. My family was already seated a couple of benches behind the prosecutor when I arrived. Other than a single reporter behind them, with a yellow notepad in her hand, the rest of the courtroom benches were empty. I took a seat on the side of the defense bench between Mr. Watson and Ms. Knight.

Judge Schell began with a brief hearing outline and called the participants of both the prosecution and the defense counsel.

First up was Mr. Jent, who wasted no time referring on several occasions to 3553(a), the defendant's right of allocution, and the *United States vs. Booker* ruling, where the Unites States Supreme Court decision concerning criminal sentencing stated that the maximum sentence a judge could impose was a sentence based upon the facts admitted by the defendant.

This was the legalistic lingo Mr. Jent was very familiar with, but then, for some reason, he opted to go on a tangent about my state case, which not only confused the issue but was factually incorrect in many instances. An eloquent speaker he was not, as he struggled to explain how Dianne and I had planned our elopement to begin a new life in the U.S. under different identities. He seemed unsure about many details we had gone over in Kalispell a few months back. I wasn't sure if he didn't remember or was trying to pad the story for the benefit of the judge. In either case, there were now several confused listeners in the courtroom trying to follow his embellished story.

Awkwardly transitioning to the PSI report, he pointed out a correction in my criminal history points, which dropped my recommended custody of between six and twelve months based on the sentencing guidelines, before following up with a correction to my writ. It was dropped three days after being filed, but it made no difference, he argued, and I should be credited for being in federal custody for the past year.

The judge listened patiently to his choppy, erratic arguments, and when he ineptly finished, Mr. Watson took over.

Always striving for composure, he too fumbled through his confusing recollection of my history as he presented his version of the arguments. Like his counterpart, he mentioned the 3553(a) and the Booker cases, noting that although everyone was aware of the rulings, he was not there to reiterate the law but simply to point out that the federal sentencing guidelines were no longer mandatory for the judge to follow.

But within minutes, he found himself in the same position as Mr. Jent—expounding inarticulately on our state elopement case. No one, including Judge Schell, had any idea where he was going with his visceral narrative. But when he mentioned the passport as one of the documents I had obtained, Judge Schell stopped him and asked for clarification.

"Why did your client feel the need to get a new ID and passport rather than just use his own?"

Mr. Watson seemed unsure and struggled to come up with a viable explanation.

It was an awkward moment that would eventually reflect on me and my credibility, so I stepped in. With my hands still cuffed in chains, I leaned over to Ms. Knight and whispered, "It was because of work in Japan."

She quickly scribbled "Japan" in large block letters on her notepad, before passing it on to Mr. Watson, who was still stumbling around for an answer.

But even with that hint, he could not connect the dots. Eventually, he simply skirted the question altogether and awkwardly transitioned to his closing remarks about why I deserved probation instead of incarceration.

With his slow, drawn-out diction he noted that the judge had several options at his disposal, including releasing me with time served because of my commendable character and my aging parents' health.

When he was done, Judge Schell turned to me and asked if I had anything else to say to the court.

Eager to make my own defense and clear up some of the ambiguous questions my attorneys had struggled with, I walked to the podium and started with the most obvious and logical statement:

Your honor, first I'd like to say that I take full responsibility for my actions, specifically applying for and obtaining a U.S. passport.

Although I understand that this is not an excuse, I did it for no other reason than to travel to Europe and Japan because of an IT consulting project. My intention was never to deceive or commit a crime in the country where I have lived for the past twenty-four years.

Unlike the state case, I was guilty of the charge and I had no problem taking responsibility. All I asked in return was that the justice system take my earnest admission into consideration.

Hearing me out, the judge reminded me that since the 9/11 tragedy, Homeland Security took passport fraud very seriously.

I acknowledged the caution with a nod before he started his inquiry into the confusing case details that my attorneys had grappled with earlier: the reasons behind our elopement, and how I obtained my alias. Briefly summarizing and explaining that I had gotten my new identity from an obituary, the judge appeared satisfied with my sincerity and candidness, before moving on to the final stage of the hearing—the sentencing.

Joined by Mr. Watson and Mr. Jent on either side of me at the podium, the judge called on Mr. Shipchandler to give the court his recommendation. In a quiet tone, the prosecutor agreed with my attorneys and said the four and a half months' time served would be appropriate.

Turning to the probation officer to ask the same, Ms. Carlson quoted from her PSI report and recommended nine months in custody with three years of supervised release, and a fine of $10,000.

Taking all this into consideration and noticing the complaint for forfeiture in rem civil lawsuit listed in the PSI report, the judge looked in our direction for clarification. No one seemed eager to explain—especially my attorneys now cautious about asking the judge for an additional hearing to resolve the alleged double jeopardy after the prosecutor's warning in his rebuttal letter.

This would have been the perfect time to throw myself at the mercy of the court and explain how there was no real crime committed; how I had given hundreds of people jobs; how I prospered over the years through hard work; how I had paid hundreds of thousands of dollars in taxes; and how I thought the federal government was unreasonable with their forfeiture and accusations of fraud. But I was also mindful how that might be interpreted by the judge who was just about to sentence me for my passport charge. Ms. Knight once told me that of all the federal judges she knew, Judge Schell was one of the more fair and considerate. I was not about to gamble with my possible probation, and therefore I said nothing, leaving my forfeiture fate in the hands of Mr. Shipchandler, who briefly explained the circumstances to the curious judge.

When it finally came to my sentencing, Judge Schell didn't care that the probation officer had recommended nine months in a penitentiary; he didn't care that I had spent months trying to convince my own attorneys I should be at the lower Category I in the sentencing guidelines; and, least of all, he couldn't care less about the little old prosecutor from Montana on a sanctimonious crusade to get me two more years in federal prison as stipulated in his state plea agreement. All Judge Schell cared about was what he thought was fair. He looked up at me, said, "I believe him!" and with a rap of his gavel, gave me time served and a $10,000 fine (see Document: 3729 @ www.ambrozuk.com).

The $10,000 fine I could have done without, but in retrospect, I was finished with my federal case and on my way to Immigration! After a long four and a half months, it felt invigorating to walk out of the courtroom with a smile on my face, knowing that my next stop would be my final at INS.

When I walked out of the hearing and briefly met with all three attorneys in the pass-through booth, they were in a festive mood—including Mr. Jent who sported a rare grin from ear to ear. One by one they congratulated me enthusiastically, but what I was most interested in was what to expect next.

Mr. Watson explained that although no one seemed to know for sure, he had been told by an immigration officer it would most likely take a couple of weeks before I was sent back to Canada. After spending over fourteen months in state and federal detention centers, I had no illusions about their promises or estimates, but I remained optimistic knowing that I would soon be back with my family.

When I called Renata, my parents, and Carolyn, everyone was relieved and excited about the latest court ruling. My sister was going to call INS to find out when I would become the property of Immigration and Customs Enforcement (ICE), and if there was a way to expedite the deportation process. According to their own detainer filed the day I was arrested (see Document: 3901 @ www.ambrozuk.com), they had forty-eight hours to pick me up and move me to wherever they housed illegal aliens for deportation.

Act III: Immigration Case

CHAPTER FIFTY-NINE

ICE Giveth and ICE Taketh Away

October 12 – 21, 2007
Day 409 – 418

AFTER SEVERAL FALSE alarms in as many frustrating days, I was officially in INS custody.

On Tuesday morning at nine o'clock, an ICE officer transported me and two Mexicans to the immigration headquarters for processing. Dressed in my orange jumper suit and a cheap pair of tennis shoes I came in with, we were checked out, handcuffed, and within an hour, standing inside the INS temporary holding facility located a few miles north of downtown Dallas off highway I-35E (see Document: 3917 @ www.ambrozuk.com).

A long counter, on the left of a walkway, divided a book-in area with a dozen ICE officers in front of computers from the four cells on the right that contained close to 100 people. Everyone was waiting their turn in the overcrowded and unsanitary holding tanks that reeked with the stench of sweat, urine, and B.O.

The larger cell, where approximately forty of us were corralled, contained a no-privacy toilet and a single concrete bench for ten people, with everyone else forced to either stand or sit on the dirty floor to give their legs a rest. Even our lunch was nothing short of pitiful, with only a small Styrofoam cup of water, and two sandwiches made from a single slice of baloney wrapped in white bread.

It was definitely not the amazing immigration facility with great food I had been told about by many in Denton County. Fortunately, this was only a staging area until they relocated us to Haskell, Texas, a state prison that doubled as an immigration detention center.

Mexicans comprised 95 percent of the detainees, and most were undocumented aliens. After being offered the option to sign their deportation papers, they were loaded onto one of the two buses that made nightly trips to the U.S.-Mexico border.

For the rest of us with more complicated cases that required a court appearance, it could take months before an audience with an immigration judge was granted. In either case, everyone had to be processed and evaluated, and that took considerable time.

I spent my entire first day in that filthy cell without seeing a single ICE officer before everyone was transported by van to the local Euless City Jail for the night where we ate dinner, took a shower, and got some rest.

It wasn't until mid-afternoon on the second day when I finally met with my "ICE freedom champion," Adam Koeneman. He took me to his office cubicle in the back to go over my paperwork, my cases, and my options after being fingerprinted and photographed at the front counter.

Curious about why a Canadian from Poland was sitting among the Mexicans ready to be deported, we spent over an hour discussing my state and federal case details, while he cross-referenced each of my charges in his INS legal books.

"Not all crimes at the state and federal level are considered felonies in the eyes of immigration, and they often get downgraded to a misdemeanor charge," he said. Because I never received any prison time—other than time served in detention centers—he seemed confident that I would still be eligible for voluntary departure. As my newly acquired federal sentencing was still not showing up on his computer, he wanted to verify the charge with the federal government in Sherman, Texas. If everything was as we discussed, he would talk to his supervisor to confirm his recommendation of voluntary departure.

But when he came back twenty minutes later, he had good news and bad news. The bad news was that his supervisor would not approve voluntary departure, but the good news was that I could post bond and wait to appear in front of the immigration judge from the comfort of my own home.

Voluntary departure was preferable to administrative removal—as I would be eligible to reinter the U.S. almost immediately—and therefore it made sense to take him up on the bond offer while I waited for my court appearance. Initially, the bond he proposed was $30,000, but after I explained my Merrill Lynch situation, he dropped it to a more reasonable $10,000. With a couple of quick phone calls to resolve logistical issues, Renata sent an overnight FedEx containing my Canadian identification and a $10,000 cashier's check to Carolyn, who would then post the bond on Wednesday. When I called my sister a couple of hours later, the money was already on its way. According to Officer Koeneman, if they received the bond first thing in the morning, I would most likely walk out a free man that same afternoon.

But as quickly as my bond offer materialized, it evaporated just as fast the next day after returning to the INS holding facility. Agent Koeneman called me out of the line while they were still removing everyone's handcuffs to give me the disappointing news.

Digging deeper into the charges, and discussing my case with the other officers, he confirmed that my criminal endangerment charge was considered an aggravated felony by immigration, and therefore remained a cause for executive removal without bond.

I was back to square one, my two options being: sign the Warrant Of Removal-Deportation he presented me with (see Document: 3904 @ www.ambrozuk.com), and be deported to Canada in less than two weeks; or fight to remain in the United States, which could not only take months, but I would have to do it within the confines of INS detention centers. Looking at my options from a logical perspective, my choice seemed clear: in less than two weeks I could be back in Canada with my family. I saw no reason to spend months just to see an immigration judge who *might* be sympathetic enough to grant me voluntary departure. I had lived in the United States for over twenty-five years—longer than anywhere else in the world combined—so it seemed only fitting I now return home without further delays.

"Unlike the state and federal governments, we don't want to keep you behind bars," the ICE officer amicably pointed out as he handed me the deportation papers to sign. During the last couple of days he had gone out of his way to get me the best deal, and that was all I could ask for. After signing the papers, they loaded us onto the Greyhound bus heading for Haskell, Texas.

The Rolling Plains Regional County Jail and Detention Center was over four hours away from downtown Dallas. Centrally located in the middle of nowhere, it served not only the state of Texas, but also several other surrounding states. The facility was visible from a distance, even in the dark, when we arrived, with bright lights on the towering poles illuminating the enclosed buildings. It was the closest to a classic prison look I had the pleasure of experiencing so far, with the concertina barbed wire covering the double fences that surrounded the entire complex.

Unlike the state and federal detention centers, here things seemed much more lax, albeit everything still moved at the same snail pace when it came to processing the detainees. It was 9:00 p.m. the following day when I was assigned to an eight-man pod after being fingerprinted, medically screened, and tested for TB once again—literally in the same location on my arm where a red mark was still clearly visible from the previous test.

Other than the meals being similar to Shelby before the lockdown, what this facility offered, comparable to no other, was REC twice a day with various sports equipment, including access to a multilane Olympic-type outdoor track field for those eager to stretch their legs for an hour. Next to the main building entrance door was a volleyball net that stood empty because of cold weather, two asphalt handball courts, a basketball hoop, and three awnings covering the picnic tables with weight machines in between. But the most popular was the track enclosing the soccer field where most of the sport enthusiasts congregated.

With horses grazing in the distance, I made it a point to walk twice a day every day in the fresh air while talking with others about their cases. A few were from Russia, several others from various African countries, and even one from Canada, who was also scheduled for deportation in the coming week.

Although a few were still there six months later fighting INS to remain in the U.S. because of their businesses and/or families, I saw no reason for me to delay my departure longer than necessary. Once all my paperwork was complete and my travel voucher from the Canadian Embassy arrived, I was more than happy to leave—without a dispute—and begin the next chapter of my new life back in my home country of Canada.

CHAPTER SIXTY

Is That Your Final Offer?

October 22 – 24, 2007

Day 419 – 421

AFTER A WEEK of shuffling between Dallas, Euless, and Haskell to eventually accept the immigration offer of administrative removal, on Monday ICE presented me with yet another option I simply couldn't refuse.

Up at 3:00 a.m. to catch the transport back to Dallas, it wasn't until two o'clock in the afternoon when Agent Koeneman finally called me out to tell me that after their attorneys looked into my case again, they couldn't make the aggravated-felony charge stick. Instead, they replaced it with the following four immigration provisions (see Document: 3908 @ www.ambrozuk.com):

1) for a crime involving moral turpitude

2) for being in the U.S. at any time or place other then as designated by the Attorney General

3) for getting a passport, and

4) for falsely representing myself as a citizen of the United States.

Because they were considered lesser offenses, I could bond out if I decided to contest the administrative removal by appearing in front of the immigration judge to plead for voluntary departure.

I was enthusiastic about being deported back to Canada in a couple of weeks to see my family in person after so many years, but the idea that I could be with them in a matter of days while entertaining the possibility of voluntary departure left me ecstatic.

Wasting no time, my sister sent another $10,000 cashier's check via FedEx to Carolyn so she could post bond, then booked a flight back to Dallas on Thursday in anticipation of my release from immigration custody.

It has been a while since my last hearty meal and a cold beer, so I very much looked forward to breathing free air again, giving Carolyn and my sis a great big hug, and being able to carry on a conversation that lasted longer than fifteen minutes.

CHAPTER SIXTY-ONE

Let's Just Stay Friends . . . NOT!

April 2006

AFTER AN EXHAUSTING ten days with Genea in Japan, our relationship had deteriorated to the point of tolerance. I didn't know what the future held, but I had no reason to part ways in anger. Genea, on the other hand, was not as forgiving.

During our two-hour wait to board the plane in Tokyo, and again while we were waiting for our luggage at the airport in Dallas, she made sure I understood that, at best, our relationship was downgraded to friendship only. Hinting I should take another girl the next time I had a business trip was only one way she tried to get her message across. They were not-so-subtle hints she delivered calmly and with control, but they appeared necessary for her closure. I imagined these reminders were there because of her ex-boyfriends who refused to part ways amicably, but I had no intention of repeating their mistake. I kept my options open but accepted the fact that Genea and I were through, and that we would both be better off with other people.

As arranged, Kim picked us up at the airport, and after quickly loading our bags into the car, we headed back to my house. It was refreshing to see Kim with her always upbeat attitude. After spending weeks with Genea walking on eggshells, I had missed the camaraderie that Kim and I shared.

She asked about our trip, but when I summed it up with, "It was nice to have some company," she knew exactly what I meant. To celebrate our return and go over the adventures in Japan, we decided to meet with Ken for drinks. Out of courtesy, I even invited Genea, but when she declined, we dropped off my luggage at my house, I drove Genea home, and on my way to our favorite Mexican restaurant, I called Carolyn to say hi.

For the last month and a half with Genea, I felt like I had been suffocating. Carolyn was the breath of fresh air I needed to cheer me up. We talked for only a few minutes before agreeing to meet at a pub to catch up after I was done with Kim and Ken.

When I arrived at the restaurant, Kim and Ken were already waiting on the patio with three large, frozen margaritas. They were obviously curious about our trip but not very surprised when I humorously summarized it with, "After further consideration in this most important matter, I can only conclude that travelling with Genea sucks!" Recalling Genea's outburst ten days ago during their drive to the airport, and again noticing her demeanor during our drive back from the airport, I think Kim already knew how it all went down but wanted to hear it from me directly.

When I left the restaurant, I headed for my rendezvous with Carolyn. Always giggling and bouncing with energy, she made me realize I could never be happy with someone like Genea who drained the life out of me.

But despite what appeared to be a cordial parting of ways, there was still a dark cloud hanging over my head—Genea knew about my past and seemed spiteful enough to do something about it.

I had already experienced some of her indiscretions when she confided in her co-worker the day after I told her about my past. She justified herself by explaining her co-worker also knew people in similar situations—people who were living in the U.S. illegally using an alias—but her lack of judgment seemed very irresponsible, if not downright alarming. Getting an approval from her co-worker may have put her mind at ease back then, but that was weeks ago when our relationship was in its infancy and everything was grand. After Japan, things were not so cozy between us; I was beginning to worry about her emotional state and the damage she could do simply out of malevolence.

By her own account, she had a track record of ill-parted relationships, and since I couldn't ignore that, I decided to call her the next day at work to schedule our workout at the gym. We had previously agreed to start working out together, whether in a relationship or just friends, and therefore this seemed like a good excuse to smooth any issues left between us.

When she answered with, "What's up?" in a cold, standoffish tone, I knew things were not going to be easy. She didn't appear excited about working out, at least not until I mentioned her presents, including the DVD I made for her with all the photos she had taken in Japan.

Before hanging up, I also politely asked that she not tell anyone else about my past and, to my surprise, she seemed very receptive. Her voice sounded sincere and so at that point I considered the matter closed.

As promised, I called her the following Tuesday morning to confirm our gym plans, and within an hour she showed up at my house, dressed in her not-so-conservative workout clothes—a snug T-shirt and a pair of skimpy tight shorts that appeared two sizes too small.

I had laid out all the presents I bought her, her mother, and her co-workers—including the photo DVD I made—on my kitchen island for her to take home after our workout. But as soon as she walked in, she grabbed everything off the island and carried it down to her car, there and then, once again without a thank-you. With her gifts safely locked in her car, we left for the Plano Community Recreation Center in my Firebird.

As with our vacation, the workout was just as miserable with very little conversation between us. When we did talk, everything she said had an annoyed tone to it. Staying optimistic, I periodically tried to lighten up the mood with some witty comment, but her incorrigible attitude was icy cold.

During our drive back, I tried one last time to make peace. When we agreed to stay friends in Japan, I was under the impression we would at least remain on speaking terms, but now even that seemed too presumptuous. The more I tried talking to her, the more closed off and irritated she appeared, so I just let the matter drop. I held no animosity toward her, but it was obvious I had become just another guy she gave enough rope to hang himself.

Returning to my house, she quickly made her way from the garage to the front door. With undeniable tension in the air, it was one of those awkward departures where neither of us knew what to say. She appeared anxious to leave, so I simply said, "I guess I'll see you around" as she opened the door and walked outside. Watching her stroll down the walkway toward her car parked on the street, I added "Good luck to you," with a sincere and pleasant voice.

And I meant it.

I could tell from her attitude this was probably the last time I would see her, and I honestly wanted to wish her the best. I carried no ill-will, but after so many attempts to fix us, I finally realized that day would never come. We tried; it didn't work out—it was time to move on with no hard feelings.

But Genea did not hold the same sentiments, as I would find out later that night when I received an email from her explaining why we weren't meant to be. Just like all her previous breakups, this one was also in the format of three strikes and you're out. Carolyn was over at my house and read it over my shoulder (see Document: 7240 @ www. ambrozuk.com).

In summary the email read:

Strike 1: The lying

Strike 2: Kinda of a progressive thing... (referring to our intimacy, sex, her PMS, and her irritation when we were in Japan)

Strike 3: You went too far when you said, "Hoyt's moved on. Genea wasn't good enough"

Carolyn and I kept reading the email over and over again, and neither one of us could understand why all the anger. Breakups are never easy, but there should have been little reason for her hostility. She got wined and dined for two months, got an all-expense paid vacation to Japan, and now she was free to find her "next man" as she used to refer to her boyfriends. It seemed that between the two of us, she got the better deal and had come out ahead in the greater scheme of things.

Leery of her spitefulness, I tried one last time to bury the hatchet. "Don't go away mad, just go away!" was always my motto, so I wrote to her the next day, hoping it would make her rethink our friendship status—or at the very least take the edge off her animosity (see Document: 7241 @ www.ambrozuk.com). Unlike the letter I read at her house from one of her ex-boyfriends—who still blamed her for their breakup—my email was much more Genea-friendly and apologetic. I carefully pointed out all the things we had in common, and how I still thought we could get over our problems while leaving an open door in case she changed her mind.

But unfortunately my attempt to reconcile was all for naught, because four months later Genea contacted Sheriff Jim Dupont in Kalispell, Montana to tell him my whereabouts (see Document: 3114 @ www.ambrozuk.com). Despite my letter and my generosity throughout our relationship, eventually her bottled-up anger got the better of her, just like it always had with her previous relationships. She was damaged goods, and I was simply the next statistic in a long list of men to feel her wrath.

But why wait four months to turn me into the authorities? Why not turn me in as soon as I had told her about my past?

During her interview on *America's Most Wanted* (see Document: 6802 @ www.ambrozuk.com), she justified herself by suggesting she did it not only because she wanted the Babcock family to have closure, but also because she didn't want others to find out about me and my past like she did. But those reasons seemed like excuses she created for herself each time a relationship ended badly.

I was not the one who did all those things to her, and I was not the one responsible for her current mental state, yet somehow it felt like I was being punished for it. She had no problem going to Japan with me after I told her about my past, and she definitely didn't have a problem being intimate right up to the last day of our vacation, so why the deception? It makes a lot more sense to realize that her hostility—rather than nobility—was responsible for her change of heart after so many months.

I was truly saddened to hear about Genea's history and the psychological trauma she endured over the years, but that does not give her the right to go on national TV and spread lies about me, my character, our relationship, or why she betrayed my privacy and trust. No one except Genea herself will ever know the truth behind why she turned me in, but I do know it was more than to appease the Babcock family. Whether it was her anger and resentment of men, or perhaps the fact that Carolyn and I were back together again—much like Hoyt eventually left her for his ex-girlfriend—the reality was that the damage was done, and I would have to deal with the consequences.

In hindsight, I should have taken the initiative years before to close out all my affairs in the U.S. and return to Canada, but I never did. Without Genea, I would still probably be living in Texas as Michael Smith. And therefore, in retrospect, as much as I should be mad at her for ratting me out, I cannot help but be grateful to be back with my family after almost a quarter of a century.

They say, "Every cloud has a silver lining," and, in this case, that could not be more true—a fitting ending to an ominous relationship with a blessing in disguise.

CHAPTER SIXTY-TWO

Freedom at Last

October 25, 2007
Day 422

AFTER 421 DAYS in the state, federal, and immigration detention centers, Thursday they finally let me out.

Despite what everyone was saying—including, and especially all my attorneys who were confident there was no way in hell I would be allowed to walk on United States' soil before being deported—today Carolyn posted the $10,000 bond and I was released from INS custody.

It was early in the afternoon when she completed the paperwork, and we walked out of the INS detention center into a warm sunny day that felt nothing short of exhilarating. After fourteen months—and no physical contact—Carolyn's tender hug, bubbly personality, and infectious smile were just what the doctor ordered. We got into her convertible, took the top down, and after a brief pit-stop at Burger King to welcome me back to civilization, we headed for my house to begin what would be the first of many reunions and celebrations with my friends and family.

It felt good to take a shower, get cleaned up, and put on some normal cloths after so many months of going commando—but the best part was still yet to come.

It was close to six o'clock when my sister finally knocked on the front door, dropped everything in the walkway, and gave me the nicest, warmest, and most heartfelt embrace ever. We stood there for what seemed like eternity, taking in the moment in silence, as if trying to atone for lost time. She had been God sent ever since my arrest and our first conversation, and now she was finally here in the flesh after all these years.

Other than my pending immigration fate, most of my legal battles were over. There were still a few outstanding issues to address—my Corvette release, the jury consultant refund, Merrill Lynch frozen accounts, the civil forfeiture case, and Kim and Ken—but at least I was free to deal with all that from the comfort of my home and with my family by my side.

After a twenty-four year absence, and despite all I had endured, the only thing that mattered was reconnecting and spending time with my family. I had been away for far too long; it was time to embrace the next chapter in my life. And what better way than to start with Canadian hockey, Canadian bacon, Canadian maple syrup, and Polish pierogies to pave the way for my overdue welcome home.

Act IV: Summary and Conclusions

CHAPTER SIXTY-THREE

State (Criminal) Case

WHO COULD HAVE imagined that two high school sweethearts in love would find such immeasurable tragedy as their life was about to begin? Who would have thought that during their innocent elopement such a horrific accident would end one life and leave the other emotionally crippled for years with the penance of mourning?

But on August 22, 1982, that was exactly what happened.

What was unbelievable was that the Flathead County investigators, led by the outspoken Sheriff Jim Dupont, would look at all the evidence collected, and all the recovery photos taken, and conclude this was a crime.

The Canadian justice system, the Crown Counsel, didn't think so. In their eyes, this was a case of two kids in love eloping when the tragic accident occurred. They filed no charges (see Document: 3002 @ www.ambrozuk.com), despite Dianne and I being both Canadian citizens, and the aircraft having been rented in Canada.

So why would that same sentiment also not ring true with the Flathead County authorities in Montana? How could they look at the exact same facts and evidence, but conclude the exact opposite of the Canadian authorities?

When a passenger in a car assumes a safe journey from point A to point B then perishes when a careless driver hits a tree along the way, that is grounds for a potential negligent homicide charge because the occupant was unaware of the impending danger. But when Dianne and

I plan our elopement—gathering supplies for months in preparation for our departure—that same argument cannot be made so easily. Because Dianne was a willing participant and well aware of the inherent dangers of landing a fixed-wheel aircraft on water, this was no different from a tandem skydiver, a weekend racecar driver enthusiast, or an X-games athlete who chose to put their life in peril while being fully aware of the potential risks.

Ed Corrigan knew that, as Dianne's younger sister had mentioned inadvertently in her victim impact statement submitted to court:

> *Ed Corrigan has told me that there was a possibility that Jerry could have gotten off of the negligent homicide charge should it have gone to trial and it been shown that Dianne was a willing accomplis [sic] in the event.*

That, along with the remark Dianne's father made to my attorney, where he mentioned the prosecutor and his intent to postpone my March 12, 2007 trial date, only reaffirmed the state case had nothing to do with justice and due process of the law. Denying me the right to a preliminary hearing, pulling out of my first signed plea agreement, and even adding two more baseless charges to my case, served as cunning tactics by a prosecutor wanting to delay the state case resolution as long as possible.

It is unfortunate that people like the presumptuous Sheriff Dupont and Ed Corrigan had the authority, and the audacity, to take something as innocent as our elopement and turn it into a media spectacle for their own political and personal gains. Fair and unbiased men they were not, given that this was not a case of "he said, she said." All the evidence was available for twenty-four years—showing how Dianne and I had planned our getaway, how she went voluntarily, and how her tragic death was nothing more than a ghastly accident—but to Flathead County authorities, that version was not good enough. There had to be something more sinister at play. There had to be someone who had to pay.

Flathead County Deputy Jim Dupont, the initial investigator on the case in 1982, spent twenty-four years telling the media how I casually had landed the plane, taken the bag with the money, and exited the aircraft without helping Dianne with her seatbelt.

But that was the furthest thing from the truth.

I often wondered what their prejudgment might have been if this were not an elopement, but an incident with similar circumstances. What if Dianne and I had been returning to Vancouver that afternoon and faced engine trouble, forcing us to land on a lake with the same outcome? Would that be considered an accident, or would it still be negligent homicide?

But after so many years of exaggerated stories and conjecture by the Flathead authorities in front of the media, there had to be someone responsible. There had to be a scapegoat. From Mr. Babcock, who, to the very end, refused to acknowledge that Dianne was a voluntary participant in our elopement, to Ed Corrigan, who used the media as a tool to echo the Babcock family sentiments ("Their belief, if true, means that essentially she was kidnapped and murdered . . ."), they collectively roused the public, hoping to turn the tables on something that should have been easily resolved through my denied preliminary hearing.

In the end, as their final justice, I ended up with two state charges, along with a hefty restitution that included paying David Oliver $20,000 for an aircraft worth $7,000.

Perhaps to Sheriff Dupont, Ed Corrigan, and Judge Stadler, their conduct seemed justifiable. But it shouldn't have been. The Eighth Amendment of the Constitution of the United States of America should have been reason enough for them to dispense justice without prejudice.

When prosecutors and judges are given the freedom to manipulate and delay court cases because of political reasons or unsound, self-righteous stances, it is not just plain wrong but goes against everything the law is meant to stand for: the right to a speedy trial and remaining innocent until proven guilty.

In 1982, Sheriff Dupont and the Flathead County authorities may have gotten away with speciously labeling the tragic accident as negligent homicide, but since then the playing field has changed. Today, with the advent of the Internet and social media, they can no longer cast aspersions or hide behind false conjectures and allegations, because now the world is watching, and it can judge for itself.

CHAPTER SIXTY-FOUR

Federal (Criminal) Case and Probation

AT THE CONCLUSION of my state case, I was taken into custody by U.S. Marshals and eventually transported to Denton County, Texas. There I spent the next four-and-a-half months waiting to appear in front of the judge for my federal passport sentencing. But unlike my state case, I had no problem taking responsibility for my indiscretions. Although the passport was used strictly for business, no matter how justifiable the reason seemed, it was still wrong.

I had spent twenty-four years educating myself, starting a business, providing jobs for over 230 people in seventeen years through my company, paid hundreds of thousands of dollars in personal and corporate taxes, and, for all intents and purposes, was a model U.S. citizen. Perhaps that was why my exemplary record was enough for the judge to rule in my favor—unbiased. After letting me explain my circumstances, he succinctly said, "I believe him," gave me time served, and let me move on to Immigration.

Suffice to say, his compassionate sentiment was not echoed by the U.S. federal probation officer, Bill Gallimore, who would eventually catch up with me after I bonded out. A month and a half after I was released from immigration custody, I got a phone call at my house from Gallimore, wondering why I hadn't reported to the probation office for supervision.

Supervision seemed pointless as I was about to be deported back to Canada, but it was obvious that the probation officer took his job seriously. If he couldn't reach me by the end of the week, he said, he would issue a warrant for my arrest.

With the federal government seizing my cars, I borrowed Kim and Ken's Hummer and made my way to the probation office for my initial orientation and screening, complete with urine tests for drugs. But after complying unconditionally with their requirements, I was surprised when he and his supervisor, Myra Kirkwood, denied me the chance to spend the holidays with my family.

We had planned to celebrate our first Catholic Christmas reunion in Bellingham, Washington, a small town near the Canadian border where everyone would join me as I waited for my immigration case to be resolved. But Mr. Gallimore and his supervisor didn't share our Christmas spirit.

Instead, after a quarter century, I would spend my first Christmas and New Year's with my family on Skype. It wasn't what everyone was hoping for, but this was one more hurdle we had to get past in the interim. Thankfully, the following year, with the entire family at my side in Canada, it would be a celebration to remember, filled with nothing but elation, contentment, and the delightful joy of the holidays.

CHAPTER SIXTY-FIVE

Immigration Case

AT THE CONCLUSION of my federal case, I was picked up by ICE officers and taken into INS custody to deal with my illegal entry into the Unites States. This was my final stop before being deported to Canada, and the only question was whether I would leave by voluntary departure or administrative removal. Treating my state and federal convictions as non-aggravated felonies, they allowed me to bond out for three months as I waited for my day in court to ask the immigration judge for leniency.

I very much appreciated my temporary release despite unforeseen challenges, including obtaining legal documentation. Other than my Canadian Citizenship Card my sister had applied for while I was still in Montana, I had none. This posed a problem with even the simplest of tasks, including driving a car.

What I did have was a complete set of "Michael Smith" alias IDs that no one seemed to care about or want back. Using a copy of my certified indictment and plea agreement papers that contained both my alias and legal names as proof of identity, Renata and I went to the nearest Texas Motor Vehicle Branch to apply for an official Texas driver's license with my proper name. But to our surprise, when we met with the constable in charge, he sounded indifferent. "As far as I'm concerned, you are Michael Smith," he said, and all but approved me driving around town using the alias responsible for my problems in the first place.

It was a curious reply from an official but not as ironic as the fact that, twenty-four years earlier, I had been able to get alias IDs more easily than the legitimate documents I was applying for now.

Fortunately, I wouldn't have to drive without a valid driver's license for long before I found out my immigration fate. My master hearing date was set for January 23, 2008, and after hiring attorney Garry L. Davis, we appeared in front of the immigration judge confident that ICE would not take me into their custody again.

For those still keeping score, we're up to ten attorneys: Clancy (dismissed), Davis (Texas State), Sherlock (Montana State), Palmer (Corvette release), Cohen (Merrill Lynch), Watson and Jent (Montana State, and Texas Federal cases), Knight (Texas Federal), Mickelsen (Texas Federal civil), and now, Mr. Davis.

But even Mr. Davis, who seemed knowledgeable about my options and chances in court, was wrong. With a ruling from Judge D. Anthony Rogers of Administrative Removal, I was once again taken into INS custody (see Document: 3913 @ www.ambrozuk.com). It was not the decision I had hoped for but the good news was that in a couple weeks, once all the paperwork was complete, I would finally be going home to my family in Canada.

And sure enough, on the morning of February 19, 2008, two ICE officers escorted me to the Dallas/Fort Worth Airport—this time without restraints—where we boarded a direct flight to Vancouver. When we eventually landed at YVR and got to Customs, the ICE officers showed the airport official my papers, wished me luck, and I continued on to the arrival gates where my family was waiting with large bouquets of flowers and smiles from ear to ear.

Unlike the airport fiasco in Flathead County fifteen months ago, no reporters were there to dampen my Canadian homecoming. After a few warm hugs, along with the traditional three European kisses on the cheeks from everyone, we left for my parents' house to begin what would be the first of many celebrations of my long overdue return home.

An auspicious new beginning, indeed!

CHAPTER SIXTY-SIX

Corvette Release Case

DESPITE REPEATED ATTEMPTS to get my 1981 Corvette repairs properly completed, six years later the car was still with John Bodnar, owner and operator of JB's Corvette Specialists body shop. After my arrest, Carolyn had tried to contact Mr. Bodnar to pick up my car using power of attorney. Instead of being cooperative, he refused to speak with her and referred her to his attorney, Mr. Parker, who was already in the process of repossessing the car based on the grounds that it had been abandoned.

Forced to deal with their attempted larceny, I hired Mr. Palmer, yet another attorney, to pursue legal action. On December 6, 2007, I received a registered letter from Mr. Bodnar's lawyer to pick up my vehicle once I paid the tab of $874.39 for final repairs, storage fees, and towing (see Document: 3620 @ www.ambrozuk.com). The law stated that, before my vehicle could be considered abandoned, they had to send a final notice to the owner before they could apply for a new car title. What Mr. Parker was not counting on was my release from the immigration detention center on bond and readiness to oblige. Fortunate with the timing was an opportunity to put an end to Bodnar's ridiculous scam.

Under the instructions of my attorney, I contacted Mr. Parker and got him to agree to release the Corvette without paying a dime. I showed up two days later at Mr. Bodnar's body shop with a release contract in my hand that we signed (see Document: 3619 @ www.ambrozuk.

com) before I took my stripped—and in dire need of further repairs (see Document: 3612 @ www.ambrozuk.com)—vehicle home.

Looking back at the condition of my Corvette after six years of restoration, one can quibble about whether I should have abandoned the car and moved on. But after all my disappointments with prosecutors, judges, and attorneys during my tenure in detention centers, this was one victory I was determined to not let slip through my fingers. If for no other reason than principle, after failing to make the proper repairs I had already paid for, I was not about to let Mr. Bodnar swindle me out of my Corvette too.

CHAPTER SIXTY-SEVEN

Merrill Lynch Case

SHORTLY AFTER MY arrest, and without as much as a single court order, Merrill Lynch took it upon themselves to freeze all my personal and corporate assets. Their actions would have cascading effects as they prevented me from paying my attorneys, house utilities, and yearly property taxes.

It seemed unbelievable that a financial institution—a bank if you will—could lock up my money for over a year and a half and not be liable for compensatory or punitive damages. I lost thousands of dollars not only on attorney fees and the market—my stocks had continued to depreciate over time—but adding salt to injury, Merrill Lynch also continued to charge me maintenance fees on all my locked accounts during the entire time.

My only recourse was to hire a civil attorney, Mr. Cohen, to fight this absurdity. But the release of my accounts and my money was not that simple. Despite the option of paying him to fly to New York and sue Merrill Lynch, there was a very good chance we would lose. Their corporate lawyers had already covered their bases when I initially had opened the accounts and signed their contracts.

The only upside was that my money was never in peril because it was all legally earned. Unlike my properties, there was no alleged mail, wire, bank, or loan-and-credit application fraud tying me to my money. The best they could do was delay its release.

And sure enough, when I finally returned to Canada, Merrill Lynch seemed much more cooperative as long as I signed their release contract prohibiting me from suing them for damages in the future (see Document: 3516 @ www.ambrozuk.com).

Despite all the unnecessary hardships endured because of Merrill Lynch, there is a hard lesson to be learned in dealing with financial institutions: it may be your money, but they think it's theirs to do with as they please. Nobody reads the fine print when opening a new account, but perhaps they should rather than believe the well-dressed, smooth-talking, professional who assures you that your money is safe in their possession.

CHAPTER SIXTY-EIGHT

State (Civil) Case: Foreign Judgment

BACK IN CANADA after my state, federal, and immigration cases were completed, I received a court document in the mail from Tarrant County, Texas that read: Notice Of Filing Of Foreign Judgment (see Document: 3401 @ www.ambrozuk.com). Conveniently timed to arrive just after Merrill Lynch had released my frozen assets, the foreign judgment was filed by David Oliver, owner of the defunct Canadian aircraft rental company. He filed the motion on behalf of himself and the other judgment creditors: Flathead County Sheriff's Office, Flathead County Attorney's Office, David Firth, and Gerald Babcock, in order to place liens on my properties so that I would be forced to pay back the $41,577.08 state restitution.

To ensure he got his money, David Oliver flew to Texas, hired an attorney, somehow managed to take up residence in Fort Worth, Texas so he could legally file the judgment against me, and then demanded reimbursement for his travel expenses to Texas as well (see List: 9010 @ www.ambrozuk.com).

All this happened after my house went on the market and my receiving a serious offer from a buyer. Because of the inconvenient timing, I was forced to spend more money on an attorney, specifically Mr. Sherlock, to pay off and redistribute the restitution monies to the appropriate parties so that I could sell my house.

In the end, the profitable sale of my home did go through, but I am still bewildered by David Oliver, the same man awarded $20,000 by

Judge Stadler in Flathead County to fix an aircraft worth $7,000 without any proof or receipts, who then went out of his way to fly to Texas to make sure he got his money. If only this kind of effort went into his business in 1982, then perhaps he too could have been successful without needing to blame our elopement, or the media attention, for its failure.

CHAPTER SIXTY-NINE

Federal (Civil) Case: Complaint for Forfeiture In Rem

WHILE IN THE Denton County Detention Center dealing with my federal passport case, I was served with a complaint for forfeiture in rem lawsuit from the federal government. The summons stated they were in the process of repossessing all my properties—my cars, my house, and my lakefront lots—because of alleged fraud.

To fight what appeared to be double jeopardy with respect to my pending passport charge, I hired my ninth attorney. He seemed optimistic that we could not only win the case but set precedence for how the government seized personal property in the future.

But when it was over, there would be no precedence set, and I would have no choice but to settle out of court for the sake of time and money. According to my attorney, Mr. Mickelsen, if we decided to go to trial, it would be months, if not years, before the case was finally resolved. At a judge or a jury trial, whichever party lost, they would appeal the decision and thus further prolong the case resolution. In the meantime, I would continue to pay monthly utility bills and yearly taxes for my properties that would eventually amount to tens of thousands of dollars.

Weighing all my options, and as much as I thought the federal government was being inequitable in their pursuit of my hard-earned possessions based on petty technicalities, I had no choice but to settle out of court. Cutting my losses, I paid the federal government $100,000 to release my assets before I put them on the market for sale (see Document:

3838 @ www.ambrozuk.com). Although their appreciation value over the years overshadowed the government's extortionate fine, it was small consolation for what seemed like a perfect example of federal resources and priorities gone wrong.

In the end, I learned a valuable lesson about the federal civil court system and my attorneys. For thirteen months after my arrest, they were all confident that because I had bought everything legally and without drug money, my property was never in peril. As reassuring as all eight were before the federal government filed the lawsuit, every single one of them turned out to be wrong. If along the way even one had expressed doubt, I would have sold off everything in a heartbeat. By doing so, I would not only have saved myself the expense of hiring another attorney to deal with the forfeiture in rem case, but also $100,000.

And thus was my school of hard knocks—a disappointing ending to my federal civil case, where I had been surrounded by unshakably confident attorneys who appeared as resourceful as they were knowledgeable but, in the end, obviously were not!

Act V: The Closure

CHAPTER SEVENTY

I Came, I Saw, I Went Back to Canada

IN 1982, WHEN Dianne and I embarked on our intrepid adventure, neither of us contemplated the possible fallout if something went wrong during our carefully planned elopement. We were not the first, and surely will not be the last to come up with such grandiose plans. Sometimes that's just what teenagers in love do. They don't think about the consequences first; that reasoning is reserved for the latter years of life. We were in love, excited about our future, and simply wanted to leave without hurting anyone.

So before going any further, let's just stop and think about that!

We were young, carefree, and only wished for a better life. There was no malicious intent and plenty of evidence to show that despite what the prosecutor insinuated, and all that the Babcock family refused to believe, Dianne was a willing participant in our elopement.

And therefore, it is preposterous to think there are people like Sheriff Jim Dupont and prosecutor Ed Corrigan who had access to a foot-thick stack of evidence and chose to ignore it because of their preconceived judgments. Everything was in the evidence—the RCMP interviews with our families, the contents of the garbage bag recovered from the aircraft, corroborating our plan and Dianne's participation—yet they cherry-picked what they wanted to feed to the public and discarded the rest.

The irony of the entire state case was that everyone involved chose to pretend Dianne was an innocent bystander, that there was no love between us, that she didn't spend months planning the elopement with me, and that there must have been some sinister reason behind the unfortunate accident. It is human nature to choose a side and follow through at all cost. More often than not, once you form an opinion and make a choice, you stand by your conclusions and convictions to the very end, no matter what the evidence may later show, and no matter what the actual truth is.

But what if you were wrong?

What if the Flathead County authorities made false assumptions and conclusions and fed their bias to the media and the public for twenty-four years, whether by ignorance or on purpose?

How can one possibly look at all the evidence and not conclude this was nothing more than two high school sweethearts in love who did the unthinkable?

But, unfortunately, as I learned over the course of nine months, Ed Corrigan, the lead Flathead County attorney prosecuting my case, was on a mission. No stranger to controversy, he had already been reprimanded by the Montana Supreme Court for unethical conduct on several occasions and was the subject of an ongoing investigation by the ACLU, according to my attorneys. In the corporate world, he would have been fired long ago for such misconduct, yet here he was again following the same patterns. How was that possible? Apparently not that unheard of in a town where collusion begets collusion, with no one there to "police the police" and hold them accountable for their palpable absurdity.

Like it or not, that is how the law works in reality. This is not TV and things rarely are as they appear. As much as one would like to believe that ultimately justice will be done, there is always someone in law enforcement ready to prove you wrong.

Throughout my ordeal in Flathead County, I had the distinct feeling that many, including my own attorney, Patrick Sherlock, felt I should have pleaded guilty to the negligent homicide charge right from the beginning. He spent months trying to manipulate me through our many talks, eventually bringing in clinical psychologist, Dr. Edward Trontel, to coerce me. After a few months in state detention, I was bound to come around, they thought. But I had no misapprehension about what Dianne and I regrettably had done, and it was definitely not negligent homicide.

In 1982, the Royal Canadian Mounted Police looked extensively into the accident and, along with the Canadian justice system, the Crown Counsel, ultimately concluded there was no basis for criminal charges, despite Mr. Babcock's campaign of retribution (see Document: 3003 @ www.ambrozuk.com). But the same could not be said for the "alternate facts" gun-slinging lawmen of Flathead County, who all but united against the Canadian authorities by taking justice into their own hands. Their jurisdiction transcended borders as they conveniently overlooked the fact that Dianne and I were both Canadian citizens, and the aircraft was rented from a company in Canada.

But irrelevant to their misguided perspective, and despite the Babcock family and Ed Corrigan trying to vilify our 1982 conduct in front of the media twenty-four years later, I can honestly say I have never felt like Dianne's tragic death was anything but an accident.

To say otherwise would serve only to belittle her. She was not a twelve-year-old child—she was a grown woman who was not only passionately in love, but also intelligent, logical, and rational. We worked together to plan our elopement, and therefore her decision stands on its own merit. She had months, and plenty of opportunities, to speak with Tom and her family if she had any doubts or concerns. But she didn't. And so one needs to ask: why?

The brutal truth is that we were deeply in love and, despite the unforeseen dangers, our elopement made sense to both of us at the time. We were a team, as close as a couple could possibly get, and our decision—although irrational in hindsight—seemed like the best option for our future and our rare, exuberant love.

But sadly, on that tragic night, when our lives were about to enter a new chapter, I lost the only woman I ever truly loved.

After the accident, I was broken. In the days, weeks, and months that followed, I couldn't care less if I lived or died. It was the hardest and darkest of times I would ever live through, spending years getting over my grief before a slow return to becoming a productive citizen. And all that I did in silence—without drugs, without sympathetic friends to talk to, without family members to console me, and without counselors or psychologists to help with the nightmare I relived night after night.

Just because I didn't act the way people expected doesn't mean I was guilty of negligent homicide. Just because I didn't stay after the accident, was traumatized, in mental turmoil, and out of my mind after losing the one person I intended to spend the rest of my life with, doesn't give the Flathead County authorities the convenience of speculation and blame, especially when it's wrong.

Why didn't I stay at the scene of the accident? Why didn't I call the authorities that night? Why didn't I return home? All these are valid questions, but when you're in complete shock, you operate on instinct like a tormented animal. There was no rhyme or reason for my behavior at the time and no logical explanation as to why I would even continue on to Mexico without Dianne.

But slowly, over a period of years, things would start to make sense again. Initially, I applied for my new identity simply out of necessity, but in time I would also find a purpose. Partly for myself, and partly because of all the encouragement from my parents over the years, I would eventually return to school, graduate, and join the workforce before starting my own company as I slowly returned to a productive life.

But unlike an identity thief, my purpose was never to harm anyone or use it for any malicious or illegal activity. Not unlike someone in a witness protection program, I simply borrowed a deceased name so that I could survive.

No one is saying it was the right thing to do, especially after the repercussions that eventually followed, but there is a difference. Perhaps that was why, after four and a half months in detention, the federal judge lowered my recommended sentence and gave me time served before sending me on to INS, expediting the reunion with my family in Canada after so many years.

That is not to say my long journey home was anything short of arduous during the fifteen months I spent in detention centers awaiting my day in court.

At long last I had my family back, and our daily conversations were instrumental in helping me stay upbeat and positive, but the reality was that things were slowly crumbling around me. Like vultures circling a dead carcass, I found myself fending off attacks from institutions and people alike looking to capitalize on my current circumstances.

There was my 1981 Vette that JB's Corvette Specialists body shop tried to confiscate after six years rather than properly finishing repairs. There was the jury consultant, who refused to refund our deposit because of a technicality. There was Merrill Lynch, who decided to freeze my accounts without so much as a court order. There was the civil forfeiture case with the U.S. federal government trying to repossess all my assets because of alleged fraud. There was the foreign judgment case from which David Oliver, Ed Corrigan, and the Babcock family were determined to get their restitution money. Even my best friends, to whom I had loaned $70,000, stopped making payments so that I couldn't pay for the most trivial things like my utility house bills. And all this was happening while I dealt with prosecutors, judges, and even my attorneys who seemed to have their own agendas in the state, federal, and immigration cases.

At times it felt like I was slowly being poisoned from the inside, ready to give up and let everyone have their way. Fortunately, there was an antidote to their acrimonious intents. I had Carolyn and my family in my corner from the start, and a plethora of friends who offered their support throughout with the odd letter, a postcard to wish me well, or the kind words in their character reference letters. In the end, it was their understanding and reinforcement that carried me through the court systems with a positive attitude, up until my return home to Canada.

Many years have passed since Dianne and I started all this, but it would not be fair if the truth could not be told because of people like Sheriff Dupont and Ed Corrigan, who cunningly manipulate public opinion, and the law, to get away with deception.

No one is denying that what Dianne and I did was irresponsible and foolish, but immature stupidity is not the same as negligent homicide. This is not about the prosecutor's self-righteous justice or the Babcock family's requital—this is simply about Dianne and I, pure love, and our elopement gone wrong.

Everyone has an opinion or is an expert on love, but how many have truly experienced it and would be willing to sever all ties with their friends and family for the rest of their lives for it, as we did?

Only with the right frame of mind, in the right place, and with the right two people is such altruistic love possible. Dianne taught me that. She showed me how to love someone more than life itself, and ever since I have been a prisoner of our unconditional passion that forever changed me.

You can love your pet, and you can love your friends, siblings, and parents more. But when you meet that someone so remarkably unique who turns your entire world upside down—where you discover you cannot bear to live a single day without them—that is what the love of your life is made of.

It's not about your friends and their advice, it's not about money or security, and it's definitely not about your parents trying to selfishly protect you because they think they know best. It's only about you and that extraordinarily fragile bond you both share.

If you never had it, you will never understand. If you always had hamburger, you will never know what steak tastes like. But if you ever have a chance at such precious, under-your-skin closeness—to feel like you're part of something more than just comfortable security—don't squander it, because odds are you will never have that opportunity again.

It stands to reason that the older we get, the harder it is to leave the drama of past relationships behind. In a lifetime of dating, there are sure to be few opportunities at true love, but if you hesitate and never let your guard down to take that leap of faith, all you will ever know is mediocre hamburger.

Life is about following your heart with the one who will rock your world. And for a brief moment, I had that. I was blessed to have met the love of my life who was my other half, and I would give anything to experience that again.

I will forever hold a special place in my heart for the one who spoiled me. And if I am not fortunate enough to find such rare love again, I will be content with what we shared during our year and a half together, because those incredible moments, in that brief glimpse of time, were enough to last me a lifetime.

I feel much better now...☺

Acknowledgments

This book exists in its current form because of the many people who not only helped shape it, but also supported me along the way.

My first and biggest thank-you must go to my family who stood by me through thick and thin. I didn't know what to expect after twenty-four years, but, undeniably, blood is thicker than water, and they could not have been more instrumental in keeping me focused and motivated. If not for them, I can honestly say that things would not have turned out as well as they did.

The same sentiment goes to all my friends who put a smile on my face each and every day while I remained in detention centers. Through their letters, jokes, phone calls, visitations, and character reference letters, their understanding and support went a long way when dealing with the U.S. legal system.

As ironic as it may seem, I also want to thank Ed Corrigan, the state prosecutor, who, through his unrelenting pursuit of Flathead County justice, motivated me to tell my story as it really happened. Without his persistence, there would be neither a book nor a website to at long last explain the circumstances surrounding my elopement with Dianne.

And finally, I want to express my deepest gratitude to the people who contributed, and were largely responsible, for the current state of the book. From editors like Irene Kavanagh, who rightfully questioned, debated, and corrected many a topic, to the legal counsel of Daniel Steven, who pointed out and explained every legal aspect and ramification of the memoir and the website, I will be forever grateful for their influence, hard work, and dedication.

Thank you all, and I hope you enjoy the book as well as the interactive website, both of which we labored over for years to bring my story to life.

29085734R00267

Made in the USA
Columbia, SC
19 October 2018